BETWEEN YOU AND ME

BETWEEN YOU AND ME

A MEMOIR

MIKE WALLACE

WITH

GARY PAUL GATES

NEW YORK

Book design by Richard Oriolo

LIBRARY OF CONGRESS CATALOGING-IN-PUBLICATION DATA

Wallace, Mike
Between you and me : a memoir / Mike Wallace with Gary Paul Gates.—1st ed.
p. cm.
Includes index.
ISBN 1-4013-0029-4
1. Wallace, Mike.   2. Journalists—United States—Biography.
I. Gates, Gary Paul.   II. Title.

PN4874.W283A3 2005
070.92—dc22
[B]   2005046259

FIRST EDITION

10 9 8 7 6 5 4 3 2 1

TO DICK SALANT, WHO,

BACK IN 1963 AS PRESIDENT OF CBS NEWS,

GAVE ME THE JOB AND THE LIFE HE

KNEW I YEARNED FOR

CONTENTS

INTRODUCTION   1

ONE   Presidents   5

TWO   First Couples   37

THREE   Race in America   67

FOUR   The Middle East   99

FIVE   Icons and Artists   133

SIX   Con Men and Other Crooks   159

SEVEN   The General and the Whistle-blower   187

EIGHT   Valentines   221

NINE   . . . And Other Celebrated Characters   249

EPILOGUE   275

ACKNOWLEDGMENTS   279

INDEX   281

BETWEEN YOU AND ME

INTRODUCTION

BACK IN THE 1950s, WHEN television was black-and-white and still a relatively new late-night diversion for folks who wanted a news update followed by some entertaining talk in their bedrooms, my colleague Ted Yates came up with a notion for an interview show that just might get their attention.

At the time I was anchoring and Ted was producing the eleven o'clock news on Channel 5, the New York station that also carried two showbiz icons of the time, Ernie Kovacs and Soupy Sales. The station manager agreed that it was probably worth a try. (Back then it seemed everything was worth a try.) So in October of '56, we combined our news update with the experiment we called *Night Beat*.

It was Yates who came up with the title, and it was also he who gave our innovative venture its spark. A lanky ex-marine, Ted had the manner and fearless temperament of a cowboy. He came by it honestly. Born in Wyoming, he had spent much of his childhood in Cheyenne, close to the open land and cattle herds of the region that used to be known as the Wild West. But his family eventually moved east, and so instead of a life in the saddle and a home on the range, he wound up in New York, pursuing a career in television news.

By the time *Night Beat* went on the air, the two of us had been working together at Channel 5 for about a year. We'd also become close friends, and that continued through the years ahead, even after he and I went our separate ways in TV journalism. But I'm sad to say that Ted's life came to a tragic end in 1967. In June of that year, when he was filming a story for NBC News on the Six-Day War in the Middle East, and while under fire in East Jerusalem, he was shot in the forehead and died the next day. I thought of him then—and remember him now—as the bravest man I've ever known.

Night Beat was a radical departure from the usual pablum of radio and television interviews. We agreed that, properly primed with solid research, I would ask our guests the kinds of questions that folks in the TV audience might want to ask for themselves if they had the chance: nosy, irreverent, often confrontational. Within just a couple of months, we knew we were on to something special. The viewers told us so, the TV critics did the same, and best of all, the famous and infamous figures of the time—politicians, tycoons, entertainers, athletes, just about everyone of any consequence in New York, it seemed—wanted the chance to test themselves against our role-playing arrogance.

Night Beat quickly became a prime topic of conversation—a lot of it noisy and argumentative—at dinner tables, cocktail parties, and saloons all over the city. My anonymity during prior years of radio and television work suddenly morphed into shouts from cabdrivers: "Give 'em hell, Mike, go get 'em." The reigning queen of TV at the time, Faye Emerson, said it best: "There is no such thing as an indiscreet question." And for our M.O., we appropriated a dictum from playwright-cum–social critic George Bernard Shaw:

"The ablest and most highly cultivated people continually discuss religion, politics, and sex. It's hardly an exaggeration to say that they discuss nothing else with fully awakened interest. Common and less cultivated people, even when they form societies for discussion, make a rule that politics and religion are not to be mentioned, and take it for granted that no decent person would attempt to discuss sex."

Sid Caesar parodied us on his NBC show, then the most popular comedy series on television. We got into public hassles, one of the biggest triggered by a Q&A with the fiery union leader Mike Quill, who bristled when I asked about his Catholicism—he still bore scars from the labor battles of the 1930s, when he'd been accused of greater fidelity to Moscow than to Rome. (He was often referred to in those days as "Red Mike.") The sublimely gifted Irish actress Siobhan McKenna helped us no end by making an offhand remark that infuriated Jews; her apology doubled our audience.

Within six months ABC came calling to offer us a network slot for a weekly nationwide broadcast. What we gleaned from all this and what followed at ABC, and later at CBS, is what you'll read about here: tales from all manner of characters we've persuaded to talk to us down the years, presidents and First Ladies, dictators and demagogues, preachers, painters, musicians, movie stars and comedians, con men and other assorted crooks.

This is the second memoir I've done with Gary Paul Gates, a former CBS News colleague and longtime friend. Our first was called *Close Encounters,* published in 1984, and while the main focus in that book was on my earlier career in broadcasting, this new one deals almost entirely with the famous and infamous I've interviewed, and with behind-the-scenes stories that relate to those encounters.

Of course, some overlap has been unavoidable. When we've revisited a subject we wrote about earlier, mainly we've added new information not previously available; we've also brought to it a fresh perspective. After all, people change and so do their reputations, some for better, others for worse. Gary and I have changed, too; we're twenty years older, and at least one of us claims to be a little wiser.

Anyway, I hope you'll enjoy the tales we tell, for we've had a helluva good time reporting them.

ONE

PRESIDENTS

JOHN F. KENNEDY
DREW PEARSON
CLARK CLIFFORD

IN MAKING THE JUMP FROM a local program to the showcase of a coast-to-coast broadcast, Ted Yates and I were determined to maintain the candid, sometimes combative style we'd introduced on *Night Beat*. But that proved easier said than done. Part of the problem was that we'd lost the element of surprise we'd enjoyed when *Night Beat* burst on the scene the previous fall. Our reputation had preceded us to ABC, and more than a few of our prospective interviewees were wary of being grilled on network television by a guy who had been described by one captious critic as "Mike Malice" and by another as "The Terrible Torquemada of the TV Inquisition." This meant we had to work that much harder to find the kind of characters who might interest a national audience. But I'm happy to say that during our first few months at ABC, we were able to book a diverse gallery of guests for *The Mike Wallace Interview,* ranging from the highbrow (Philip Wylie, Margaret Sanger, and Frank Lloyd Wright) to the lowbrow, a group that included a mobster (Mickey Cohen), a stripper (Lili St. Cyr), and a pair of Hollywood sirens (Jayne Mansfield and Zsa Zsa Gabor).

Still, there were problems to confront. It didn't take us long to discover that in moving up to a network broadcast, we'd ventured into terrain far more treacherous than what we'd been accustomed to at Channel 5. Now that we were playing to a national audience, the stakes were higher, and there were times when we ran into the kind of dicey situations that provoke threats of libel suits.

One such dustup occurred when I interviewed the muckraking Washington columnist Drew Pearson. In those days, almost all the media power was in print, and no one was more powerful than the syndicated columnists. While many Washington columnists saw themselves as pundits and preferred to pontificate instead of investigate, Pearson was a journalistic throwback to the old school. He specialized in finding skeletons in Beltway closets, and he found enough of them to make him the most feared reporter in Washington. To go along with his zeal for exposure, Pearson had a reputation for shooting from the hip. At least two presidents—Franklin D. Roosevelt and Harry Truman—had publicly accused him of being a chronic liar, but when it came to that particular allegation, nothing came close to matching the extravagance of a Tennessee senator named Kenneth McKellar. In a speech on the Senate floor, McKellar denounced

Pearson as "an ignorant liar, a pusillanimous liar, a peewee liar, a liar during his manhood, a liar by profession, a liar in the daytime and a liar in the nighttime."

In our interview, I naturally asked Pearson if any of those pungent adjectives accurately described him, and he naturally denied that he was any kind of liar. We then talked about politics and the next presidential election. The two of us shared the conventional wisdom that Richard Nixon was the probable Republican nominee, and when we turned our attention to who was likely to oppose him in the general election, I noted that "the Democratic glamour boy would seem to be Senator Jack Kennedy."

Although I didn't know the senator from Massachusetts well, I felt a certain kinship with him because we shared a common background. As boys growing up in the Boston suburb of Brookline, Jack Kennedy and I had lived in the same neighborhood. Let me digress a moment here to elaborate on that connection.

Over the years I've often described the Brookline of my youth as "an O'Connor and Goldberg town," and our two families exemplified that. I was the fourth and last child of Frank and Zina Wallace, both of whom were Jewish immigrants who came to America from the shtetls of Tsarist Russia in the late nineteenth century, some four decades after Kennedy's forebears emigrated from Ireland. My father eventually became a successful insurance broker, and by the time I was born in 1918, our family was settled in Brookline, which had become a haven for upwardly mobile Jews and Catholics who were still not welcome in the snootier sections around Boston, a city then notorious for its class-conscious snobbery. Rather than storm the social citadels erected by the haughty Brahmins and other Yankee Protestants, the families of immigrants from Ireland and Italy and Eastern Europe chose to converge on communities that were more tolerant, and none was more attractive in those days than the upscale suburb of Brookline.

Joseph and Rose Kennedy moved to Brookline shortly after they were married in 1914, and began raising their large family just a block or so away from our home on Osborne Road. Jack Kennedy was one year older than I was, and we attended the same neighborhood school. More often than not, when I've told people that Kennedy and I went to the same elementary school and that its name was Edward Devotion, they've assumed it was a Catholic school, which reveals how little they know about Brookline's glorious history.

Edward Devotion was an early hero in the American Revolution. On the night Paul Revere made his legendary ride through Boston and neighboring towns, his friend and fellow patriot Devotion mounted his horse and went on a similar gallop to sound the alarm that the British were coming. The course he followed took him through Brookline. I suppose the main reason why Devotion's ride of warning has been so overshadowed is because many years later, when Longfellow sat down to write his famous ballad, Revere happened to be the horseman he chose to immortalize.

At a social function a few years ago, I was approached by Robert Kraft, the enterprising owner of the New England Patriots, the first team to win three Super Bowls in the twenty-first century. Since I hardly knew him, I wasn't aware he was from Brookline and was surprised to hear him say that he, too, had grown up in my old neighborhood and was a pupil at Edward Devotion, although his time there came long after Kennedy's and mine. He then asked if I'd been back there in recent years. I said I had not, and he told me it was worth a visit because the school had chosen to honor three of its most famous graduates—Kraft, Kennedy, and me—by putting our pictures on a wall near the main entrance.

"My picture is on top," Kraft declared with some relish, "because of the three of us, I had the best grades. Then comes your picture, because you had the second-best. Then below you is Kennedy's picture."

I thanked him for sharing this bit of hometown lore, and proceeded to suggest that it was probably the only time in his life that John F. Kennedy finished third and last in anything.

Even though Jack Kennedy and I were about the same age and lived in the same neighborhood and attended the same elementary school, our paths seldom crossed during the years he lived in Brookline. I'm sure that in time, I would have gotten to know him better if he hadn't moved away. After Joseph Kennedy made his fortune as an investment banker and in other enterprises, he began to set his sights on greener pastures, and in 1927, when Jack was ten and I was nine, the Kennedys relocated to Riverdale, then a posh and exclusive section of New York City.

From there, Jack Kennedy went on to his impressive achievements, which included heroism in the Pacific during World War II, then election to Congress in 1946 and to the Senate six years later. His political star then rose so rapidly that by 1957 he was on the short list of Democratic contenders for the White House. Which brings me back to my interview with Drew Pearson in December of that year. My reference to Kennedy as his party's "glamour boy" led to a question about the senator and his controversial father.

WALLACE: In your column on October twenty-seventh, you wrote that Senator Kennedy's—and I quote—"millionaire McCarthyite father, crusty old Joseph P. Kennedy, is spending a fortune on a publicity machine to make Jack's name well known. No candidate in history has ever had so much money spent on a public relations advance buildup." Unquote. What significance do you see in this, aside from the fact that Joe Kennedy would like to see Jack Kennedy president of the United States?

PEARSON: I don't know what significance other than the fact that I don't think we should have a synthetic public relations buildup for any job of that kind. Now, Jack Kennedy's a fine young man, a very personable fellow. But he isn't as good as the public relations campaign makes him out to be. He's the only man in history that I know who won a Pulitzer Prize for a book that was ghostwritten for him, which indicates the kind of a public relations buildup he has had.

WALLACE: Who wrote the book for him?

PEARSON: I don't recall at the present moment.

WALLACE: You know for a fact, Drew?

PEARSON: Yes, I do.

WALLACE: That the book *Profiles in Courage* was written for Senator Kennedy?

PEARSON: I do.

WALLACE: By somebody else?

PEARSON: I do.

WALLACE: And he, Kennedy, accepted a Pulitzer Prize for it?

PEARSON: He did.

WALLACE: And he has never acknowledged the fact?

PEARSON: No, he has not.

Kennedy's office called the next day and asked for a copy of the transcript. A day or so later, a meeting—to which I was not invited—was held in the executive suite of my boss, Oliver Treyz, the president of ABC Television. Among those present were Bobby Kennedy and the esteemed Washington lawyer Clark Clifford, whose honor roll of prestigious clients included the Kennedy family. Their purpose in setting up the meeting with Treyz was to get an on-air apology from Pearson and/or me for what had been said in our broadcast about the authorship of *Profiles in Courage.*

In the meantime, I'd urged Pearson to specify who had ghost-written the book. After checking with his sources, he called to tell me it was written by a member of the senator's staff, a young man named Ted Sorensen. A few years later, Sorensen would acquire a certain derivative glory as one of President Kennedy's top advisers and his primary speechwriter, but in 1957 he was unknown to the general public. In the preface to *Profiles in Courage,* Kennedy credited Sorensen for "his invaluable assistance in the assembly and preparation" of the material on which the book was based, and that was the extent of his acknowledgment. Pearson refused to make the desired apology and so did I, but the network brass failed to back us up. Faced with the threat of a libel suit, Treyz chose to deliver the apology himself, and to make the capitulation complete, he agreed to let Clifford write it for him. So, prior to our next broadcast, the president of the ABC television network appeared on-camera and read the mea culpa composed by Kennedy's lawyer. Among other things, Treyz said, "We deeply regret this error and feel that it does a grave injustice to a distinguished public servant and author."

I was incensed that my employers had caved in to the Kennedys. The way I saw it, the ABC apology was a humiliating insult to Pearson, who, for all his reputation as a loose cannon, was a seasoned journalist and no stranger to litigation; through the years he had weathered more than a few libel suits with no serious damage to his career. As for the Kennedys, I believed they were bluffing.

There is a postscript to this episode. In the spring of 1991, I interviewed Clark Clifford on *60 Minutes.* He was eighty-four years old and in the deep twilight of his long and extraordinary career. In his prime, Clifford had been one of the most influential advisers ever to move through the corridors of power in Washington, and when I talked to him that spring, he'd just written his autobiography, *Counsel to the President*. Most of the interview focused on his very close relationship with three of our most dynamic Democratic presidents: Harry Truman, John F. Kennedy, and Lyndon Johnson. But what the viewers of *60 Minutes* did not see that evening was the part of our conversation dealing with the 1957 Drew Pearson controversy. Thirty-four years later, Clifford revealed to me just how angry the Kennedys had been:

"My phone rang, and it was Senator Kennedy. He said, 'I must see you at once.' He then came to my office and said, 'I've written a book, as you know, *Profiles in Courage*. Drew Pearson said I didn't write the book, and it's terribly upsetting to me.' About that time, the phone rang for Senator Kennedy. It was his father. He listened to him awhile and then said, 'Father, I'll put Clark on.' I get on the phone. He said, 'This is Ambassador Kennedy.' I said, 'Yes, Mr. Ambassador.' He said, 'Sue the bastards for fifty million dollars.'"

As he recalled that brusque order, Clifford let out a hearty laugh. He then said he assured the former ambassador that "we are going to look into it," but the senior Kennedy's only response to that was to repeat his previous command: "Sue the bastards for fifty million dollars."

Even after I heard that story, I was not convinced that if push had come to shove, the Kennedys would have sued us. In the context of the elaborate preparations he was making to run for president, the last thing the senator and those close to him would have wanted was a highly publicized court fight over the question of who had written *Profiles in Courage*.

Whatever the case, the Kennedy camp stuck to its guns. A few weeks after my interview with Pearson, the senator invited me to his office on Capitol Hill, where he showed me his notes for the book and insisted that Pearson had it all wrong. Over the years, Sorensen has been steadfast in his assertion that he was not the author of *Profiles in Courage*. But his disavowal has not gone unchallenged. In a 1980 book called *Jack: The Struggles of John F. Kennedy*, the historian Herbert Parmet detailed his thorough investigation of the creative process that produced *Profiles in Courage* and came to the conclusion that it was essentially ghostwritten. "The research, tentative drafts and organization were left to the collective labors of others," Parmet wrote, "and the literary craftsmanship was clearly the work of Ted Sorensen."

CLINT HILL

THE FLAP OVER THE PEARSON interview was my only contact with the illustrious politician who had been my boyhood neighbor. During the years when Kennedy was in the White House and leading us across the New Frontier, I had various assignments that took me to cities at home and abroad, but Washington was seldom one of them. Fact is, I was going through a series of twists and turns as I jumped around from one job to another, and I didn't settle down until March 1963, when I went to work for CBS News, which has been my professional home ever since. In September of that year, CBS launched a new midmorning news show, and I was assigned to anchor it; that's what I was doing on November 22, the day the shots rang out in Dallas.

Many of us who lived through the shock and the grief of that day were inclined to view the Kennedy assassination as a ghastly aberration, the kind of horrific deed that simply did not happen in a civilized society and would never occur again in our lifetime. That naive assumption was shattered by subsequent events, for instead of being an isolated tragedy, Kennedy's murder was the first in a wave of comparable assaults on political leaders that persisted over the next decade and beyond. The two most charismatic black leaders of the civil rights era were gunned down by assassins, Malcolm X in 1965 and Martin Luther King, Jr., three years later. And just two months after King was killed, a second Kennedy was slain in the midst of his own campaign for president. In 1972, at another campaign stop in another presidential race, Alabama governor George Wallace was shot. He survived that attack, but the wounds he suffered left him paralyzed for life. And in September 1975, President Gerald Ford was the target in California of two assassination attempts that took place within seventeen days of each other.

Every fresh act of violence rekindled memories of the first Kennedy assassination, and not long after the attempts on President Ford's life, I interviewed the Secret Service agent who had been assigned to Kennedy's car on that dreadful day in November 1963. His name was Clint Hill, and over the years he'd refused to talk in public about what had happened in Dallas, or about any other aspect of his work with the Secret Service. But Hill had been granted early retirement in the summer of 1975, and now that he was no longer on active duty, he agreed to appear on *60 Minutes* to answer questions—for the first time—about the assassination he had witnessed from such close range.

In preparing for that interview, I learned that the shooting in Dallas had left Hill deeply troubled and stricken with guilt. Nonetheless, I was caught off guard by the raw, visceral anguish he displayed when I brought up the subject.

WALLACE: Can I take you back to November twenty-second in 1963? You were on the fender of the Secret Service car right behind President Kennedy's car. At the first shot, you ran forward and jumped on the back of the president's car—in less than two seconds—pulling Mrs. Kennedy down into her seat, protecting her. First of all, she was out on the trunk of that car—

HILL: She was out of the backseat of that car, not on the trunk of that car.

WALLACE: Well, she was— She had climbed out of the back, and she was on the way back, right?

HILL: And because of the fact that her husband's—part of his—her husband's head had been shot off and gone off to the street.

WALLACE: She wasn't— She wasn't trying to climb out of the car? She was—

HILL: No, she was simply trying to reach that head, part of the head.

WALLACE: To bring it back?

HILL: That's the only thing—

At that point, Hill broke down; tears streamed down his face. I sat in silence for a moment or two and then gently asked if he would prefer to move away from this painful memory and talk about something else. But he made it clear that he wanted to go on, and so, after he'd regained his composure, I continued to question him about that day.

WALLACE: Was there any way— Was there anything that the Secret Service or Clint Hill could have done to keep that from happening?

HILL: Clint Hill, yes.

WALLACE: "Clint Hill, yes"? What do you mean?

HILL: If he had acted about five-tenths of a second faster, or maybe a second faster, I wouldn't be here today.

WALLACE: You mean you would have gotten there and you would have taken the shot?

HILL: The third shot, yes, sir.

WALLACE: And that would have been all right with you?

HILL: That would have been fine with me.

WALLACE: But you couldn't. You got there in less than two seconds, Clint. You couldn't have gotten there. You don't— you surely don't have any sense of guilt about that?

HILL: Yes, I certainly do. I have a great deal of guilt about that. Had I turned in a different direction, I'd have made it. It's my fault.

WALLACE: Oh, no one has ever suggested that for an instant! What you did was show great bravery and great presence of mind. What was on the citation that was given you for your work on November twenty-second, 1963?

HILL: I don't care about that, Mike.

WALLACE: "Extraordinary courage and heroic effort in the face of maximum danger."

HILL: Mike, I don't care about that. If I had reacted just a little bit quicker, and I could have, I guess. And I'll live with that to my grave.

I've never interviewed a more tormented man. Hill's agony was so deep, so poignant, that I couldn't resist getting swept up by it, and there were times during our conversation when I could feel my own tears welling up. Many of our viewers were no less affected, as we learned from the letters that flooded into our office in the days following that broadcast.

In our interview, Hill said that a "neurological problem caused by what happened in the past" had prompted his doctors to urge him to accept retirement from the Secret Service at the still-youthful age of forty-three. When the camera wasn't rolling, he was even more candid. What our audience wasn't told was that he was suffering from severe depression.

In the years since our 1975 interview, I've inquired about Hill from time to time to see how he was doing and to pass along my best wishes. But I didn't have any direct contact with him again until the fall of 2003, when all the media were turning their attention to the fortieth anniversary of the Kennedy assassination. I wanted to know if Clint would be willing to revisit the subject in another interview with me. When I called him at his Virginia home just outside Washington, he greeted me warmly, and although he made it clear he did not want to talk any more about that day in Dallas, he assured me he was fine and that the misery he'd gone through was now behind him. He had finally managed to put his demons to rest, and he no longer blamed himself for the death of John F. Kennedy.

LYNDON JOHNSON

THAT TRAGEDY IN DALLAS ELEVATED Lyndon Johnson to the presidency, and I had a memorable encounter with him two years after his stormy reign in the White House had come to an end. The occasion was a *60 Minutes* piece on the opening of the Lyndon Baines Johnson Presidential Library in the spring of 1971. The event was considered so major that Don Hewitt, the executive producer of *60 Minutes*, elected to fly to Texas with me and our production crew to take part in our coverage of the story.

Johnson had been practically hounded from office by the groundswell of opposition to his war policies in Vietnam. By the time he left the White House, he had become an almost desolate figure, no longer welcome in the high councils of his own party. Since then, he'd been living as a virtual recluse on his ranch in the Texas Hill Country, where, according to some reports, he was so consumed by bitterness that he spent a lot of his time brooding over his fate and nursing his grievances.

Johnson's resentment extended to the press, which he blamed for having fanned the flames of protest that undermined his presidency, and for the most part, he had turned a cold shoulder to reporters. But the opening of his presidential library put him in a more receptive mood. The library had been conceived as a lasting memorial to the great achievements of his domestic policy, and now that it was ready to be unveiled to the public, Johnson was not only willing but eager to cooperate with the media. So much so that when he learned we were planning to do a *60 Minutes* story on the opening, he invited Hewitt and me to be his guests at the ranch. Nor was that all. When we arrived at the airport, Johnson and his wife, Lady Bird, were on hand to greet us and take us under their wings. Even by the larger-than-life standards of Texas hospitality, it was an expansive, even effusive welcome, which we appreciated.

The next morning we were roused from our beds bright and early. Johnson, reveling in his role as über-host, was eager to give us a tour of the ranch. Along with two other guests, we were herded into his white convertible, and with LBJ himself at the wheel, we took off on the sightseeing ride at an alarmingly high speed. At one point, as we careened around the large spread, the former president swerved off the road and hit the brakes. He'd seen something that clearly distressed him. "Hewitt," he barked, "you want to pick up that candy wrapper?"

Hewitt, sitting next to me in the back, snapped to attention. "Mr. President?" he exclaimed in a startled tone.

Johnson turned and glared at Don, then gestured toward the offensive object. "That candy wrapper," he reiterated. "How about picking it up?"

It was obvious he had no intention of resuming our tour until his order had been carried out, and so, while the rest of us sat in the convertible and watched with amused approval, Hewitt sheepishly got out and did his part to combat the crime of littering at the LBJ ranch. He stuffed the candy wrapper into his pocket and returned to the car. But before he had a chance to get in, Johnson began to pull away, with Hewitt trotting along behind us in pursuit. This antic sideshow did not last long; once Johnson realized he had been a bit too hasty, he stopped the car again and let Don back in.

On reflection, the candy-wrapper incident shouldn't have surprised us that much, for throughout his long career in Washington, Lyndon Johnson had a well-earned reputation for being almost compulsive in his need to exert authority and dominate all who came into his presence. While it was true that he was no longer the political force he'd been during his years in power, he continued to rule his own turf. At the LBJ ranch, he was still the commander in chief.

Back in 1964, when LBJ was in the exuberant early days of his presidency, reporters covering him wrote and broadcast vivid accounts about his harrowing high-speed rides around the ranch. On at least one of those occasions, Johnson drove with just one hand on the wheel, while in the other one, he clutched a beer can from which he heartily guzzled. Once a can was empty, he invariably flung it out the window. In writing about that, some reporters observed that the president's behavior was hardly in keeping with the campaign the First Lady had recently adopted as her pet project: a major effort to clean up and beautify the nation's parks and highways. In light of our experience with the candy wrapper, I can only conclude that by 1971, Lady Bird had brought her husband around to her way of thinking. As students of formal religion are well aware, there is no greater passion than the zeal of a convert.

Later that day we drove over to the new library, situated on the campus of the University of Texas at Austin. Hewitt and I had decided to structure our piece in the form of a tour, with President Johnson as our guide. We went through a couple of informal rehearsals that afternoon to get the feel of things and set up camera angles. Even in those dry runs, the former president displayed understandable pride as he led us past exhibits honoring his achievements in civil rights, Medicare, and other landmark programs that fell under the heading of the Great Society. When we moved into a much smaller area in the library that dealt with foreign policy, he called our attention to an exhibit on the 1967 Six-Day War in the Middle East. But in glancing around, we couldn't help noticing that the war in Vietnam was conspicuously absent. When I asked Johnson about that, he turned somber and spoke almost in a whisper. "We don't have that one filled in yet," he said. "Besides, I've already talked about Vietnam over and over again. So there's no need to talk about it here."

Hewitt and I looked at each other in disbelief. Don began to argue that we couldn't ignore Vietnam, that it was an essential part of LBJ's presidency. Johnson refused to budge. "I don't want to talk about Vietnam," he snarled. Turning to me, he said that if I brought up Vietnam while the cameras were rolling, he would cut off the tour on the spot and "send you boys packing."

That was enough to alarm Hewitt, who promptly walked away, leaving me alone with Johnson. After a brief silence, I decided to try to persuade him from a different angle, one that would be both ingratiating and combative, a dual tactic Johnson himself had often employed to great effect. I told him that I'd been a fervent admirer of his ever since the Eisenhower years, when he had demonstrated his political genius as majority leader in the U.S. Senate. I said that even back then I thought he was exactly the kind of president the country needed—a white southerner with progressive views on the race issue—and that when the forces of history and fate later conspired to put him in the White House, he had more than lived up to my high expectations. In particular, I said, he deserved the highest praise for the strong civil rights legislation he maneuvered through Congress during his first two years in office, since there was no question in my mind that he had done more to advance the cause than any president since Lincoln. "But then," I said, "everything turned sour, Mr. President, and you know why?"

"Why?" he rasped.

"Because you let that war get out of hand." I took a deep breath and then forged ahead, man-to-man. "Vietnam fucked you, Mr. President, and so, I'm afraid, you fucked the country. And you've got to talk about that!"

Johnson glared at me with startled fury and then stalked off. In retrospect, I'm not sure why I asked the question in that manner.

I suspect my thought process went something like this: Okay, if he refuses to talk about Vietnam, then I'll remind him, using his own forceful and graphic language, about the terrible damage that war did to him and, through him, to the American people.

The reaction to my intemperate remark was not what I had feared. Even though Johnson was steamed (to put it mildly), he did not go to Hewitt to complain that I had stepped out of line. Nor did he go through with his threat to send us packing. We proceeded to film our story, and when the time came for Johnson to guide us past the exhibits, I honored his request and did not ask about Vietnam. But to my astonishment, he brought it up himself. We'd just finished talking about the critical challenges that a commander in chief had to confront in the nuclear age when, out of the blue—without a hint or warning of any kind—the words came pouring out of him in a torrent:

"Throughout our history, our public has been prone to attach presidents' names to the international difficulties. You will recall the War of 1812 was branded as Mr. Madison's War, and the Mexican War was Mr. Polk's War, and the Civil War or the War Between the States was Mr. Lincoln's War, and World War One was Mr. Wilson's War, and World War Two was Mr. Roosevelt's War, and Korea was Mr. Truman's War, and President Kennedy was spared that cruel action because his period was known as Mr. McNamara's War. And then it became Mr. Johnson's War, and now they refer to it as Mr. Nixon's War in talking about getting out. I think it is very cruel to have that burden placed upon a president, because he is trying to follow a course that he devotedly believes is in the best interest of his nation. And if those presidents hadn't stood up for what was right during those periods, we wouldn't have this country what it is today."

A few minutes later, after we'd finished shooting and were preparing to leave, Johnson turned to me and said: "Well, goddammit, Mike, I gave you what you wanted. I hope you're satisfied."

"Oh, I am, Mr. President, I am," I assured him.

Johnson's outburst provided the climax of our story, and when we aired it in a few days, I concluded the piece with the following comment on the man and his presidency:

"What he hopes most is that he will be remembered for his Great Society and not for Vietnam. But the tragedy of Lyndon Johnson is that, although he accomplished so much for so many while he was in office, historians are bound to write of him principally as the president who bogged his country down in Vietnam. It is some measure of the man, I think, that on that matter—Vietnam—he has not wavered. He still believes that he was right, and that history will prove it."

As we would later learn, it was not quite as simple as that. Throughout the mid-1960s, as he ordered one escalation after another, Lyndon Johnson projected the image of a confident president who deeply believed he was pursuing a course that would ultimately lead to a U.S. victory. All his public statements echoed the smug optimism of his military commanders, who kept assuring us that we were winning the war in Vietnam. Although many of us eventually became disillusioned with Johnson and his war policies, we did not question his credentials. We assumed that his various decisions to expand the war were driven by sincere convictions.

Now, alas, we know how brazenly he lied to the American people. The stunning transcripts in a 2001 book called *Reaching for Glory: Lyndon Johnson's Secret White House Tapes, 1964–1965,* compiled by the historian Michael Beschloss, reveal that as early as 1965—the year he ordered the huge buildup in Vietnam that, in effect, transformed the conflict into a full-scale American war—Johnson had reached the despondent conclusion that the war was unwinnable. In a conversation with one of his aides, he lamented that sending "good American boys" to their deaths in a futile war made him feel like a pilot who has to fly a flaming aircraft without a parachute. In an anguished exchange with his onetime mentor, Senator Richard Russell of Georgia, he said that "a man can fight if he can see daylight down the road somewhere. But there ain't no daylight in Vietnam. There's not a bit."

So why did Johnson act against the grain of his own instincts? Why did he make the decision to lead America into an all-out war that he privately believed could not be won? Politics? To judge from the tapes that Beschloss assembled and other evidence, he did so mainly because he was convinced that if he abandoned the military commitment he had inherited from the Kennedy administration, right-wing Republicans and other militant anti-Communists would destroy him politically. What a sad irony that is, for in the end it was the war—and the fierce opposition it provoked—that demolished his presidency and left an enduring stain on his place in history.

But in my judgment, that doesn't mean Vietnam is destined to be LBJ's ultimate legacy: We should keep in mind that Lyndon Johnson's presidency was an epic drama that produced both tragedies and triumphs on a grand scale. It's entirely possible that in the long view of history, the disastrous blunders of his policies in Vietnam will be eclipsed by the towering achievements of his Great Society programs, especially in the areas of civil rights and health care.

RICHARD NIXON

I OBSERVED THE COLLAPSE OF Lyndon Johnson's presidency from the vantage point of the campaign waged by the man destined to succeed him. Covering Richard Nixon's triumphant run in 1968 turned out to be my last major assignment as a general correspondent for CBS News. In September of that year, *60 Minutes* made its debut and I began the best, the most fulfilling job a reporter could imagine.

When I hooked up with the Nixon campaign in the early fall of 1967, the public's prevailing view was that he was damaged goods, a political has-been. There was no doubt that he had serious image problems. During his years as Dwight Eisenhower's vice president,

Nixon was a favorite target of pundits and cartoonists, many of whom routinely portrayed him as a devious opportunist, "Tricky Dick." Others saw him as a ruthless hatchet man who concealed his natural malice behind a facade of pious platitudes. And to go along with that baggage, he had to bear the stigma of sore loser, which stemmed in part from his narrow defeat by Kennedy in 1960 and even more from his far more decisive loss when he ran for governor of California in '62. It was on the night of that humiliating setback when he held his "last press conference," where, with bitter sarcasm, he told the assembled reporters, "Just think how much you're going to be missing. You won't have Nixon to kick around anymore. . . ."

Of course, that prophecy turned out to be extravagantly premature, for here he was, five years later, making another run for the White House. For some reason, I had a hunch that Nixon's prospects were not as dismal as they were judged to be by the heavyweight political reporters who worked out of Washington, and so I found myself drawn to his candidacy. At the least, I was curious to see how far his comeback attempt would carry him. There was a lot of talk that fall about the so-called New Nixon, and no one preached that born-again sermon with more fervor than Len Garment, a partner at the Wall Street law firm that had been Nixon's professional base during the years when he wasn't actively engaged in politics. Garment was a key player on Nixon's newly formed campaign team, and in an effort to learn more about that operation, I had lunch with Len one day in September of '67. By chance, it happened to be Yom Kippur, the holiest day on the Jewish calendar. Here were Garment and I, two backsliding Jews, breaking forbidden bread together while our more pious brethren observed the traditional rites of prayer and fasting.

"You're looking at a lifelong Democrat," he told me that day. "A couple of years ago I would have been the last person in the world to support Richard Nixon. But he's changed. The years in exile have made him a better man, a more thoughtful and more compassionate man. But don't take my word for it. Judge for yourself. All I ask is that you come to us with an open mind."

I assured Garment that I did my best to bring an open mind to *every* assignment I undertook. I also reminded him that, unlike the Washington press corps, I had not been exposed to Nixon during the "Tricky Dick" phase of his career, so my coverage of his comeback campaign would not be burdened by all those biases and preconceptions.

Not that it seemed to matter much, because at the time hardly anyone was paying close attention to Nixon. In fact, his campaign had attracted so little notice that I was one of a mere handful of reporters bothering to cover it. In that early autumn of '67, most of the big media guns were trained on the acknowledged front-runner for the Republican nomination, the popular governor of Michigan, George Romney. And that was exactly how Nixon wanted it. In the early stages of the campaign, he clearly welcomed our neglect. When one of his aides expressed concern about all the coverage Romney was attracting, Nixon replied, "Good, I want him to get the exposure. We have to keep him out at the point."

To sharpen the contrast, Nixon maintained such a low profile that through most of that fall, his was almost a stealth campaign. Because the atmosphere was so subdued and laid-back, gaining access to the candidate was not the problem it would become in later months, after the campaign had shifted into high gear and begun to move with bandwagon force. I recall in particular a long flight to Oregon one day in November. (That state's primary loomed as a pivotal test the following spring.) As it happened, I was the only reporter who made that trip, and not long after we took off from New York,

Nixon invited me to sit with him. For the next hour or so, he and I talked in a relaxed and rambling vein about the campaign, the various issues, and what he hoped to accomplish as president. I had other casual conversations with him from time to time, and I gradually began to form my own impressions of the man and his candidacy.

Most of them, I must admit, were favorable. The Nixon I came to know in 1967 did not strike me as devious or ruthless or any of the other negative things I'd heard or read about him over the years. I had no idea if this was because he had undergone some radical change—had actually metamorphosed into a "New Nixon"—and frankly, I didn't care all that much. But I can say that if it was a new persona, it did not include the kind of warm and ebullient disposition we normally find in politicians. Nixon was always courteous and sometimes even cordial, in his stiff and formal way; still, when it came to charm or charisma, he was a far cry from contemporary rivals like Hubert Humphrey and Nelson Rockefeller, both so congenitally outgoing that either could—and invariably did—brighten and invigorate a room simply by entering it.

Nixon had other strengths. I was especially impressed by his penetrating intelligence, his broad and sophisticated view of history, and his profound grasp of the difficult challenges he would confront in the White House. And at that point, I saw no reason to doubt his sincerity or question his character.

I also had respect for his political savvy. He certainly had the right take on poor George Romney, who was indeed flummoxed by all the glare and pressure of the day-to-day scrutiny that is inevitably directed at a front-running candidate for president. All through the waning weeks of 1967 and the first two months of 1968, Romney committed one blunder after another, and more often than not, when he tried to talk his way out of some gaffe, he only made it worse. His campaign was so inept that it prompted a fellow Republican governor—James Rhodes of Ohio—to observe that "watching George Romney run for the presidency was like watching a duck try to make love to a football."

Meanwhile, Nixon was charging out of the shadows, and as the campaign approached its first critical test—the New Hampshire primary—he had built a commanding lead over Romney. Moreover, other polls indicated that he had substantial leads in states where primaries were scheduled for later that spring, and although George Romney may not have known how to run for president, he did know when to quit. Rather than go through the ordeal of getting trounced by Nixon, the governor abruptly pulled out of the race just two weeks before the voters in New Hampshire registered their official verdict.

So all of a sudden, Richard Nixon—the notorious loser and presumed has-been—had the Republican playing field to himself. It's true that in the months to come, he would have to withstand the challenges of two other Republican governors, Nelson Rockefeller of New York and Ronald Reagan of California, but by the time they announced their candidacies, it was too late to enter any of the primaries—and thus too late to inflict any serious damage on Nixon.

A week or so after Nixon cruised to his undisputed victory in New Hampshire, Len Garment came to me with a proposition: "The boss would like you to join up, to come aboard and work with us."

I was flabbergasted. I had never given any thought to a move in that direction. "To do *what,* exactly?" I asked.

"I'm not sure," said Garment. "You know we're not that well organized yet. But I imagine it would be press secretary or communications director, or something like that."

I admit that I seriously considered accepting the offer. I was now convinced that Nixon had a virtual lock on his party's nomination and a better-than-even chance of winning the election in November. If that proved to be the case, then I'd be joining the team headed for the White House. I was intrigued by the prospect of becoming involved in the adventure of a new presidency. I talked it over with my wife and also with a few close friends and colleagues whose judgment I respected.

In the end, I decided it was not for me. I wrote Nixon a letter thanking him for the offer, but said I couldn't accept it because I didn't think I had the proper temperament to serve as a spokesman or apologist for any politician. Elaborating, I wrote that I would find it difficult to "put a good face on bad facts." Only later, when the Nixon White House was rocked by scandal and crisis, would I fully realize just how sound—and lucky—my decision had been. I've often shuddered at the thought of how I might have fared if I'd been the president's spokesman when the Watergate dam broke in the tumultuous spring of 1973.

I continued to cover the Nixon campaign as it glided serenely through the spring primaries and across the summer of 1968. In early August, the Republicans assembled at their convention in Miami Beach, where Nixon had to contend with the late challenges by Rockefeller and Reagan. Though their strenuous efforts to pry delegates away from Nixon enlivened the proceedings with a certain superficial suspense, I remained convinced that neither governor had a chance of wresting the nomination away from the old pro. From my front-row seat on the Nixon bandwagon, I had seen enough to appreciate how thorough and adept the candidate and his team had been in putting together their broad coalition of moderates and conservatives from all regions of the country. So, while others seemed surprised by how easily Nixon won the nomination on the first ballot, I was not.

Once the convention was over, I left the Nixon campaign. Don Hewitt had been given the green light to proceed with his innovative plan for a magazine show, and I'd accepted his offer to cohost the new program with my good friend Harry Reasoner. I confess that when Hewitt first came to me with his proposal, I was so unimpressed that I nearly turned him down. At the time, the idea of a magazine for television was an alien concept that was not easy to envision. The TV journalism that existed then was neatly divided into two distinct and traditional formats. One was the daily or nightly news show, and the other was the documentary, and never the twain did meet. Hewitt's scheme was to merge the two formats into some kind of multisubject hodgepodge, and I didn't believe he could make it work; even if he did, I thought, he'd be lucky to keep the new program going through one full season, two at the most. (So much for my prophetic talents.)

Still, I was reluctant to say no to Hewitt, who already had a reputation for being one of the most creative producers in the history of television news. As a young pioneer in the early days of the medium, he'd invented the evening news show at CBS and had nurtured it through its formative years. What's more, when Don Hewitt is delivering a sales pitch at full cry, it is almost impossible to resist him. Once he had brought all of his evangelical powers into play, he soon won me over, and I agreed to be part of his experimental new broadcast, which he had decided to call *60 Minutes*.

At some point during the week of the Republican convention, I informed Garment and some of Nixon's other deputies that I was moving on to another assignment, but that message must not have been relayed to the candidate himself. When Nixon came to the hall on the last night of the convention to deliver his acceptance speech, I was standing near the podium with some other reporters. As he passed by, he peered into our group looking for familiar faces and tossed personal greetings to some of us who had been with him since—as he liked to put it—"the snows of New Hampshire and before." When his gaze fell on me, he said, "Hi, Mike, I'll see you in California next week. We'll be out there planning the campaign."

"No, Mr. Nixon, I thought you knew. I'm peeling off the campaign after tonight to work on a new television series."

Nixon was dumbfounded; he looked at me as if I'd gone bonkers. Clearly, he could not comprehend how I, one of the first reporters to take his political comeback seriously, could walk away from the campaign at this triumphant juncture. He seemed almost insulted, as if I were casting a vote of no confidence in his ability to beat the Democrats in the general election, and had thus made up my mind not to waste time covering him after the convention. He seized the moment to set me straight on that score.

"We're going to win this thing, Mike," he predicted. "And later, after we get to Washington, we're going to take some great trips."

I had no idea what to make of that bizarre non sequitur. After all, every American president since World War II had felt obliged from time to time to visit other countries for one reason or another, and I assumed Nixon would be no exception. Well, so what? Was I supposed to be tempted by that travel-agent come-on? But a few years later, when Nixon became the first U.S. president to set foot in the Communist capitals of Beijing and Moscow, it occurred to me that those breakthrough missions had been on his secret agenda since before his election, and that was the cryptic message he'd been trying to get across to me that August night in 1968.

The premier edition of *60 Minutes* was scheduled for September 24, and I spent the rest of the summer and early fall preparing stories for that show and subsequent broadcasts. The next time I saw Nixon again in person was in early October, when I interviewed him for *60 Minutes*. He was then moving into the final month of his long campaign, and recent polls were showing him with a solid lead over his Democratic rival, Vice President Hubert Humphrey. One of the votes he'd be getting in November was mine, which was a fairly radical step for a guy who had never voted for a Republican in a national election.

Covering the Nixon campaign that year no doubt helped nudge me toward that sharp break with my past. There's no denying that proximity to a candidate is an occupational hazard that can affect the judgment of even the most scrupulous reporter. (In spite of Aesop's famous dictum, familiarity does not *always* breed contempt.) But more than anything else, it was the war in Vietnam that drove me into the Nixon camp.

By 1968 the country was so bitterly divided over the war that it seemed to me that only with fresh leadership in Washington could we begin to heal the psychic wounds tearing us apart. It's true that the prime target of the antiwar protests—President Lyndon Johnson—had removed himself from the political line of fire when he chose not to run for a second term, but the way I saw it, his decision did not let the Democrats off the hook. They still had to bear responsibility for the war, especially since their nominee, Humphrey, had been such an enthusiastic supporter of LBJ's policies. In my view, a Republican coming into the White House with a clean slate would be in a stronger position to lead us out of the morass, and in covering Nixon that year, I came to believe he had the qualities needed to meet that challenge.

However, most of my friends and CBS colleagues did not agree with me. In spirited arguments that fall, they kept insisting that I'd been duped by all the talk about a New Nixon, which they dismissed as so much malarkey. To them, he was still "Tricky Dick," a master of deception who would say or do anything to get elected. Their antipathy was very much on my mind when I interviewed Nixon in October at his New York apartment, and I put the question to him directly.

WALLACE: The name Nixon is anathema to millions of American voters. To them, Richard Nixon is a political opportunist to whom the desired political end has justified just about any political means. How does Richard Nixon, if elected, go about reconciling the doubts of the skeptics?

NIXON: I do have, based on a hard political career going back over twenty-two years, some people in this country who consider me as anathema, as you pointed out. But on the other hand, I believe that I have the kind of leadership qualities that can unite this country and that at least can win the respect if not the affection of those who have a very bad picture of Richard Nixon.

The theme of respect must have been paramount in his thoughts that day; at another point in our interview, he made a similar observation that, in light of later events, would take on an even deeper irony. Here is what he said:

"If I do win this election, I think I will conduct the presidency in a way that I will command the respect of the American people. That may not be the same style of some of my predecessors, but it will enable me to lead. Let me make this one point: Some public men are destined to be loved, and other public men are destined to be disliked. But the most important thing about a public man is not whether he's loved or disliked, but whether he's respected, and *I hope to restore respect to the presidency at all levels by my conduct*." (Italics are mine.)

Looking back at that pious pronouncement, it's almost too easy to feel scorn. We hardly need to be reminded that instead of restoring respect, Richard Nixon brought disgrace to the presidency. Yet even before he was engulfed by the Watergate deluge, I'd become disillusioned with his leadership. Rather than taking decisive steps to bring an end to our disastrous misadventure in Vietnam, he allowed that war to drag on and on. Four years after he became president, young Americans were still fighting—and dying—in Vietnam. In retrospect, I could only conclude that I, along with millions of other gullible voters, had gravely misjudged Richard Nixon.

But I would rather not end this reminiscence on such a sour note. I still prefer not to think of Nixon as the president who betrayed the trust of those who had believed in him; instead, I remember him for something he did on the night of the 1968 New Hampshire primary.

My assignment that night was to cover his New York headquarters, where he was awaiting the returns. The big news from New Hampshire was not that Nixon had won (by then he had no serious opposition) but that he had received more votes than any candidate in any presidential primary in that state's history, a stunning show of support for a man who, just a few months earlier, had been dismissed as a chronic loser. At one point that evening, Nixon emerged from a back room with his wife, and I was able to bag a short interview with him for our election broadcast. After getting his reaction to the heavy primary vote, I put the microphone in front of a visibly nervous Pat Nixon, who tautly but dutifully answered a couple of innocuous questions about the huge victory. I thanked her and dashed off to the CBS studio to do a live report. No sooner was I off the air than a phone call came in from Nixon. "I just wanted to thank you, Mike, for being so nice to Pat," he said. That was all, but it revealed a thoughtful and caring side of Nixon I had never seen before and would not see again.

For many of Nixon's detractors, the disdain they felt toward him extended to his wife. She was often derided as "Plastic Pat," a term coined, I believe, by Gloria Steinem. But I did not view her that way.

It's true that Pat Nixon usually came across as aloof and wary and even, at times, a little stilted and artificial (hence the "plastic" label), but there were reasons for that. For one thing, she was even more reserved than her husband and almost painfully shy. And for another, unhappy memories of personal attacks on her family in past campaigns had left her feeling bruised and vulnerable; as a result, she hated being thrust into the limelight and put on display. Yet even though Mrs. Nixon had no stomach whatsoever for the raucous commotion that is so much a part of American politics, she joined her husband on the campaign trail and did her best to be seen as a loyal and supportive wife. From what I observed, she was unfailingly courteous, in her tense and self-conscious way, to the reporters and other pests who swarmed around her in one public forum after another. Finally, there was the way she conducted herself during the Watergate crisis. Having to cope with all that must have been a terrible ordeal for her, and yet from beginning to end, she invariably projected a quiet dignity and forbearance.

TWO

FIRST COUPLES

ELEANOR ROOSEVELT

OF ALL THE FIRST LADIES who have graced the White House in my lifetime, there was one who towered over all others, just as her husband towered over all other presidents who came to power during the last century. When I interviewed Eleanor Roosevelt on my ABC show in November 1957, twelve years had passed since her husband had died in office. Yet his bold leadership and progressive New Deal policies continued to cast a strong shadow across our political landscape. And Franklin D. Roosevelt was still a polarizing figure, as his widow readily acknowledged when I asked her about the passions FDR aroused in the hearts of so many Americans.

WALLACE: Mrs. Roosevelt, I'm sure that you understand the sense in which I put this question to you, but I think that you would agree that a good many people hated your husband. They even hated you.

MRS. ROOSEVELT: Oh, yes. A great many do still.

WALLACE: Why? Why?

MRS. ROOSEVELT: Well, if you take stands, in any way, and people feel that you have success in a following, those who disagree with you are going to feel very strongly about it.

WALLACE: There's more than just disagreement involved. There are people who disagree with President Eisenhower, and yet they do not hate him. I lived in the Middle West for a good many years while your husband was president, and there was a real core of more than just disagreement.

MRS. ROOSEVELT: There was a real core of hatred. The people would call him "that man." I remember one man who rejoiced, actually, when he died. But I suppose that this is just a feeling that certain people had that he was destroying the thing that they held dear and touched them. And naturally, you react to that with hatred.

What was left unsaid—but clearly understood by the two of us and most of our viewers—was that for all those who despised Roosevelt, there were millions more who revered and loved him. That was certainly the case in my family. I was fourteen when FDR was elected president in 1932, and along with my brother and two sisters, I was caught up in the pro-Roosevelt fervor that swept through our household. My parents' admiration for Roosevelt bordered on hero worship.

There were several reasons for this ardor. Like millions of other

Americans, our family was struggling to cope with the miseries of the Great Depression, and Roosevelt's New Deal seemed to offer hope and opportunity where none had existed before. Beyond that, my parents and other immigrants of that era felt a special bond with Roosevelt. They sensed that unlike the run-of-the-mill politicians who had preceded him in the power centers of Washington, he respected their ethnic and religious diversity, traits that already were starting to redefine our national character. In both his message and manner, FDR made people like Frank and Zina Wallace feel more at home in this new land of milk and honey.

Roosevelt's sensitivity in this regard was even more impressive in light of the fact that he himself was so far removed from the immigrant experience. He was the scion of a patrician Dutch-American family whose roots in the Hudson Valley could be traced back to the colonial days of the seventeenth century. FDR was denounced by his fellow blue bloods as "a traitor to his class," and he relished their disapproval. One time, while delivering a speech at a convention of the Daughters of the American Revolution (a blue-blooded group if ever there was one), Roosevelt began his remarks with two words guaranteed to ruffle the feathered finery of the ladies in the audience. "Fellow immigrants" was how he greeted them.

But that was nothing compared to the controversy that flared up in 1939 when Eleanor Roosevelt renounced her long-standing membership in the Daughters of the American Revolution. She resigned in protest of that organization's refusal to allow the African-American singer Marian Anderson to perform at Constitution Hall, which was owned by the DAR. In her public comments, Mrs. Roosevelt made it clear that she was offended by that decision and could in no way be a party to it, even by implication. Nor was that all. She then helped organize a campaign to promote a concert by Anderson at the Lincoln

Memorial, and there—on Easter Sunday 1939—the world-renowned contralto sang before an estimated crowd of seventy-five thousand, far larger than a capacity audience at Constitution Hall.

Taking a strong stand on a highly charged issue was typical of Mrs. R, as she was sometimes called, and that was what distinguished her so sharply from her predecessors. For the most part, the previous First Ladies had been content to be national hostesses. Rarely, if ever, had they injected themselves into the public debates and political storms that swirled around them. Such matters were deemed beyond their proper range of concerns.

From the beginning, she was a vigorous missionary for her husband's policies. She seemed to be constantly on the march across America, carrying the banner of the New Deal on her visits to factories and mine shafts and sharecropper farms. She traveled so much that she came to be known as the president's eyes and ears, and because FDR was crippled with polio, she was often said to be his legs as well.

Eleanor Roosevelt's influence extended long beyond her reign as First Lady. After leaving the White House, she continued to dedicate her life to public service with her work at the United Nations, where, among other posts, she was chairman of the UN Commission on Human Rights. By the time I interviewed her, she had achieved even more stature than she had enjoyed during her years in Washington. She had become a moral force on the global stage, our special ambassador to the world, a woman respected even by our cold-war enemies in the Communist bloc.

But she still had her critics, and none more caustic than Westbrook Pegler, the hard-hitting columnist who was the conservative scourge of that era. Pegler had made almost a career out of bashing the Roosevelts, husband and wife, and in our 1957 interview, I asked for Mrs. Roosevelt's reaction to some accusations I quoted from one of his columns. "This woman is a political force of enormous ambitions," Pegler wrote. "I believe she is a menace, unscrupulous as to truth, vain and cynical—all with a pretense of exaggerated kindness and human feeling which deceives millions of gullible persons."

This was her response: "Well, it seems to me a little exaggerated, let us say. No one could be quite so bad as all that. And as far as political ambition goes, I think that rather answered itself, because I've never run for office and I've never asked for an office of any kind. So I can't have much political ambition. . . . I think it must be terrible to hate as many things as Mr. Pegler hates. I would be unhappy, I think, and therefore I am afraid that he's unhappy, and I'm sorry for him, because after all, we all grow older and we all have to live with ourselves, and I think that must sometimes be difficult for Mr. Pegler."

Mrs. Roosevelt had her own newspaper forum, the "My Day" column she'd been writing since her White House years, and in it she did not hesitate to express her own opinions. Later in our conversation, I brought up a speculative column she had written about President Eisenhower's eventual successor, in which she asserted that of all the likely Republican contenders, Vice President Richard Nixon "would be the least attractive." Not content to leave it at that, she went on, "Mr. Nixon's presidency would worry me."

When I asked Mrs. Roosevelt why she had singled out Nixon for special criticism, she replied, "I think that in great crisis, you need to have deep-rooted convictions, and I have a feeling from the kind of campaigns I have watched Mr. Nixon in, in the past, that his convictions are not very strong."

Among her fellow Democrats, her big favorite in those days was

Adlai Stevenson, who had been the nominee in the two losing campaigns against Eisenhower. She had some misgivings about the rising young star in her party, Senator John F. Kennedy, and offered her own tart comment about *Profiles in Courage*. She didn't challenge Kennedy's authorship, as Drew Pearson had, but she did suggest in a mischievous way that the title was not altogether seemly. Taking into account the senator's movie-star looks and alleged timidity on such cutting-edge issues as McCarthyism and civil rights, Mrs. Roosevelt said she would feel more positive about "young Senator Kennedy if only he had a little less profile and a little more courage."

But Mrs. Roosevelt eventually came to admire Kennedy, and when he emerged as the Democratic nominee in 1960, she actively supported his candidacy. Which is hardly surprising in view of the fact that JFK's opponent that year was the man she regarded as the "least attractive" Republican. Two years after Kennedy's election, Eleanor Roosevelt died at the age of seventy-eight, and for those of us who lived through the years of crisis and triumph that defined FDR's presidency, her passing truly marked the end of an era.

Yet there's a postscript of sorts. Many years after Eleanor Roosevelt's death, I met her grandson David Roosevelt. We had mutual friends, and through them he and I became friends. He was a member of the FDR Memorial Commission, and for years he had devoted much of his time to the long-stalled effort to erect a monument to his grandparents in Washington.

The Roosevelt Memorial Commission had been established in 1955, when David was a boy of thirteen, and four years later, land was set aside on the hallowed ground around the Tidal Basin, not far from the White House. Only three other presidents have been honored with memorials at that location, and their names are Washington, Jefferson, and Lincoln. Pretty strong company, to be sure, but in my view, Franklin D. Roosevelt deserves his place in that pantheon.

For a variety of reasons—the usual combination of red tape, inertia, and disagreements that had to be resolved—the memorial was not completed until 1997. The dedication was scheduled for May 2 of that year and, to my utter astonishment, David asked me to serve as master of ceremonies at the event. It was a glorious occasion, a historic milestone if ever there was one, and being invited to take part in it was an honor and a privilege I will always cherish. My only regret is that my parents were no longer around to see their boy Myron up there on the podium with President Clinton and the other big shots as we all paid tribute to the president and First Lady they so revered. They would have beamed with pride and happiness.

JIMMY AND ROSALYNN CARTER

MOST OF THE FIRST LADIES who followed Eleanor Roosevelt into the White House didn't exactly follow in her footsteps. Her immediate successors, in particular, chose to revert to the traditional role of modest hostess. Bess Truman had such a retiring personality that her public appearances were confined largely to ceremonial functions that she felt obliged to attend, and she steadfastly refused to be drawn into discussions about policy issues or political disputes. She left all that to Harry. Mamie Eisenhower was cut from similar cloth; after all, she had spent most of her adult life in a military culture, where the wives of officers were expected to know their subservient place. Jackie Kennedy, it's true, had a far more visible presence and was widely admired for her beauty and elegance and aesthetic sensibility. But the impact she had was almost entirely in style and tone (all that preening over Camelot); she, too, shied away from political conflicts and other quarrelsome matters. Lady Bird Johnson's grand passion was her beautification program, and although her husband offered lip-service support to her efforts in that area, sprucing up the nation's parks and highways was hardly a top priority on LBJ's ambitious agenda for a Great Society, as he demonstrated on those rambunctious rides around his ranch.

In contrast to those examples (and others like them), we have the two-term reign of Hillary Rodham Clinton, who, by any conceivable measure, must be regarded as the most independent and politically active First Lady since Eleanor Roosevelt. Among other distinctions, Mrs. Clinton was the first presidential wife who came of age during the women's movement, and she brought a keen feminist edge into the arena of a national election. Along with other controversial remarks she made in the course of her husband's 1992 presidential campaign, Mrs. Clinton described herself as the kind of wife who would not be content to stay home and "bake cookies." Such assertive candor was applauded by many Americans—especially women of her own generation—but many others were turned off by what they considered her pushy and arrogant attitude. As a result, she became as polarizing a figure in our politics as Eleanor Roosevelt had been, and she would continue to attract a steady barrage of both kudos and brickbats throughout her years in the White House.

But there was no denying her independence and professional status. Hillary Clinton came to Washington from a flourishing career as a lawyer, and no other First Lady ever brought to the post such impressive credentials. Like her husband, she was an indefatigable policy wonk, and from the moment she moved into the White House, she devoted her time and considerable energy to a variety of pet issues, from health care reform to equality for women and children's rights.

Mrs. Clinton had another distinction that set her apart from her predecessors, though she would no doubt prefer that it not be cited. She became the first First Lady to go through a long siege of exposure about her husband's sexual peccadilloes, most notably the hanky-panky with Monica Lewinsky that led to his being impeached—though not convicted—by Congress. Yet for Hillary Clinton, that scandal may have been a subtle blessing. As millions of Americans came to appreciate that even a tough lady can be wronged, she began to attract more sympathy and support than she had ever enjoyed before, and that helped to give her the boost she needed to pursue her own political ambitions. While still serving in the White House, she launched a campaign for major public office, a bold and radical step that no other First Lady—not even Eleanor Roosevelt—had dared to take. And following her 2000 election to the U.S. Senate, Hillary Clinton became the first former First Lady to be seriously touted as a future candidate for president.

Among the other First Ladies who have served during my life-time, Rosalynn Carter is the one I would single out who came the closest to Eleanor Roosevelt's and Hillary Clinton's political activism. I didn't meet the Carters until March 1985, when I visited them in Plains, their small hometown in rural Georgia, and by then, four years had passed since they'd left the White House. During their time in Washington, most of my journalistic focus had been on the Middle East and on investigative pieces that exposed con men and other rogues. Hence, I never got around to doing a story on any aspect of the Carter administration. Nevertheless, I had been intrigued by Jimmy Carter's unexpected rise to power. Unlike Lyndon Johnson, he was from the Deep South—the heart of the Old Confederacy—and until he made his triumphant 1976 run, I had shared the conventional wisdom that no politician from that region could ever be elected president. Carter managed to turn that time-honored maxim on its head, and that struck me as some kind of political miracle.

Yet the time was ripe for such a miracle. In 1976 millions of Americans were yearning for a change in political leadership, and one that went beyond the periodic shift in power from one party to another. The four presidents who had preceded Carter—Kennedy, Johnson, Nixon, and Ford—had cut their political teeth on Capitol Hill and had used their seats in Congress as springboards to national office. To varying degrees, they were all creatures of the Washington establishment, the power elite, and it was generally assumed that without such inside-the-Beltway status, one could not hope to make a successful run for the White House.

But by 1976, Washington politicians had lost their luster, to put it mildly. Thanks to the double whammy of our ignominious failure in Vietnam, a disaster that drove a president out of office, and the Watergate scandal, which forced another to resign in disgrace, many Americans had become convinced that what was desperately needed in the White House was fresh leadership from someone who had not been tainted by the corruption and cynicism of the Washington power game. From the moment he announced his candidacy, Jimmy Carter brilliantly exploited that discontent. He presented himself as a rank outsider—a simple, no-frills peanut farmer with a "just folks" personality—and he built his campaign around the modest promise that he would never "lie to the American people." Because his down-home approach struck such a responsive chord, he became the first governor since FDR to capture the White House.

I was also intrigued by Rosalynn Carter and her determination to take on a prominent role in her husband's presidency. She, too, asserted herself in ways that broke with tradition. Until she came along, no First Lady ever had the temerity to attend cabinet meetings, but with her husband's blessing, Mrs. Carter occasionally sat in on them. She also represented the president at ceremonial events and even served as his official emissary on a diplomatic visit to seven countries in Latin America. In her tone and manner, Rosalynn Carter came across as a typically gracious southern belle; her voice was as soft and sweet as warm molasses. But beneath that mellow surface, she could be as hard as nails, and the Washington press corps routinely referred to her as "the Steel Magnolia." In viewing Mrs. Carter from a distance, I didn't see her that way. In fact, I found her to be most attractive and appealing.

The skill and success that Jimmy Carter brought to the campaign trail in 1976 did not carry over into the White House, in large part because he had the misfortune to be president during a deeply troubled time in our history. Thanks mainly to the dislocations set in motion by the Arab oil boycott of the mid-1970s, he had to contend with soaring inflation and other economic woes. And during the last year of his presidency, he struggled in vain to bring an end to the hostage crisis in Iran. Carter's problems on the economic front and his failure to resolve the hostage crisis made him a vulnerable target when he ran for reelection in 1980, and he was soundly trounced by his Republican opponent, Ronald Reagan. Four years later, Reagan succeeded where Carter had failed and easily won his bid for a second term.

President Reagan's landslide victory in the fall of 1984 was still fresh in everyone's minds when I flew down to Georgia the following March to interview the Carters for a 60 Minutes story that we called "Plain Talk from Plains." When I sat down with the former president,

I promptly referred to the man who had ousted him from the White House.

WALLACE: You must be very jealous, in a sense, of Ronald Reagan.

CARTER: Not really.

WALLACE: Jealous of the fact that he is— I mean, if his is the "Teflon presidency," nothing sticks—

CARTER: Mine was the opposite.

WALLACE: Yours was the "flypaper presidency."

CARTER: I think that's true. When I was there, there was no doubt who was responsible. I was responsible. And now there is a great deal of doubt about who's responsible, and Reagan has been extremely successful, more than any of his thirty-nine predecessors, in not being responsible for anything that's unpleasant or not completely successful.

WALLACE: How does he manage that, Mr. President?

CARTER: Well, he's blamed me for his two-hundred-billion-dollar deficits. He's blamed me and Ford and Nixon for his lack of understanding of the Lebanon crisis, saying that this intelligence network was not adequate for him. He's blamed the Congress for his withdrawal of the marines from Lebanon under, you know, very damaging circumstances, and—and he has never accepted responsibility for lack of progress in Middle East peace or a lack of progress on alleviating the problems of the poor and so forth. . . .

Throughout our interview, the former president kept coming back to what he regarded as Reagan's lack of moral leadership in foreign policy, and that led to the following exchange.

WALLACE: You think we're closer to war today than we
should be?

CARTER: I think we have let the world know that our country
is no longer the foremost proponent or user of negotiations
and diplomacy, and that our country's first reaction to a troubled area on earth is to try to inject American military forces
or threats as our nation's policy.

WALLACE: Human rights under Ronald Reagan.

CARTER: Well, Reagan has basically abandoned our
nation's commitment to the human rights policy that we
espoused.

WALLACE: Why? Because he's a callous man?

CARTER: I don't know what his motivations are, but the result
has been that the world now sees our country as not being a
champion of human rights, but as being dormant, at best, in
the face of persecution.

The plain talk in Plains became even more pungent when I interviewed Rosalynn Carter. On the subject of Reagan, she was even
more critical than her husband had been.

MRS. CARTER: I think this president makes us comfortable
with our prejudices.

WALLACE: That's not very nice, what you're saying.

MRS. CARTER: But it's the way I feel, and I think it's true. . . .
I think he's been devastating to the country and—

WALLACE: How? How has he devastated the country?

MRS. CARTER: Well, I wouldn't trade places with him in history, with Jimmy and Ronald Reagan, for anything in the
world.

As she spoke, her face was clenched in anger. She obviously despised Ronald Reagan, and to judge from her frosty response to my presence, she didn't care much for me, either. (Perhaps she'd heard that Nancy Reagan was a friend of mine.) Whatever the case, on that day Rosalynn Carter was pure steel; the magnolia facade had disappeared. But that was not my last encounter with the former First Lady, and the next few times I saw her, the context had nothing to do with partisan politics.

At the time of my 1985 visit to Plains, I was recovering from a severe bout of clinical depression. Thanks to a wise and caring psychiatrist and the medication he prescribed, I was able to break out of that terrible darkness. I'll be writing more on that episode in a later chapter, but for the moment let me just say that for years afterward I didn't tell many people about my affliction. Except for my doctor and family and two very close friends, nobody knew what a painful ordeal I had gone through. And there was a reason for such reticence; given my fishbowl line of work and my reputation for being a tough and abrasive reporter, I was ashamed to be identified as the sort of "pathetic wimp" who had suffered from depression. For that, I knew, was the popular (though completely erroneous) perception of the disease.

But as time passed, I gradually came around to the view that if I talked about my experience in public, it just might help others come to a better and more accurate understanding of depression. Thus, for the past ten years or so, I've done just that, on Larry King's television show and similar interview programs, as well as at other public forums. Though I've resisted the various efforts to depict me as a poster boy for depression, I have agreed to speak at occasional fund-raising events, and it was at these fund-raisers that I began running into Rosalynn Carter. As I soon learned, she has been vigorously engaged in programs to eradicate the stigma attached to depression and similar afflictions ever since her years in the White House, when she served as the honorary chairperson of the president's Commission on Mental Health.

I should point out that her dedication to helping the less fortunate is a moral imperative she shares with her husband, who is living testament to the belief that presidents can go on to serve their country with impressive distinction even after they're voted out of office. In fact, Jimmy and Rosalynn Carter have been such paragon role models that they may have set the gold standard for conduct and achievements by former first families. Since leaving Washington, the ex-president has been in the forefront of the vigilant effort to assure honest elections in emerging democracies around the globe, and that is only part of his larger commitment to the cause of human rights. In addition, he has brought his own hammer-and-nails labor to the task of building habitats for humanity.

As for the commitment I shared with Mrs. Carter to combat the ordeal of depression and other threats to mental health, I must say that the more we saw of each other, the warmer and more cordial our relationship became. The last time our paths crossed was at a fund-raiser in Atlanta. In what can only be regarded as an eerie, even morbid coincidence, two of the best friends I've ever had—Art Buchwald and William Styron—were stricken with depression around the same time that I was. Their ordeals were just as harrowing as mine, and because Art and Bill and I enjoy a certain celebrity status, we're sometimes asked to appear together at fund-raising events as a kind of depression team or trio, and that was what the three of us were doing in Atlanta in the spring of 2004. By then we had begun to bill ourselves as "the Blues Brothers." That, I grant you, is not the most clever pun ever coined, but it did help to attract attention. About eight hundred donors showed up that night to hear us relate our tales of woe, and as we walked out on the stage, I spotted Rosalynn Carter sitting in the front row. I still find her attractive, so I waved to her and said, "Hi, good-looking." She rewarded me with a radiant smile: On that occasion, she was all magnolia.

RONALD AND NANCY REAGAN

WHILE ROSALYNN CARTER WAS A relatively new friend, the woman who succeeded her as First Lady was a dear old friend. In fact, I'm certain I was the only working journalist who could boast that I had known Nancy Reagan longer than her husband had.

Throughout most of the 1940s, when I was in the early phase of my career in broadcasting, I had lived and worked in Chicago, where I jumped around quite a bit from one radio job to another. One of my regular assignments was to announce and narrate programs at the CBS station WBBM, and there I was befriended by an actress named Edie Davis, who performed on various network soap operas that originated from WBBM. She was not only talented but versatile; on one show called *Betty and Bob,* Edie played both the society grande dame and the black maid Gardenia. And though she was old enough to be my mother—I was then twenty-four and she was forty-six—we became close pals. Edie was gregarious and high-spirited and, at the time, the bawdiest woman I had ever met. I frequently ran into her in the station's green room, where we all gravitated for coffee and gossip, and invariably, she would greet me with some choice obscenity and then proceed to relate, with lip-smacking glee, the latest dirty joke she had heard. She was a pip, and since I was a new kid on the block of big-time broadcasting and still a little intimidated by the challenge, I treasured her warmth and friendship.

Edie was married to an eminent neurosurgeon, Loyal Davis, and she had a daughter from a prior marriage to a car salesman. In fact, six-year-old Nancy had been the flower girl at her mother's wedding to Loyal. By the time I met her, Nancy Davis was a student at Smith College, and I remember her as a prim and proper young lady who often wore white gloves and Peter Pan collars. Although I didn't know her well in those days, she struck me as being shy and reserved— almost the opposite of her exuberant mother—and so I was rather surprised when I later learned that "sweet little Nancy" (as I then thought of her) had gone off to Hollywood to seek her own fame and fortune as an actress. While she managed to land a few roles in minor films, her dream of becoming a star didn't pan out, at least not in the conventional Hollywood way. But the path she chose did lead to real-life romance. The next thing I heard, she was getting married to the well-known actor Ronald Reagan. I didn't give much thought to that at the time except to harbor the hope, as I would for any friend, that her marriage would bring her a lifetime of happiness.

Years passed. I moved on to New York, where I continued to bounce from one news job to another, among other chores, until I finally settled down in 1963 as a correspondent for CBS News. In California, meanwhile, Reagan's acting career lapsed into decline. The more it languished, the more time and attention he devoted to politics. By the early 1960s, he had become an eloquent spokesman for the conservative wing of the Republican Party. For a long time, Reagan's political speeches were largely dismissed as another ego trip by a Hollywood star who believed his celebrity gave him the authority to pontificate on Soviet aggression and other burning issues of the day. Then came his 1966 campaign for the governor's chair in California.

It was Reagan's first run for public office of any kind, and he confounded the experts by defeating the two-term Democratic incumbent, Edmund G. (Pat) Brown. Just like that, a rank political amateur had become governor of our largest state and, by definition, a political force on the national stage.

Still, I didn't imagine Reagan had much chance of capturing the White House, or even had the ambition to run. For one thing, his brand of conservatism had been thoroughly discredited in Lyndon Johnson's landslide victory over Barry Goldwater in 1964. For another, there was the question of credentials, or lack of them. Reagan's professional identity may not have been viewed as a liability in California, where actors are as plentiful as geezers in Florida or oil barons in Texas, but I found it hard to envision voters across the country entrusting the nuclear trigger and complex questions of foreign policy to a man who was known primarily as "the King of the B Movies."

Needless to say, I kept those reservations to myself when I ran into Edie Davis and her daughter at the 1968 Republican convention in Miami Beach. They were there to voice support for Reagan's eleventh-hour effort to wrest the nomination from Nixon. Our brief reunion took place on the convention floor, and with the CBS cameras rolling, I asked Edie if she offered Nancy and her husband advice on how to raise their children.

"Oh, heavens no," she replied. "I want them to still speak to me."

"Well," I reminded her, "you did such a good job yourself."

"You helped me."

I have no idea what she meant by that, because as I said, I hadn't met Nancy until she was a college student, and even then I didn't really know her well.

Reagan completed his second term as governor in 1974. That was also the year the Watergate crisis reached its boiling point and brought the end to Nixon's presidency. That disruptive change did not deter Reagan from going ahead with his plan to run for president in 1976, even though such a move now meant challenging the new White House incumbent, Gerald Ford, for the Republican nomination.

In the fall of 1975, shortly after he announced his candidacy, I did a profile of the Reagans for *60 Minutes*. Part of the story dealt with such predictable matters as Reagan's campaign strategy and his political philosophy. At the time, most Americans didn't know very much about the Reagans as a couple, so most of what we filmed was a family portrait. We showed them relaxing at their 640-acre ranch near Santa Barbara, where I talked to them at some length about the life they shared and their rapturous devotion to each other. I had heard a charming story about the circumstances that first brought them together in Hollywood, and so I asked Nancy about that.

WALLACE: Mrs. Reagan, I understand that you met this fellow first about twenty-four years ago because you were a subscriber to the *Daily Worker*. The Communist Party newspaper?

MRS. REAGAN: I wasn't, but there was a Nancy Davis who was. I was doing a picture for Mervyn LeRoy, and I complained to him about it. And he said, "I know Ronald Reagan. He's president of the Screen Actors Guild, and he'll be able to straighten out your problem."

WALLACE: You didn't want to get on any blacklist or anything of the sort? Nancy Davis, *Daily Worker* subscriber.

MRS. REAGAN: (Laughs) Well, at that point I just wanted to meet Ronald Reagan.

She had recently been quoted as saying that "my life began when I met Ronnie," and I mentioned that when some people heard that, they were inclined to chuckle. And she replied, "Well, then they chuckle. But it did." For his part, Reagan was no less rhapsodic in his comments about their relationship.

> REAGAN: For all the years we've been married, it's been "we," not "you and I." It would be inconceivable to me to go my own way on something without her. And I think it would be the same with her.
>
> WALLACE: She's your Lady Bird?
>
> REAGAN: (Laughs) No, no. There's no Lady Bird in Nancy.
>
> WALLACE: What do you mean?
>
> REAGAN: Well, you've known her longer than I have. And you know her as a very private person, and a very vulnerable person.

Although Reagan did not succeed in his insurgent campaign against President Ford, he came a lot closer to winning the GOP nomination in 1976 than many of us had anticipated. And if, as expected, he chose to run again in 1980, he was likely to be even more formidable. Like many other Americans, I'd underestimated Reagan's appeal as a national candidate, and for me, this was starting to pose a problem. There was no doubt in my mind that Nancy (and, to a lesser extent, her husband) looked upon me more as a friend than as a reporter.

In fairness, they had little reason to think otherwise. The only major story I had done on them was the 1975 profile, which turned out to be not much more than a soft-touch feature piece. That, of course, had been our intention; we had purposely set out to do a "getting to know you" story. But with the arrival of 1980 and another campaign, one that could easily put the Reagans in the White House,

I decided the time had come to make it clear to them that being their friend did not make me their toady. And the best way to get that point across would be to interview the candidate and confront him with questions I was certain he wouldn't like. In other words, no more Mr. Nice Guy.

The opportunity came in July 1980, when I sat down with Reagan at his home in Pacific Palisades a few days before the Republican convention opened in Detroit. Having breezed through the primaries that spring, he had a firm lock on the nomination. In our interview, I asked him about his lingering reputation as a super-hawk, an inflexible foe of détente with the Soviet Union and China. I alluded to recent polls that indicated many Americans still viewed the prospect of his presidency with alarm and apprehension. Some of them had told pollsters they were actually scared to have him in the White House. I also reminded him about the outlandish stand he had taken back in 1965, when he declared, "It's silly talking about how many years we'll have to stay in the jungles of Vietnam when we could pave that whole country, put parking stripes on it, and still be home for Christmas."

I then brought up another hot-button issue: Reagan's reputed lack of rapport with the African-American community. Just a few days earlier, he had incurred the wrath of many blacks when he disregarded an invitation to speak at the NAACP's annual convention. The head of that organization, Benjamin Hooks, called the lack of response a snub, and one more example of Reagan's "racial insensitivity" and avoidance of public appearances with black leaders. After Reagan and I had talked a little about that, I decided to bring the issue closer to home.

WALLACE: How many blacks are there on your top campaign staff, Governor?

REAGAN: I couldn't honestly answer you. No.

WALLACE: That speaks for itself.

REAGAN: Huh?

WALLACE: I said, that speaks for itself.

REAGAN: No, because I can't tell you how many people are on the staff.

WALLACE: But you can tell black from white.

REAGAN: Oh yes, but I mean we've got a mix of volunteers and staff members and—

WALLACE: I'm talking about top campaign staff.

REAGAN: Well, let me put it this way—

WALLACE: Let me not belabor it. I mean, apparently, there are none.

REAGAN: No, I don't think so. I mean, I'm— I don't— I don't agree with you on that.

In addition to being flustered, Reagan was miffed. And so was his wife. While I pressed him about blacks and his reputation as a belli-cose cold warrior and other sore points, I was acutely aware of Nancy, across the room, in an agitated state, beyond the range of the camera; I could almost feel her glaring at me. When we paused briefly to put a new roll of film in the camera, she marched over to me, eyes ablaze, and opened fire: "Mike Wallace, what kind of ques-tions are you asking? Why are you doing this to Ronnie?"

I responded, wearily, with the standard reporter's explanation that in asking the kind of questions that upset her, I was merely do-ing my job. Her reaction to my little lesson in Journalism 101 was swift and sure: The next thing I knew, Nancy had flung herself onto my lap and was giving me a big hug. That may have been nothing more than an impulsive show of affection, but I suspect it was more likely a move calculated to underscore our long friendship and thus remind me that no friend of hers should be "doing this to Ronnie." In any event, we all burst out laughing, and that eased the tension a bit. But I obviously had hit a nerve or two, and over the next few days, I kept hearing comments about how much I had upset Reagan, Nancy, and his people. The reports of their displeasure were, of course, music to my ears.

Reagan went on to his nomination at the GOP convention, and from there he marched through his victorious campaign against President Carter. Although Nancy and I kept in fairly close touch with each other during her eight years in Washington, it was mutually understood that our telephone conversations were strictly off the record; even now it would not be proper for me to violate that confidence. I can say, however, that she was a very savvy politician in her own right, and she had firm—often critical—opinions about some of the president's top advisers. But much to my regret, not once did she steer me toward an inside story that I could report on *60 Minutes*. Most of the time we simply nattered on in the familiar manner of two friends who'd known each other for decades.

More than anything else, perhaps, we talked about our kids. Nancy was somewhat estranged from her daughter, Patti, and son, Ron, and I tried to help her deal with that. Actually, she probably saw more of my son Chris in those days than she did her own children, because he was then covering the White House for NBC News, and doing a first-rate job on that beat. I know from what Chris told me that Nancy always greeted him warmly, but when it came to getting inside scoops about life and work in the White House, he had no better luck than I did.

Over the past three decades, Chris has built up his own solid reputation as a television correspondent. I'm obviously proud of the fact that he decided to pursue a career in broadcasting, even though it wasn't his first choice. When he graduated from Harvard in 1969, his sights were set on print journalism, and he landed a job covering city hall for *The Boston Globe*. After some gentle prodding from me and his stepfather, my good friend and longtime colleague Bill Leonard (who later became president of CBS News), Chris crossed over to our branch of the media. Following the usual path, he started out in local news and moved on to the networks, first NBC, then ABC, and, most recently, Rupert Murdoch's domain, where, on *FOX News Sunday,* he demonstrates week in and week out that he's better at anchoring a news show than I ever was.

Getting back to Nancy, the difficulties she went through with her children were all the more poignant because they were in such sharp contrast to the warm and loving relationship she had with her own mother. Edie Davis died in 1987 at the age of ninety-one. I wrote a farewell tribute to her for *The Washington Post,* and in putting it together, I was struck by how fortunate my old friend had been. Not only had she enjoyed a long and full life, but during her golden years, she experienced the deep satisfaction of seeing her daughter live in the White House as First Lady to an extremely popular president who also happened to be a most devoted son-in-law. One of the joys of Edie's life was that every year on her daughter's birthday, Reagan would send her flowers to thank her for having given birth to Nancy.

The last time I interviewed Reagan on *60 Minutes* was in January 1989, just before his two-term reign came to an end. Among the questions I put to him on that occasion were several about decisions and policies that had provoked serious criticism and thus were apt to leave blemishes on his legacy. In particular, I brought up the Iran-Contra affair, the big-time scandal that shook up the White House power structure and even threatened to destroy his presidency. Reagan acknowledged that 1987—the year the scandal dominated the political headlines—had been "a very tough year," but he said he could not discuss the specifics of the elaborate deception because some of the legal cases had not yet been resolved. However, he did make a point of saying that "the whole Iran-Contra affair has been terribly distorted by the media up and down," and he expressed confidence that the misadventure would have little or no lasting impact on his reputation.

Self-confidence had often been cited as one of Reagan's political strengths, so I asked him about the almost jaunty optimism and bonhomie he had projected throughout his eight years in Washington.

WALLACE: We've heard the presidency called the loneliest job in the world, a splendid misery, whatever, and I have never sensed that you have been the least bit miserable or the least bit lonely in this job. Why hasn't this job weighed as heavily on you as it has on some other occupants of the Oval Office?

REAGAN: Well, Mike, I don't know what the answer to that would be. Maybe none of them had a Nancy. But I came here with a belief that this country, the people, were kind of hungering for a, call it a spiritual revival. The whole thing of the sixties and the rioting and so forth and the disillusionment with Vietnam, it seemed that the people had kind of lost faith in the destiny of this country and all. And I came here with, as I say, plans, and set out to implement them. No, we didn't get everything we asked for, but you don't fall back in defeat.

There was no doubt in my mind that Reagan had infused the White House with a pride and self-assurance that had not been seen there since the invigorating years of Kennedy's New Frontier and the early days of the Great Society, when LBJ was still a commanding presence. In the process, Reagan made millions of Americans feel better about their government, their country, and even themselves. After all the disruptions and setbacks we had been through, we needed an emotional uplift, and Reagan gave us that. Intangible though it was, I regard that as one of his most impressive triumphs.

As for substance, I think Reagan deserves a large share of the credit for one of the towering achievements of our time: the collapse of Soviet power in Europe that brought an end to the cold war. It's true, of course, that by the time he became president, the Soviet system was already sliding into serious dysfunction. But Reagan's decisions to beef up the U.S. military and expand the frontiers of nuclear technology put so much pressure on the Russians that they came to realize that a peaceful solution was their best option. When the time came for critical discussions at the summit meetings with Mikhail Gorbachev, Reagan proved to be an adept and flexible negotiator. To the astonishment of many—especially his detractors—the old cold warrior, who had once denounced the Soviet Union as "an evil empire," transformed himself into an ardent peacemaker.

In our interview, Reagan recalled how that transformation began in earnest in 1985, at his first summit meeting with Gorbachev. At one point, he said, the two leaders slipped away from the arms negotiations and went off by themselves to a lakeside cottage, accompanied only by their interpreters. For over an hour, they sat in front of an open fire and chatted. Here's part of that conversation as Reagan remembered it four years later:

"I said, 'We don't mistrust each other because we're armed. We're armed because we mistrust each other. And while it's all right to talk about arms and limitations on arms, why don't you and I see if we can't eliminate the things that caused the mistrust.' I further said to him that here we were, two men in a room together, and we probably had the power to start World War Three. But by the same token, we had the power to bring world peace."

By the time their tête-à-tête came to an end, Reagan and Gorbachev had agreed to visit each other in their respective capitals, and the president recalled with relish the reaction of his negotiating team to that startling development: "I want to tell you, when the general meeting was over, and I told our people that it was already agreed upon that there were going to be two more summits in the United States and in Moscow, they fell down. They couldn't believe it!"

I am hardly the only member of the journalism fraternity who awards high marks to Reagan's presidency. At the time of the millennium, *Time* magazine and CBS News collaborated on a most ambitious undertaking: to select from all walks of life the hundred most influential men and women of the twentieth century. Along with renowned world leaders and scientists and artists and captains of industry, three U.S. presidents made the final cut. That's all, just three. Two of them are named Roosevelt. And the third is Ronald Reagan.

After the Reagans left the White House and returned to California, Nancy spent the next several months finishing a book, and I interviewed her when it was published in the fall of 1989. The book was called *My Turn,* and the title could not have been more apt, because many of its pages were devoted to settling scores with high-ranking members of the Reagan administration who, in one way or another, had triggered her criticism, especially Don Regan, the president's chief of staff. Her provocative book induced a provocative interview, and there were times when Nancy expressed irritation at my approach. When I brought up an incident that strongly implied she "felt that George Bush lacked political courage," she asserted in a scolding tone: "You're putting words in my mouth, Mike Wallace!"

Toward the end of our interview, I mentioned how the Reagans were cashing in on their first-couple status by attracting very handsome lecture fees. That led to my comment on an extravagant junket they were about to take.

WALLACE: You're going to be in Japan, and I'm told it's a two-million-dollar two weeks.

MRS. REAGAN: They're getting two of us. They're working us like crazy. We're taking the wives of servicemen over there so that they can see their husbands.

WALLACE: But it's going to be a well-recompensed two weeks.

MRS. REAGAN: It is for everybody who goes there, which you probably know. Now, you really didn't need that question.

I could tell from her icy stare and the metallic tone in her voice that this time she was really sore at me. I later learned that Nancy felt I had sandbagged her because I didn't let her know in advance that I intended to ask her about the Japanese junket. This, alas, is an all too familiar complaint: guests who happily appear on *60 Minutes* to plug their latest book (or whatever) and then are angered when we stray from that subject and bring up matters they would prefer not to discuss.

In any event, when Nancy passed the word that she was no longer speaking to me, I could only assume that was the end of our long friendship. Then one night some two or three months later, she was a guest on Larry King's show, and I happened to be watching when King mentioned our falling-out and asked her if we were still estranged from each other. In reply, she asked Larry if she could send a message to me over the air. He said sure. Nancy looked directly into the camera and asked me to call her, which I did the next day. The upshot was that we patched everything up, and since then, I'm happy to say, our friendship has been as strong as it ever was.

My last *60 Minutes* interview with her took place in 2002, eight years after her husband wrote a letter to his fellow Americans, informing us that he had begun his descent into the dark oblivion of Alzheimer's disease. In that letter, Reagan wrote, "I only wish there was some way I could spare Nancy from the painful experience." After quoting that line to Nancy, I suggested that he had been more anguished about her future sorrow than his own. And she agreed.

Much of that interview was an exercise in nostalgia. The two of us looked at excerpts from the 1975 story, at the ranch in the mountains above Santa Barbara. We talked about how happy their life together had been in those days and about the joy that awaited them a few years later on the way to the White House. What made 2002 an especially sad time for Nancy was the fact that in March of that year, she had observed her fiftieth wedding anniversary. Yet by then her husband was deep in the abyss of his dread disease, so she was unable to celebrate it with him. I asked her about that.

WALLACE: What did you do that day?

MRS. REAGAN: Nothing. And how I'd love to be able to talk to him about it. And there were times when I had to catch myself, because I'd reach out and start to say, "Honey, remember when . . ."

WALLACE: Yeah. Do you think he knows you still?

MRS. REAGAN: I don't know . . .

WALLACE: What are your days like? What do you do all day?

MRS. REAGAN: Well, I see friends. Not every day. I stick pretty close to home, really.

WALLACE: Lonely?

MRS. REAGAN: Yes, it's lonely. Because really, you know, when you come right down to it, you're in it alone, and there's nothing that anybody can do for you. So it's lonely.

WALLACE: It was back in 1975 [when] you said that your life began with Ronald Reagan, and you've also said that you can't imagine life without Ronald Reagan. And now you're in the midst of what you call your long good-bye. Have you said good-bye?

MRS. REAGAN: No, not really. He's there. He's there.

For a year or so after we did that story, I would hear rumors from time to time that Reagan was on the brink of death. I would then call Nancy, who would quickly assure me that in spite of his terrible illness, her husband was still holding firmly on to life. But when I called her on the first Saturday in June 2004 and asked if the latest reports I had heard about him being near death were the usual false alarms, she replied no and quietly confirmed that this time he was indeed dying. She went on to say that her son, Ron, and daughter, Patti, were with her at his bedside and that they did not expect him to last through the weekend. Of course, I offered my deepest condolences, and after we finished talking, I called the CBS News desk to alert them to the situation. About three hours later, the bulletin came in from California that Ronald Reagan had died. And in the stately rituals and tributes that extended through the following week, millions of her fellow Americans, along with dignitaries from other countries, joined Nancy Reagan in the final chapter of her long good-bye.

THREE

RACE IN AMERICA

ELDON LEE EDWARDS
JAMES EASTLAND
ORVAL FAUBUS

THE STRUGGLE FOR RACIAL EQUALITY has pulsated through the American bloodstream since the early abolitionists launched their crusade to eradicate slavery. And of all the stories that have engaged my attention over the years, none was more significant or compelling than the civil rights movement that began in the mid-1950s and extended through most of the '60s.

My first professional dealings with America's racial conflict came in 1957, when I interviewed a couple of die-hard segregationists who staunchly defended the Jim Crow laws that were still in effect throughout the South. When our *Night Beat* team made the move to ABC in the spring of that year, one of our first guests on the network program (rechristened *The Mike Wallace Interview*) was a fellow named Eldon Lee Edwards, who made his living as a paint sprayer in Atlanta. But that was merely his day job, for he much preferred to be identified by the title that defined his nocturnal activities: Imperial Wizard of the Ku Klux Klan.

The KKK had been around since the days of Reconstruction, when its night riders, dressed in white robes and hoods, roamed across the rural South and spread terror among the recently freed slaves in an effort to discourage them from exercising the rights of citizenship they had been granted by new federal laws. But by the 1950s, the Klan was no longer the menacing force it had been in earlier decades. Even in the South, there were signs that it was not taken seriously; to many southerners, the Klan had become an embarrassment, even a bit of a joke.

Eldon Edwards struck me as a cartoon figure when he arrived at our New York studio in full Klan regalia. With his ankle-length robe, conical hood, and emblematic cross stitched across his heart, he looked for all the world like someone who had just stumbled in from a Halloween party. But his manner could not have been more earnest, and he was not amused when I asked him if the Klan was now perceived as an object of mirth.

WALLACE: Do people regard it as something comical, as kind of a comic opera?

EDWARDS: No, they do not.

WALLACE: You feel that the South respects the Klan?

EDWARDS: Well, they do, they respect the Klan for the principles for which it stands.

To challenge that assertion, I quoted from an article that had recently appeared in *The New York Times*. According to the *Times* story, when three Klansmen showed up on a busy street corner in Montgomery, Alabama, in their robes and hoods, "several Negroes looked unflinchingly at the robed men and began to smile and then to laugh." White onlookers also greeted the Klansmen with "grins of amused incredulity," and one of them said in a mocking tone, "Looks like they've been lost out of one of them old movies."

Edwards dismissed the story as propaganda, claiming that the *Times* and all other major American newspapers—including the two in his hometown, *The Atlanta Constitution* and *The Atlanta Journal*—were "controlled" by the NAACP and the Anti-Defamation League of B'nai B'rith. When I asked him if he had any evidence to support such an irresponsible charge, his only response was a knowing smirk. From the look in his eyes, I inferred that Edwards regarded me—a northern Jew who worked in the New York media—as part of the sinister conspiracy. He was far less reticent when I asked him about Klan dogma on the subject of racial purity.

WALLACE: In one piece of Klan literature that you furnished us, it is charged, quote, "One drop of Negro blood in your family destroys your white blood forever." I take it that you believe that?

EDWARDS: Well, I wouldn't define it down to one drop now. But here it stands to reason, as common sense, that mongrelization means destruction. It means the destruction of the white race. It means the destruction of the Nigra race. I sure will believe in segregation for the simple reason we believe in preserving and protecting God's word. He created the white man. He intended for him to stay white. He created the Nigra. He intended for him to stay black. And we believe that mongrelization destroys both races and creates a mongrel which is not a race.

Although the opinions he expressed were repellent, Edwards and his fellow Klansmen could be dismissed as beyond-the-fringe extremists whose heavy-handed racist views were not shared by respectable, law-abiding southerners, even those who supported segregation. What I found far more disquieting was an encounter I had later that year with another ardent segregationist who was also a prominent and influential member of the southern power bloc in Washington—Senator James Eastland of Mississippi.

It was our custom in those days to announce at the end of each broadcast who was slated to be next week's guest. On the Sunday before Eastland's scheduled appearance, I closed the show with the following promotional pitch: "Next week we go after the biggest fight the Confederate states have had since Bull Run—the battle for civil rights. We will get the story from the controversial, outspoken senator from Mississippi. He's James Eastland. We will try to find out why Senator Eastland charges that, quote, 'the Negro is an inferior race,' unquote, and why he described the United States Supreme Court as, and I quote again, 'a crowd of racial politicians in judicial robes.' Unquote."

I received a call from Eastland's office the next morning to inform me that the senator had seen my promo and wasn't going to answer "those kind of questions." I was told he was having second thoughts about appearing on our show under any circumstances, but he was willing to discuss the situation with me in his office. So Ted Yates and I quickly caught a flight to Washington. Known for his courtly manner, Eastland greeted us with suave courtesy, and for the next several minutes we gingerly talked around the subject of what questions might be appropriate if he decided to go ahead with the interview. Then, shifting abruptly to another tack, the senator inquired, "Mr. Wallace, who is your sponsor?"

"I don't know why you ask, Senator. You know it's the Philip Morris Company."

But I had a pretty good idea why he'd asked. Philip Morris had built a reputation as an equal-opportunity employer, a policy that did not win the tobacco company many friends in the South during that era of mounting racial tension. Moreover, Philip Morris had not only supported Negro newspapers with advertising dollars, they had also donated money to the Urban League and other civil rights organizations.

"Yes, Philip Morris," Eastland said in response to my answer, "yes, that's what I understand." With his soft voice and honeysuckle smile, he continued to project an amiable demeanor, but his words were anything but friendly. "Mr. Wallace, should you ask me questions which I find inimical, I just might find it necessary to point out that Philip Morris, that cancer-bearing agent, is regarded in the South as a Nigra-lovin' cigarette." He paused for a moment to let that sink in, and then said, "So perhaps you would now care to be guided by that in framing the questions which you intend to put to me."

Yates and I could hardly believe what we had just heard. "Nigra-lovin' cigarette"? I had to remind myself that this was a United States senator talking, not some Ku Klux Klan wizard who pranced around in a goofy costume. In any event, Eastland must have concluded that his boorish threat was enough to intimidate us, because he did agree to appear on *The Mike Wallace Interview* the following Sunday. When the time came, I didn't pull my punches; our interview did indeed revolve around the "kind of questions" I had previewed, and Eastland, to his credit, did not dodge them or sugarcoat his position as a strong segregationist. Nor did he go through with his threat to take a shot at Philip Morris and its alleged reputation in the South.

WALLACE: Senator, if a Negro maid or nurse is good enough to care for a white infant in the South—live with that infant, feed that infant, et cetera—why is not the same Negro maid allowed to eat in the same restaurant with southern whites?

EASTLAND: It's a matter of choice.

WALLACE: Choice by the whites?

EASTLAND: No, it's a matter of choice by both races.

WALLACE: Are you suggesting—?

EASTLAND: You know that in Mississippi, it was a Reconstruction legislature composed principally of Negroes that enacted our segregation statute.

WALLACE: Are you suggesting the Negro—?

EASTLAND: I'm suggesting that the vast majority of Negroes want their own schools, their own hospitals, their own churches, their own restaurants . . .

WALLACE: Are you saying that the Negro in the South wants segregation?

EASTLAND: Ninety-nine percent—yes, sir!

At another point in our interview, I asked Eastland if he thought "the day will come in your lifetime when we will see an integrated South."

"No," he replied without hesitation.

But James Eastland and his fellow segregationists were on the wrong side of history, for by 1957 there were already signs that the tide was turning against the status quo they were trying to preserve. Three years earlier, in one of the pivotal events in the advance toward civil rights, the U.S. Supreme Court had ruled in *Brown* v. *Board of Education* that racial segregation in public schools was unconstitutional. That historic decision set in motion the long and difficult process of integrating schools in communities throughout the South. The first major confrontation in that struggle took place in September 1957, and the battleground was Central High School in Little Rock, Arkansas.

In many ways, Little Rock was an unlikely setting for the racial violence that erupted there. Arkansas had a reputation for being more moderate than most other southern states, and its governor, Orval Faubus, was regarded as one of the region's more liberal politicians. (Shortly after he was elected in 1954, Faubus desegregated public transportation and appointed six blacks to the Democratic State Committee.) But resistance to legally imposed integration was hardening in Arkansas, as it was elsewhere in the South, and in the spring of 1956, the entire state legislature signed the Southern Manifesto, which denounced the Supreme Court's decision as "naked judicial power." Orval Faubus did not need a refresher course in political science to understand that if he hoped to remain in the governor's chair, he would have to come down firmly on the side of the segregationists.

In the summer of '57, the Little Rock school board put the finishing touches on its modest plan to integrate Central High School. Nine carefully selected Negro students were enrolled for the fall semester, and on September 2, the night before the new semester was scheduled to start, Faubus made his move. Citing "evidence of disorder and threats of violence," he called out the Arkansas National Guard to prevent the black youngsters from entering the school. His action contravened a federal court order, and far worse, it fomented the smoldering resentments that had been building up in Little Rock. Emboldened by their governor's act of defiance, angry segregationists converged on the school, where they jeered and cursed at the black students and any other Negroes who happened to be in the vicinity. For the better part of a month, the "Little Rock crisis" (as it came to be called) made headlines around the country and much of the world. Although President Eisenhower was reluctant to intervene, the escalating violence and rioting eventually forced his hand, and on September 25 he dispatched one thousand paratroopers to Little Rock to enforce the desegregation order.

Throughout the crisis, Orval Faubus was generally portrayed in the national press as a cynical opportunist. It was often pointed out that until recently, he had leaned toward a pro-integration position, and the prevailing view was that he had exploited the school controversy to save his own political hide. In a cover story on the governor, *Time* magazine characterized him as "a sophisticated hillbilly." We gave Faubus an opportunity to speak for himself on national television, and he took us up on it. So at the height of the disruptions, just a few days before Ike sent in the troops from the 101st Airborne Division, Yates and I and a camera crew flew to Little Rock.

In the course of our interview at the governor's mansion, I had ample opportunity to form my own impressions of Faubus; he didn't strike me as a rabid segregationist or any other kind of firebrand. His answers to most of my questions were measured and restrained, and in every other respect, he came across as a voice of moderation.

WALLACE: Governor, what's your opinion of the crowds of white adults who gather outside Central High School each weekday morning? They curse at any Negro who happens to pass by. They call Negroes animals. And almost to a man, they say Governor Faubus has done the right thing. What do you think of these people?

FAUBUS: Well, malice, envy, hate is deplorable in any place or in any circumstance. But as President Eisenhower has said himself, "You can't change the hearts of people by law. . . ." So why should we be so impatient as to want to force it? Because force begets force, hate begets hate, malice begets malice. . . .

WALLACE: Governor, we, of course, all know that the Supreme Court has ruled that there must be integration. You have said that you respect that ruling. Tell me this: Personally, do you favor Negro and white children sitting together in classrooms?

FAUBUS: I have never expressed any personal opinion as to the matter.

WALLACE: Why not?

FAUBUS: I feel that it is best not to.

WALLACE: Why?

FAUBUS: I am the governor of a state, pledged to uphold its laws, to keep the peace and order and also the laws of the nation. My personal views are not relevant to the problem.

WALLACE: You will make no further statement than that?

FAUBUS: No.

That was one of the rare occasions in those days when an interview I did was on the cutting edge of a major news event, and I remember how pleased I was the next day when *The New York Times* ran a front-page story on the exchange with the embattled governor. As for the noncommittal posture he displayed in our interview, that was typical of Faubus, who, throughout the crisis, shrewdly played his cards close to the vest. If his main goal was to hold on to his job, then the strategy worked. Faubus was reelected in 1958, and he was still running the show in Little Rock in the summer of 1960 when I paid him another visit. I was crisscrossing the country that summer on an extended election-year assignment for the Westinghouse broadcasting chain, and when I made a stop in Little Rock, Faubus gave me a cordial welcome. Altogether, he served six straight two-year terms as governor, a winning streak that came to an end when he was upset in the 1966 Democratic primary.

Orval Faubus must have truly enjoyed being governor of Arkansas, because in the years that followed, he made three futile attempts to get the job back. He ran and lost in 1970, and again in 1974, and once more in 1986. Faubus's campaign for governor in '86 was his last hurrah, and the man who defeated him that year was an ambitious politician on the rise named Bill Clinton.

MARTIN LUTHER KING, JR.

IN 1954, THE YEAR THE Supreme Court handed down its landmark decision on school desegregation, a young black minister arrived in Montgomery, Alabama, to commence his mission as pastor at the Dexter Avenue Baptist Church. He was only twenty-five years old and had just recently completed his studies at Boston University for a Ph.D. in systematic theology. Even then Martin Luther King, Jr., viewed his ministry as part of a larger crusade for racial justice and equality. But he had no way of knowing how soon he would be propelled into action as a leader of that cause.

The incident that was destined to change his life and alter the course of American racial history occurred on December 1, 1955, when a department store seamstress named Rosa Parks boarded a City Lines bus in Montgomery and took a seat. As the bus continued on its route, more white passengers got on, and in keeping with the local Jim Crow law, they had first claim on the seats. So when the driver ordered Mrs. Parks to stand up and she refused, she was arrested.

In response, King and other local Negroes organized a boycott of city buses. In the past, such attempts to challenge the status quo in Montgomery had failed due to weak leadership. But the city's black community now had a strong new voice and presence to rally around. King's church soon became the command post for the protest action, and in his first television interview, the young pastor made it clear that the boycott's primary goal was to force a change in the bus line's seating policy "to a first-come, first-serve basis . . . with no reserved seats for any race."

The boycott held firm and lasted for nearly a year, during which time King's moral strength and resolve were frequently put to the test. The worst moment came when his home was bombed; he wasn't there at the time, but his wife and infant daughter narrowly escaped death. A few weeks after that, King and other boycott leaders were arrested on charges of interfering with the normal flow of free enterprise. In the meantime, the battle was also being fought on the legal front, and that part of the struggle went all the way to the U.S. Supreme Court. Its decision—handed down in November 1956— was an unequivocal victory for the boycott and the young minister who had led it.

King emerged from the long confrontation as a hero to his people, and understandably so. Most historians agree that more than any other single event (even more than the Supreme Court's school decision), the Montgomery bus boycott spawned the civil rights movement. King was at the forefront of that movement as it spread across the South, and by the time I interviewed him in early 1961, he and his forces were assailing the citadels of segregation with sit-in demonstrations, freedom rides, and other forms of protest.

My own career had gone through a notable change. When our first year at ABC came to an end in the spring of 1958, Philip Morris decided *The Mike Wallace Interview* was more trouble than it was worth. In addition, the network brass's former ardent enthusiasm for our program had cooled considerably. It was obvious that we were on our last legs at ABC, so Ted Yates and I and the rest of our original *Night Beat* team decided to return to the less stressful confines of a local station in New York. We didn't go back to Channel 5; our new home was the small and independent Channel 13, which would later become the New York City station in the Public Broadcasting System. That was where I interviewed Martin Luther King, Jr., in February 1961 and asked him about some of the tactics he endorsed in the battle to overcome segregation.

> WALLACE: Dr. King, do you feel that there is no feeling among some Negro leaders that the methods of sit-ins and economic boycotts, which you and your group employ, have perhaps alienated many southern moderates who were formerly more sympathetic to your cause?
>
> KING: Well, I am sure there are some Negroes who feel this. I don't think it's a majority opinion. I think there are some few—
>
> WALLACE: Some older, more conservative groups, perhaps?
>
> KING: Well, there are some few, yes. But I don't think this would be the majority. I think the vast majority of Negroes and Negro leaders feel that they are good.

I then quoted from an article of his that had appeared in a recent issue of *The Nation,* in which he charged that "the intolerably slow pace of civil rights is due at least as much to the limits which the federal government has imposed on its own action as it is to the action of segregationist opposition." He went on to write that "leadership and

determination . . . have been lacking in recent years," and I pressed
him on that.

> WALLACE: Are you pointing the finger at President Eisen-
> hower on that score, Dr. King?
>
> KING: Well, honesty impels me to say that I don't think Mr.
> Eisenhower gave the leadership that the problem
> demanded. . . . I don't think he's a man of ill will, but I don't
> think he ever understood the depths and dimensions of this
> problem. And I am convinced that if he had taken a strong
> forthright stand, many of the problems and the tensions that
> we face in the South today would be nonexistent.

Eisenhower was no longer president. John F. Kennedy had been
inaugurated just three weeks before our interview, and King expressed confidence that the new president would be an active supporter of the civil rights movement. (He did add, however, "I hope I'm
not engaging in superficial optimism.") We discussed the enormous
difficulty of getting a tough anti-segregation law through Congress,
and I suggested that without such legislation, Kennedy could not be
an effective leader on the issue.

> WALLACE: What specifically can he do? You have said "the
> president could give segregation its death blow through the
> stroke of a pen." What can Kennedy do?
>
> KING: The president has the power—with a stroke of the pen,
> as I said—to end many of these conditions in housing, in em-
> ployment, and in hospital and health areas. These are some of
> the things he could end almost overnight with a stroke of the
> pen. And we must never forget that the Emancipation Procla-

mation was an executive order, as well as ending segregation
in the army, and there are many, many areas where the president can end segregation in this way.

WALLACE: You've even talked about a secretary of integration.

KING: Yes.

WALLACE: Did you make that suggestion seriously?

KING: I certainly did. I think this is vital. I think this is necessary. . . .

Another subject on King's mind that evening was the recent marriage of Sammy Davis, Jr., to the Swedish actress May Britt. Our
viewers didn't hear his concerns about that, because he and I talked
about it only off-camera. He was intrigued by the high-profile inter-
racial marriage, if more than a little apprehensive about how it would
be exploited by "our enemies." It was, after all, no secret that one of
the segregationists' favorite assertions (often expressed in rants of
apocalyptic frenzy) was that integration would inevitably lead to
miscegenation—or "mongrelization," as Eldon Edwards chose to
phrase it. Yet I had the distinct feeling that for all his misgivings, King
was personally impressed by Davis's boldness and success at romanc-
ing such a glamorous blonde.

In 1961, Martin Luther King, Jr., was already a deeply revered
figure. When I introduced him on our broadcast, I noted that as a
moral leader, he had been compared to Gandhi and Thoreau and
even to Christ. The crowning achievements of his crusade were still
to come. In 1963 he and his fellow demonstrators resisted Bull Connor's police dogs and fire hoses in Birmingham, Alabama, and at the
march on Washington later that summer, King delivered his famous
"I Have a Dream" speech. His critical role in those two events provided much of the impetus that persuaded President Kennedy and

his successor, Lyndon Johnson, to embrace a full-scale commitment to legislation banning segregation in all public facilities, and in 1964 the sweeping Civil Rights Act was passed. That was also the year King was awarded the Nobel Peace Prize. The following year he led an extensive campaign to get Negro voters registered, and Congress responded to that with another strong civil rights measure, the Voting Rights Act of 1965.

Although he was then at the height of his prestige, King and his followers would soon be moving into waters more troubled and treacherous than those they had been navigating. Over the past decade, the civil rights demonstrators had concentrated their fire on the walls of legal segregation that stretched across the South. But with the passage of the two anti-segregation bills by Congress, those walls came tumbling down. So in 1966, King shifted his battleground to communities in the North where social and economic structures were built on the rock of de facto segregation, separation of the races by custom and covert manipulation rather than by law. The primary targets of this new offensive were jobs and housing, and those areas of dispute were far more complex and elusive than the lunch counters and bus terminals and other public places that had been the sites of the protests in the South.

Along with the geography, the racial climate had also changed considerably. In the summers of 1965 and '66, riots broke out in the black ghettos of several northern cities. One effect of all that mayhem was to disenchant many white Americans who had been sympathetic to the civil rights movement. To make matters even more difficult, King's authority within his own sphere was being challenged by younger and more militant black activists. They approved of his commitment to action, but they had become impatient with the nonviolent methods he so firmly espoused.

The leader of the new militancy was a young radical named Stokely Carmichael, chairman of the Student Nonviolent Coordinating Committee (SNCC). To many white Americans, the shrill demand of Carmichael and his cohorts for what they called "black power" was nothing less than a call to arms, a summons to incite angry Negroes to commit more acts of violence. The predictable response to that perceived threat was to strengthen the bonds of white resistance all across America.

It was against this volatile background that King took his campaign for integrated housing to the town of Cicero, a working-class suburb of Chicago. Four decades earlier, Cicero had acquired a certain notoriety as the home of Mob king Al Capone and the center of his bootlegging operation. The town's reputation received another setback in the summer of 1966, when an unruly crowd of white residents greeted King's demonstration with bricks and bottles, along with racist taunts and catcalls.

I had gone to work for CBS in 1963, and for most of the next three years, I anchored the *Morning News* there. From my anchor desk, I reported regularly on King's activities and other developments in the fight to overcome segregation. In 1966, I left that post to cover civil rights stories in the field, and one of my first major assignments was as correspondent on a *CBS Reports* documentary that we called "Black Power, White Backlash."

In putting together that hour-long report on the turbulent changes in the civil rights movement, I interviewed numerous participants and observers, both black and white, and one of them inevitably was King, who was still engaged in the open-housing drive in Cicero and other white neighborhoods in the Chicago area. When my camera crew and I arrived at his motel at the agreed-upon hour for our morning interview, in response to my knock, he opened the door to his room slightly and stuck out his head. He explained that he had overslept. He asked us to wait a few minutes while he got dressed.

In our interview, I brought up a speech King had recently given in which he reaffirmed his commitment to nonviolence: "I would like for all of us to believe in nonviolence," he declared. "But I'm here to say tonight that if every Negro in the United States turns against non-violence, I'm going to stand up as a lone voice and say, 'This is the wrong way!'"

In his conversation with me, he elaborated on that point.

KING: I will never change in my basic idea that nonviolence is the most potent weapon available to the Negro in his struggle for freedom and justice. I think for the Negro to turn to violence would be both impractical and immoral.

WALLACE: There's an increasingly vocal minority who disagree totally with your tactics, Dr. King.

KING: There's no doubt about that. I will agree that there is a group in the Negro community advocating violence now. I happen to feel that this group represents a numerical minority. Surveys have revealed this. The vast majority of Negroes still feel that the best way to deal with the dilemma that we face in this country is through nonviolent resistance. . . . And I contend that the cry of "black power" is at bottom a reaction to the reluctance of white power to make the kind of changes necessary to make justice a reality for the Negro. I think that we've got to see that a riot is the language of the unheard. And what is it that America has failed to hear? It has failed to hear that the economic plight of the Negro has worsened over the last few years.

The "economic plight of the Negro" was a relatively new theme for King, and it would soon become his top priority. During the last two years of his life, the focus of his quest for equality and justice shifted more and more from racial matters to economic issues. Those were the concerns that brought him to Memphis in the spring of 1968. That city's striking sanitation workers had reached out to King for support, and he had responded. It was there that he was shot and killed while leaving his motel for an early dinner. Given all that he accomplished, I've always found it hard to believe that at the time of his death, he was only thirty-nine years old.

I've had the privilege of interviewing many public figures over the years, and on more than one occasion, I've been asked which one I admired the most. The first time that question was put to me, I gave it considerable thought, because several worthy candidates came to mind. The answer I eventually settled on was Martin Luther King, Jr.

Some of my reasons for citing King were predictable enough. He was a man who devoted his life to making America live up to its heritage as the land of the free, a country where "liberty and justice for all" was not just an empty slogan. He had the courage of his convictions, and he acted on them. From the bus boycott in Montgomery, where it all began, to the last demonstrations on the streets of Memphis, King not only preached nonviolence, he practiced it, even though the protests he led frequently put him in harm's path. Given all the risks he took, it's hardly surprising that his life came to a violent end.

But for me, King's most impressive moment came about a year before he was killed, when he took a controversial stand on an issue that was not directly related to civil rights. In early 1967, he spoke out publicly against President Johnson's war policies in Vietnam. He condemned the U.S. presence there as immoral and argued vigorously that the resources being used to fight that war should be channeled into the social goals of the Great Society programs. King's decision to break with Johnson on the war was made with considerable anguish, for no one had a more profound appreciation than King of all that LBJ had done to advance the cause of civil rights. King's public opposition to the war was another sign that he was determined to expand his leadership beyond the sphere of the civil rights movement, and more than anything else, that heroic stand crystallized my immense regard for Martin Luther King, Jr.

In 1994, I was the correspondent on a profile of King that was part of the *20th Century* series that CBS News produced for A&E. In my close to that broadcast, I offered this tribute to the man I continue to admire more than any other public figure who rose to prominence during my lifetime:

"Martin Luther King's moral passion and his ability to inspire others with his extraordinary eloquence left an indelible mark on America. And his premature death left a void in our history that has never really been filled. Like Washington and Lincoln, he was one of the very few Americans who, in the context of his time, could truly be called the indispensable man."

MALCOLM X

THE CALL FOR BLACK POWER and other militant battle cries that swept across the civil rights movement in the mid-1960s startled and frightened many white Americans. If some of us were less alarmed, it was probably because we recognized that the outburst of black rage was not a new phenomenon. In many ways, it echoed the harsh and inflammatory rhetoric I first encountered back in 1959.

At that time, America's racial climate was still fairly placid. Yes, the civil rights movement was under way, but it was just gathering steam for the major offensives to come. In addition to my interview show on Channel 13, I anchored a broadcast called *News Beat,* which had the distinction of being New York's first half-hour evening news program. All the other nightly newscasts, local and network, were still locked into the fifteen-minute format that had been in effect throughout the 1950s.

So that was my professional domain in the spring of 1959, when I met with a black reporter named Louis Lomax. He had come to my office with a proposal that began with a question: "Mike, what do you know about the Black Muslims?"

I told him I had never even heard the term. Nor, I felt certain, had any of my white colleagues and acquaintances. Remember, in those days most blacks still preferred to be called Negroes, and Moslems—spelled with an O, not a U—were Arabs who lived mainly in the Middle East. Lomax promptly enlightened me: "The Black Muslims are black separatists. They're a hate group. They hate white people."

He went on to say that the Black Muslims were "totally opposed to integration" and therefore had nothing but contempt for the civil rights movement. He described them as a rapidly growing army that already had recruited more than two hundred thousand African-Americans into its ranks. I scoffed at that claim, insisting that such a visibly large and angry force would have attracted some attention from the press. I had not seen one story about the so-called Black Muslims in any major newspaper or magazine.

"That's right!" Lomax declared. "The white press isn't covering this story because the white press can't get near these people. And that's what I want to talk to you about."

He proposed that we collaborate on a documentary about the

Black Muslims, and it led to one of the most explosive pieces I've ever been involved in. Lomax did most of the reporting, and I anchored the Channel 13 broadcast, which we called "The Hate That Hate Produced." The title sounds like tabloid hype, but the story more than lived up to its billing. Our report included film coverage of a Muslim rally steeped in an atmosphere of pure venom. One speaker after another condemned Caucasians as "white devils" who, down through the centuries, had committed every crime imaginable against black men and women. There were also interviews with the leader of the movement, Elijah Muhammad, and its New York minister, Malcolm X, who told Lomax that "the white man was the serpent in the Garden of Eden. By nature he is evil." Moreover, in his interview with Lomax, Muhammad predicted that within a decade a "general insurrection" of black Americans would erupt and inflict "plenty of bloodshed."

Nothing quite like it had ever been broadcast or published (at least not in the mainstream press), and when we aired "The Hate That Hate Produced," we struck more than a few nerves. Moderate Negro leaders, like my friend Roy Wilkins of the NAACP, charged that we had grossly exaggerated the size and significance of the Black Muslims. Even more censorious were most of the reviewers, who accused us of sensationalism and fearmongering. Our response to these criticisms from the power centers of the white media was a defiant challenge: "All right, don't take our word for it. Go see for yourselves." And they did. Over the next few months, *The New York Times,* *Newsweek* magazine, and other influential voices in American journalism published reports on the Black Muslims that verified the essence of what we had aired.

The Muslim who emerged from our documentary as the star of the movement (formally known as the Nation of Islam) was not its titular leader. Elijah Muhammad was a remote and rather shy man who, in his rare public appearances, did not come across as all that articulate and forceful. The man who did possess those qualities in great abundance was the movement's most visible and vocal spokesman, Malcolm X, an ex-convict who had converted to the Nation of Islam while serving time for burglaries. Malcolm had a magnetic presence, and even though he railed against white America in a calm, even-tempered manner, the edge to his voice revealed the depth and passion of his beliefs. When he appeared on television and vowed that black separatism and other Muslim goals would be achieved "by any means necessary," there was no mistaking the resolve and sense of menace in his message.

Since I was manifestly one of the "white devils," neither Muhammad nor Malcolm would consent to be interviewed by me. Without Louis Lomax or another black reporter, we wouldn't have gotten the story. In time, Malcolm became more accessible to the mainstream media, and I was one of the first white television reporters to interview him. Although he never confirmed this in so many words, I suspected that he had come to appreciate all the hoopla our broadcast had generated for him and the Muslims. I did a number of stories on Malcolm over the next few years, first at Channel 13 and later at CBS News. He proved an excellent source of information and insights about the black community, and however hostile his feelings were toward white people in general, I always thought he played fair in his dealings with me. In fact, there gradually formed between us a mutual respect, even a kind of friendship, although I didn't fully realize how mutual it was until I read in the autobiography he wrote with Alex Haley that he regarded me as one of the few white reporters he could trust.

As time passed, Malcolm toned down his harsh views to the

point where he was no longer driven by a visceral hatred of white America. The decisive change in his outlook occurred during his 1964 pilgrimage to Mecca, where he worshipped side by side with devout Muslims who were white. When he came home from that journey, Malcolm renounced the racism that he had been preaching for the past several years, and I asked him about the dramatic shift in his attitude when I interviewed him on the *CBS Morning News* in the early summer of '64.

WALLACE: Then the white man is no longer the devil and evil?

MALCOLM X: The Holy Koran teaches us to judge a man by his conscious behavior, by his intentions. So I judge a man by his conscious behavior. I am not a racist. I don't subscribe to any of the tenets of racism.

WALLACE: And so you feel that there are good whites and good blacks and bad whites and bad blacks?

MALCOLM X: It's not a case of being good or bad blacks and whites. It's a case of being good or bad human beings.

Even before his epiphany in Mecca, Malcolm had experienced a sharp rift in his relationship with Elijah Muhammad. The split was attributed largely to the resentment Muhammad and some of his top deputies felt about all the prominence Malcolm enjoyed in the media. He was widely viewed as the chief spokesman for the movement, and that did not sit well with other Muslim leaders. By March 1964 the discord had become so severe that Malcolm broke away from the Nation of Islam and, later that year, formed a rival group called the Organization of Afro-American Unity.

But the rupture in the relationship between the two Muslim leaders had to do with a lot more than jealousy, as I learned when

I talked to Malcolm in June 1964. He had come to my office to discuss the interview I had in mind for the *Morning News,* and when I asked him about Muhammad, he suddenly glowered and said, "Mike, he is not the man he's cracked up to be. His morals aren't what he would have you believe. This man Muhammad who paints himself as an ascetic, who paints himself as a holy prophet of God, is a lecher. I'm telling you, this man Muhammad is a *lecher!*"

"Oh, Malcolm, come on," I replied. "Be serious."

"I *am* serious. I can tell you that he takes girls as secretaries, girls within the movement, and gets them pregnant, and then farms them and their children out. Elijah Muhammad is the father of several children by several different teenage girls."

Needless to say, I found that hard to believe; yet even before I had a chance to ask if he had any proof to back up his allegation, he volunteered to telephone one of the girls Muhammad had impregnated and let me listen in on their conversation. The call was made, and I heard the young woman confirm Malcolm's story. He also agreed to disclose what he knew when I talked to him on-camera. Suddenly, the interview I'd been planning now promised to have a lot more relevance than the change in Malcolm's attitude toward white folks. When we did the interview and I asked him about his former leader's lechery, he did not hesitate to repeat and elaborate on what he had told me in the privacy of my office.

MALCOLM X: He made six sisters pregnant. They all had children. Two of those six had two children. One of those two is having a child right now. I am told that there is a seventh sister who is supposed to be in Mexico right now, and she's supposed to be having a child by him.

WALLACE: Do you feel perhaps that you should now take over
the leadership of the Black Muslims?

MALCOLM X: No. I have no desire to take over the leadership
of the Black Muslims, and I have never had that desire. . . .

WALLACE: Are you not perhaps afraid of what might happen
to you as a result of making these revelations?

MALCOLM X: Oh, yes. I probably am a dead man already.

He made that observation in such a calm, matter-of-fact tone
that I assumed he was merely being metaphorical. But in retrospect,
I'm convinced that he knew then what fate had in store for him. In
February 1965—about eight months after our interview—Malcolm X
was shot and killed while addressing a meeting of his followers at the
Audubon Ballroom in Washington Heights. His three assailants were
later identified as Black Muslims. Like Martin Luther King, Jr., he
was gunned down in his prime; it is a morbid coincidence that both
of these charismatic black leaders were assassinated at the age of
thirty-nine. The bitter irony, of course, is that unlike King, who was
slain by a white man, Malcolm was murdered by members of his own
race and adherents of the faith he had done so much to propagate.

Posterity has been kind to Malcolm, who went on to acquire
more stature in the years since his death than he ever enjoyed during
his lifetime. One of the more ambitious homages to him was Spike
Lee's feature film *Malcolm X,* which starred Denzel Washington.
When that movie was released in 1992, I did a retrospective piece on
Malcolm for *60 Minutes.* Among the people I interviewed was Alex
Haley, the author of *Roots* and the coauthor of *The Autobiography of
Malcolm X.* Haley had also engaged in extensive conversations with
Martin Luther King, Jr., so I asked him how the two leaders viewed
each other.

HALEY: I didn't know Dr. King as well as I knew Malcolm by any means, but I did do a rather lengthy *Playboy* interview of Dr. King. He would sort of hedge around awhile, and it might be forty-five minutes before he would say, in his very casual sort of southern way, "Well, what's brother Malcolm saying about me these days?" And then I would go back to New York. Malcolm, unlike Dr. King, the first thing out of his mouth was "What did he say about me?" It was so interesting.

WALLACE: Were they jealous of each other?

HALEY: I wouldn't say jealous, because I think both had a very distinct sense that they were both working toward the same objective, but different paths.

WALLACE: Opposite sides of the same coin.

HALEY: Yes, exactly.

Toward the end of that 1992 story, I said that "today his message touches young blacks in ways that even Martin Luther King's message never touched," and when I interviewed Spike Lee, I asked him why more recent black leaders had failed to measure up to the standards set by Malcolm.

"Well," he replied, "I don't want to name names. But the black masses do not feel like these other guys are doing what needs to be done. . . . But Malcolm speaks to them."

Taking that as our cue, we concluded the piece with an excerpt from a speech Malcolm gave when he was at the height of his combative power:

"We declare our right on this earth to be a man, to be a human being, to be respected as a human being, to be given the rights of a human being in this society, on this earth, in this day, which we intend to bring into existence by any means necessary."

LOUIS FARRAKHAN

ONE OF THE MANY BLACK Americans who answered the evangelical call to join the Nation of Islam was a young calypso singer from Boston who billed himself as "The Charmer." By all accounts, he had talent as well as charm, and in later years he would sometimes claim that if he had pursued a musical career, he might have become another Harry Belafonte. He was formally known in those days as Louis Eugene Walcott, but that lasted only until 1955, when, at the age of twenty-two, he became a Black Muslim and changed his name to Louis X. The minister who guided and nurtured his conversion to the Nation of Islam was Malcolm X, and Louis X soon became one of his most devoted acolytes. In 1956, on Malcolm's recommendation, he was appointed minister of the Muslim mosque in Boston, and not long after that, he adopted yet another name—Louis Farrakhan.

He continued to revere Malcolm as his mentor and role model until 1964, the year Malcolm broke away from the Nation of Islam. In that internal dispute, Farrakhan chose to pledge his allegiance to the movement's leader, Elijah Muhammad, and as a reward for his loyalty, he was appointed minister of the New York mosque shortly after Malcolm was killed in 1965. From that power base, he steadily strengthened his position within the Black Muslims, and after Muhammad died, Farrakhan took over the leadership of the Nation of Islam in 1978.

Throughout his public ministry, Farrakhan did his best to present himself as another Malcolm X. There's no denying that his inflammatory attacks on white Americans were reminiscent of his mentor's menacing diatribes during the years when he was preaching racial hatred. But try as he might, Farrakhan could never get out from under the long shadow cast by Malcolm's life, or the far more sinister shadow of his death. For years, even decades, after Malcolm was slain, Farrakhan was suspected of having been the chief instigator of the assassination. Malcolm's widow, Betty Shabazz, went to her grave believing in Farrakhan's guilt, and that belief was shared by her four children, starting with her eldest daughter, Attallah, who, as a six-year-old child, had witnessed the murder of her father at the Audubon Ballroom.

In the spring of 2000, I was able to persuade Attallah Shabazz and Louis Farrakhan to appear together on-camera and talk about the assassination. My interview with them formed the core of a 60 Minutes story we called "Who Killed Malcolm X?" At one point I reminded Farrakhan about an incendiary editorial he'd written for the Nation of Islam's newspaper a few months after Malcolm's split with the Muslims and his public revelations about Muhammad's sexual transgressions.

WALLACE: Let me read what you wrote in December of 1964: "The die is set and Malcolm shall not escape, especially after such evil, foolish talk about his benefactor, Elijah Muhammad, in trying to rob him of the divine glory which Allah has bestowed upon him. Such a man as Malcolm is worthy of death." This was only two months before he was shot down. That is why people believe that you were responsible for the death of Malcolm X.

FARRAKHAN: No, not at all. My name was not among those at that time who were considered the players.

According to Attallah Shabazz, those "players" were known to her father, for he had told his family and a few close friends that he had obtained the names of the Nation of Islam members who had been assigned to kill him.

WALLACE: Did your father not have a list of the people?

SHABAZZ: Oh, my father knew everybody personally.

WALLACE: The people who were out to kill him?

SHABAZZ: The list was longer than those who actually pulled the trigger.

Farrakhan did not go so far as to confess that he had been directly involved in the plot to kill Malcolm X, but toward the end of the tense and often wrenching encounter, he did admit to a certain culpability.

FARRAKHAN: May I, Miss Shabazz, say . . . I wish that Malcolm X were alive today and not dead. Yes, it is true that black men pulled the trigger. We cannot deny any responsibility in this. Where we are responsible, where our hands are a part of this, we beg God's mercy and forgiveness.

WALLACE: What did you expect to come out of this conversation? What did you hope would come?

FARRAKHAN: I genuinely hope that perhaps a healing can come to Miss Shabazz and her family. As I may have been complicit in words that I spoke leading up to February twenty-first [the date of Malcolm's murder], I acknowledge that, and regret that any word that I have said caused the loss of life of a human being.

When I asked for Shabazz's reaction to the meeting, she said, "He's never admitted this before publicly until now. He's never caressed my father's children. I thank him for acknowledging his culpability, and I wish him peace."

That was not Farrakhan's first appearance on 60 Minutes: I had done a story on him four years earlier. That 1996 profile aired just a few months after his most ambitious undertaking, the much ballyhooed Million Man March. The purpose of that event was to induce black men from all across America to assemble in Washington for a day of atonement and a shared pledge to embrace family values and commitments. Although Farrakhan scored some moral points for himself and his cause, he proceeded to squander them on a subsequent trip to the Middle East and Africa. During his visits to the capitals of three Islamic countries—Libya, Iran, and Iraq—he met with leaders who were sworn enemies of the United States, and he was severely criticized for making statements that indicated he shared their corrosive hatred of America. When I interviewed him in the spring of '96, I asked him about those remarks and about his visit to Nigeria, which also had sparked some controversy. While in Nigeria, he voiced support for a regime that I contended might well be the most corrupt government in the entire world. That assertion struck a nerve, and Farrakhan lit into me with a fusillade of righteous fury:

"You're not in any moral position to tell anybody how corrupt they are," he declared. "America should keep her mouth shut wherever there's a corrupt regime, as much hell as America has raised on the earth. No, I will not allow America or you, Mr. Wallace, to condemn them as the most corrupt nation on earth when you have spilled the blood of human beings."

He paused for a moment, but only to reload: "Has Nigeria dropped an atomic bomb and killed people in Hiroshima and Nagasaki? Have they killed off millions of Native Americans? How dare you put yourself in that position as a moral judge? I think you should keep quiet, because with that much blood on America's hands, you have no right to speak."

Farrakhan eventually calmed down and even offered an apology of sorts for getting "so fired up."

"Oh, no," I assured him. "That's good. That's good."

"That's my passion," he explained.

That passion had been on display in his frequent denunciations of white people in general and Jews in particular. I decided to broach the subject of his pet antagonisms in personal terms.

WALLACE: You don't trust the media—you've said so. You don't trust whites—you've said so. You don't trust Jews—you've said so. Well, here I am: white, Jewish, and a reporter. So why in the world did you trust me enough to sit down to talk to me in this way, Mr. Farrakhan?

FARRAKHAN: Well, let— Let me say this: I would not say that all whites and all Jews and all media are untrustworthy. That is not a fair characterization of my thinking.

WALLACE: That's the perception of a lot of people in America.

FARRAKHAN: Perception is not necessarily reality.

I asked him to look at some footage from one of his speeches that was directed at Jews. As the following excerpt makes clear, the message and tone of his remarks could only be construed as virulent anti-Semitism:

"You are wicked deceivers of the American people. You have sucked their blood. . . . You are the synagogue of Satan. And you have wrapped your tentacles around the U.S. government, and you're deceiving and sending this nation to hell. But I warn you in the name of

Allah, you would be wise to leave me alone. But if you choose to crucify me, know that Allah will crucify you."

Even in the face of such incriminating evidence, Farrakhan insisted that his ultimate goal was to bring about a reconciliation between the Black Muslims and American Jews. If that was his objective, then he pursued it in a strange way. In the years since our interview, he continued to rail against Jews in his vituperative fashion, and all the major Jewish organizations continued to denounce him as a contemptible bigot. Who could blame them, for with his highly charged rhetoric, Louis Farrakhan continued to live up to his reputation as an anti-Semitic rabble-rouser.

Having said that, I also know from personal experience that one does not have to be a raving anti-Semite to be rebuked by the powerful Jewish lobby. Some of the reporting I did in the Middle East back in the 1970s aroused the ire of the American Jewish Congress and similar pressure groups, and they unleashed their attack dogs in an intensive campaign to discredit my work and my character. That was when I learned that if you dare to deviate from their doctrinaire positions on Israel and other critical Jewish issues, you will surely become a target of their wrath—even if you happen to be one of their own.

FOUR

THE MIDDLE EAST

SYRIAN JEWS

THE CIVIL RIGHTS MOVEMENT WAS a big national story, a
social and political drama that unfolded on American soil. On
the international stage, the story I was most deeply involved in over
the years was the long and frustrating struggle to achieve peace in the
Middle East. Both of those subjects had the kind of historical weight
and resonance that gratify a reporter's desire to cover events that are
apt to have serious, long-range consequences. Unlike the battle for
civil rights, which had its share of triumphs and clear signs of
progress, the efforts to bring an enduring peace to the Middle East
have been largely a failure, a melancholy pattern of false starts,

BETWEEN YOU AND ME

dashed hopes, and broken promises. In the course of my career at
CBS News, I had more assignments in that troubled region than all
other foreign countries combined, and I was given the opportunity to
report on the bitter conflict from every possible angle.

My first assignment was in 1967, at the time of the Six-Day War.
Charles Collingwood and I had coanchored the CBS coverage of Israel's swift and crushing victory over its Arab neighbors from the network's "war room" in New York. As soon as the fighting stopped, I was
sent to Tel Aviv to put together an overview report on the war—an
"instant special," as it's known in the trade. I returned to Israel in
1969 and again two years later to do 60 Minutes stories on how the
victors were adjusting to their expanded borders. In the immediate
aftermath of the '67 war, Israeli officials insisted that they did not
want to maintain permanent possession of the territories they had
captured from Egypt, Syria, and Jordan. Their avowed plan was to
use the Sinai Peninsula, the Golan Heights, and the West Bank as
bargaining chips in negotiations with the Arabs toward a firm and
formal peace agreement. Arab resistance to that approach led to a
hardening of the Israeli position, as I learned on my 1969 visit when
I interviewed Defense Minister Moshe Dayan, the great hero of the
Six-Day War. He told me that his government did not intend to relin-
quish the occupied territories, which prompted me to ask him if Israel would agree to return to its pre-1967 borders in exchange for "a
real peace."

"No," Dayan replied, "not even for a real peace."

Thus were the battle lines drawn for the protracted struggle that
would persist over the next several decades.

I was also determined to present the opposite side of the dispute
on 60 Minutes. Toward that end, I made trips in the early 1970s to
four Arab countries: Egypt, Libya, Lebanon, and Jordan. Nor did I ignore other aspects of the Middle East conflict. In early 1974, not

long after the region's leading producers of petroleum engineered an oil embargo that sent shock waves of inflation through the U.S. economy, I traveled to Saudi Arabia to do a profile of that country's powerful oil minister, Sheik Ahmed Zaki Yamani. From there, I flew across the Persian Gulf to interview the shah of Iran.

I mention these assignments to underscore the point that I was well acquainted with the turmoil and volatile politics of the Middle East when I went to Syria in 1975 to work on the story that caused all the furor within the Jewish lobby. The main focus of that report was on Syria's autocratic ruler, Hafez al Assad, and his well-trained military apparatus. In both the 1967 war and the 1973 Yom Kippur War, the Syrians fought with more skill and valor than any of their Arab allies, which was why we decided to call our story "Israel's Toughest Enemy."

During our stay in Damascus, my producer, Bill McClure, asked for permission to take our cameras into the city's Jewish community. I was quite surprised when that request was granted, because I had heard depressing stories from Jewish friends in America about how miserable life was for Jews in Syria. I had been told that they were confined to ghettos and were constant victims of persecution. Among other indignities, they could not worship in synagogues or study in Hebrew, their traditional language. My overall impression was that Syrian Jews were compelled to live as prisoners in their own country.

It did not take us long to discover how untrue most of that was. Yes, there was a Jewish quarter, but Jews also lived outside of it, side by side with Muslims and Christians. We learned that there were no fewer than fourteen synagogues in Damascus, and we visited one of them. We looked in on students at two schools in the Jewish quarter and observed that at least some of their lessons were in Hebrew. When I asked one of the Jewish teachers if she had any explanation for all the stories I had heard, she replied in a caustic tone, "I think that it's Zionist propaganda." I could hardly believe that a Jewish teacher was making such an accusation; I remember thinking, Wait till the folks back home hear *this*!

I also interviewed a Jewish pharmacist. When I asked him if he had felt a divided loyalty during the wars between Syria and Israel, he declared without hesitation that he fully supported Syria. Perhaps sensing that I also was Jewish, he added a rhetorical question: "Wouldn't you feel the same if war came between the United States and Israel?"

At the same time, we reported the drawbacks for Jews who lived in Syria. They were prohibited from serving in the Syrian army, and it was rare for a Jew to hold any kind of government job. They also needed special permission to leave the country and even to travel within Syria's borders. What was more, they were required to carry cards identifying them as Jews and were generally kept under close surveillance. Yet we also noted that when it came to travel and security measures, similar restrictions were imposed on all Syrians—regardless of religion—because Assad's government was, without question, a police state, one of the most oppressive regimes in a region where dictatorship was the rule rather than the exception.

We took care to keep the story in proper perspective. In preparing the report for broadcast, we began with observations about Assad's obsessive desire to regain control of the Golan Heights, the rich Syrian farmland that had been occupied by Israel since 1967, and his regime's cozy relationship with the Soviet Union. It wasn't until we were six or seven minutes into the piece that we turned our attention to Syria's Jewish community. Even though our story was balanced and fair, I fully expected that our portrayal of Jewish life in Syria would upset some viewers who had been conditioned to believe that no Jew would ever give his allegiance to a nation that had fought wars against Israel. Nevertheless, I did not anticipate the firestorm that erupted when we aired "Israel's Toughest Enemy" on *60 Minutes* in February 1975.

I was accustomed to controversy and had even courted it from time to time, but never before had I been the target of such intense hostility. In the deluge of critical letters and telegrams that flooded into the offices of CBS News, I was vilified for having betrayed my ethnic heritage, and some of the attacks in that vein were quite personal. (One of the more polite epithets hurled at me was "self-hating Jew.") It soon became evident that an orchestrated mail campaign had been mounted against me and our broadcast. It's fairly easy to spot that sort of thing. Postcards and letters arrive in clusters with identical postmarks and even the same vituperative phrases. Nor did it take an expert in special-interest groups to figure out what the main impetus was behind all this malicious mail.

Of all the powerful pressure groups in America, none had more influence in those days than the so-called Jewish lobby. The people who ran it had the finances to marshal their forces and the savvy to use them to maximum effect. This was especially true when it came to the media. According to *The Power Peddlers,* a 1977 book about lobbying activities in America, "The Israeli lobby is unique among lobby groups with its 'clout' with the press. [No other group] has ever succeeded in making reporters look over their shoulders as much as the Israeli lobby."

One of the more militant voices within that lobby was the American Jewish Congress. In recent years, the AJC had intimidated other news organizations into retracting or revising stories that did not conform to its dogmatic views, and its zealous watchdogs now zeroed in on *60 Minutes*. The assault formally began a few days after the broadcast, when Hewitt and I met with four top officials from the AJC in

Hewitt's office. The visiting delegation was led by its president, Rabbi Arthur Hertzberg, who castigated us for having been "duped" by the Syrians. Hewitt also happens to be Jewish, and when the rabbi and his associates weren't denouncing our journalistic integrity, they were making snide remarks about our moral defects as Jews. Rabbi Hertzberg all but demanded that we do a follow-up piece, a revision based on interviews with Syrian Jews now living in the United States, all of whom would naturally be furnished to us by the American Jewish Congress. After brushing off that proposal, Hewitt and I stood our ground, stoutly defending the story on Syria in all its particulars. And that, I mistakenly thought, was that.

As we soon discovered, Rabbi Hertzberg had just begun to fight. A few days after our contentious meeting, the American Jewish Congress called a news conference, where its officials reiterated the objections and accusations we had heard in Hewitt's office. On most occasions, when we aired a piece that provoked a hostile reaction, the criticism would peter out in a few days, a week or so at the most. But the American Jewish Congress was determined to keep the Syrian story on the front burner, and its well-organized attacks on "Israel's Toughest Enemy" persisted for several months after our broadcast.

Of all the shots the AJC aimed at us, the most offensive came in an editorial that ran in its publication *Near East Report*. Drawing an analogy that I found obscene, the editorial compared our broadcast to "films in which Goebbels portrayed the clean and tidy barracks in the idyllic concentration camps." Even at its absolute worst, life for Jews in Syria didn't come close to the psychotic depravity of the Third Reich, and I felt that to suggest such a parallel was to dishonor the memory of the millions who suffered and perished in the holocaust.

A postscript: There are far fewer Jews living in Syria now, and that's because the harsh restrictions on travel were lifted in the early 1990s. Although they were not allowed simply to cross the border into Israel, Jewish residents were free to leave Syria, and many of them have moved to other countries. The most popular destination for Syrian Jews has been the United States—in particular, Brooklyn, New York—but a fair number (there are no precise figures available) chose to relocate in Israel, which they reached through transit countries.

MENACHEM BEGIN
ANWAR SADAT

WHEN I INTERVIEWED MENACHEM BEGIN in the fall of 1977, he had recently taken over as prime minister of Israel. He had come to power a few months after President Jimmy Carter was sworn into office, and there were reports that the two new leaders regarded each other with a wariness that bordered on mistrust. As a longtime member of the opposition party in the Knesset—the Israeli parliament—Begin had acquired a reputation for being an inflexible hard-liner, and that was bound to put him at odds with Carter, who had vowed to adopt a more evenhanded approach to the Arab-Israeli conflict. There was a growing concern among American Jews that Carter and his foreign-policy team were tilting toward the Arabs, and I was curious to know if Begin shared that apprehension.

> WALLACE: He is the first American president—the *first* American president—to talk of a Palestinian homeland. He is the first American president to talk of legitimate Palestinian rights.

BEGIN: Sometimes President Carter makes statements which
we cannot agree with, and then we say so openly and sincerely. Then we have our debates with him. . . .

WALLACE: You do not believe that Israel and the United
States are on a collision course?

BEGIN: No, no. No, no. I don't think that we are on a collision
course.

But it wasn't just the United States that had become disillusioned with Israel's expansionist policies, and I reminded him of how
dramatically the attitude toward his country had changed in the last
decade.

WALLACE: Ten years ago, after the Six-Day War, Israel was the
most heroic nation in—in the world, virtually. Everybody admired Israel, right? Today Israel seems to be, around the
world, pretty close to alone. Question: why?

BEGIN: Seems to be? May I tell you that these people go
around the world telling the story of the poor Palestinians,
whom we rejected, as they say, et cetera. This is the big lie of
the successful propaganda. . . . They tried to destroy our people time and again, either directly or with the help of invading
armies, and they didn't succeed because we fought them off.
And then they cry out, "But we were wronged!" They were
wronged by their own aggression.

On two occasions within the previous decade, Israel had to repel
armies from Egypt, Syria, and other Arab neighbors. But in 1977 its
main security concern was not another conventional war so much as
the sporadic and deadly acts of terrorism that were being carried out

by Palestinian guerrillas. The irony was that the Israelis had their own history of guerrilla warfare, and no one had been more deeply involved in it than Menachem Begin. With his thick glasses, which gave him an owlish appearance, and his formal sartorial taste (in contrast to the laid-back open-collar style preferred by most Israeli leaders, Begin almost always wore a conservative suit and tie in public), he may have looked like a staid economics professor, but his early claim to fame was as a warrior.

Back in the 1940s, during the years leading up to Israel's War of Independence, Begin had been commander of the Irgun Zvai Leumi, a radical guerrilla force committed to the violent overthrow of British rule in Palestine. Under his leadership, the Irgun launched attacks on Arab villages, British troop trains, and other targets throughout the region that would later become Israel. To their critics (a group that included such prominent Jews as Albert Einstein and Hannah Arendt), the Irgun commandos were terrorists. But in the eyes of their admirers, they were freedom fighters, and Begin in particular was later praised for having helped dynamite the state of Israel into existence.

Three decades later, as prime minister, Begin had to cope with the Palestine Liberation Organization and its dynamic leader, Yasir Arafat, who was spearheading a determined effort to dynamite Palestine back into existence. That led me to ask Begin the following question: "Do you—forgive me—see no similarity of purpose between the Menachem Begin of thirty years ago and the Yasir Arafat of today?"

"And who?" he stiffly replied.

"Yasir Arafat."

He glared at me in silence for a moment or two, and when he finally did speak, his first words were "I will not get angry." But he was unable to suppress his anger, and he began to berate me for having dared to draw a comparison between his Irgun guerrillas who had fought "for the survival of our people" and "the man called Arafat who wants to destroy the Jewish state and sends his henchmen to kill men, women, and children."

The interview soon came to an end, though the scolding continued even after we turned off the camera and microphones. Begin was still furious, and I was starting to get a little sore myself. It was obvious from his tone and manner that he could not understand how I, a fellow Jew, could have asked such a question. The quarrel with the American Jewish Congress over the Syrian story was still a fresh memory, and I found myself thinking: Good Lord, here we go again. I did try to explain my position. I told Begin that as the son of Jewish immigrants, I had been brought up to believe in Zionism, and I remained firmly committed to the existence of Israel. I said I had trees planted in Israel to honor the memory of my parents, and that in a number of other private ways, I had given my support to Israeli causes. However, I couldn't allow my personal feelings to inhibit my work as a reporter, and since I had heard other Israelis make the connection between the Irgun commandos of the 1940s and the PLO guerrillas of the 1970s, I considered my question fair and legitimate.

Begin wasn't buying any of that, and as our argument grew more heated, we must have started shouting at each other. The next thing I knew, the door to his office flew open and in walked Israel's defense minister, Ezer Weizman. He greeted us with a roguish grin and said, "I understand that the prime minister is having a fistfight with an American reporter." That broke the tension, and Weizman, sensing that I had no desire to continue the squabble, suggested that he and I repair to my hotel for a drink. I eagerly accepted his offer.

At the bar in the Jerusalem Hilton, we struck up a conversation with a couple of Israeli reporters, and I couldn't resist regaling them with a lively account of my encounter with Begin. I probably was not as discreet as I should have been, but I was still somewhat agitated. Anyway, a few days later, an Israeli weekly magazine published a cover story on the incident, which was boldly illustrated with a full-page photograph of Begin and me facing each other in a classic pose of confrontation. I was later told that when Begin saw the article, which featured some pungent quotes from me, he blew his stack all over again.

Although neither Begin nor I had any way of knowing it at the time, our little scrap occurred just as he was on the verge of getting caught up in a historical drama of major proportions. On November 9, 1977—three days after my interview with Begin was broadcast on *60 Minutes*—the president of Egypt, Anwar Sadat, dropped a diplomatic bombshell. In a speech before the Egyptian parliament, he said that his desire for a permanent peace in the Middle East was so strong that he "would go even to the home of the Israelis, to the Knesset, to discuss peace with them." That dramatic move was a stunning break with precedent; never before had an Arab head of state come up with such a bold proposal. The ball was now in Menachem Begin's court, and to his great credit, the reputed hard-liner responded in kind. Two days later, he announced his plan to invite Sadat to Israel to talk about an enduring peace, and on November 19, 1977, the president of Egypt stepped off a plane in Jerusalem, thus becoming the first Arab head of state to visit Israel.

That breakthrough was a step toward the most encouraging development to take place in the Middle East since Israel had joined the family of nations in 1948. One month later, Begin visited Sadat in Cairo, and in September of the following year, they both accepted President Carter's invitation to engage in face-to-face talks at Camp

David, where, after twelve days of arduous and finely tuned negotiations, they agreed on a series of accords that provided the framework for an official peace treaty between Egypt and Israel.

On two earlier trips to the Middle East in 1977, I had done stories on Egypt and the many problems that beset its president. During the second of those visits to Cairo, our focus was on the country's economic woes (we called the piece "Sadat's Troubled Egypt"), and I made a point of talking to some of Sadat's critics. When I interviewed the man himself, I said to him, "You know what they say about you? They say you're a politician, but you're no economist. You're a first-rate foreign minister, but a bad chancellor of the exchequer."

Instead of disputing that assessment, Sadat candidly conceded that "we are really suffering from a very acute economic problem. This is a fact." It was clear from his somber tone that no one was more acutely aware than he of how difficult conditions were in Sadat's troubled Egypt, and I closed our report with this observation: "It is to forestall an explosion from inside his country or from outside that Sadat labors so mightily these days for peace. . . . The peace he needs to give his country's economy a chance to flourish. The peace he may just need, in fact, to keep his job."

We aired that story in August 1977, and three months later, when Sadat returned to Cairo from his historic visit to Jerusalem, cheering crowds gave him a hero's welcome. Although many of his Arab allies had denounced Sadat's overture to Israel as an act of treachery, his daring peace initiative had clearly captured the hearts of his countrymen. It was the Egyptians, after all, who had borne the brunt of all the wars with Israel, and so it should have come as no surprise that a vast majority of them shared their president's fervent hope for a formal peace treaty.

In March 1978, I flew to Cairo to do another *60 Minutes* story on Sadat. His diplomatic triumph had greatly enhanced his stature and news value, and I wanted to give our viewers a more detailed portrait of the man. We talked about his early life and career and how, as a young army officer, he had been one of the leaders of the revolution in 1952 that overthrew the decadent regime of King Farouk and later drove the British occupiers out of Egypt. Sadat went on to serve as chief deputy to Gamal Abdel Nasser during his long reign as Egypt's ruler, and I had been told that Sadat was then disdained by some Egyptians as an obsequious bureaucrat who always treated Nasser with fawning deference. In an effort to get under Sadat's skin a bit, I asked him if he was aware that he was often referred to in those days as "Nasser's poodle, Nasser's Mr. Yes-Yes."

Puffing furiously on his pipe, Sadat managed a wan smile and said, "Yes, yes, I know. I know it."

I then brought up the general reaction in Cairo in 1970, when Nasser died and Sadat succeeded him. "No one expected you to survive. . . . Everybody said, 'Nasser's poodle will last six weeks.'"

"*Four* to six weeks," he corrected me with a merry laugh.

This was my third interview with Anwar Sadat in under a year, and I must confess that by this time I had joined the growing ranks of his admirers. I not only respected him as a statesman and a leader of his people; he had won me over with his personal charm and warm sense of humor. At the time of our 1978 interview, he seemed in particularly good spirits, and since he had rolled with the punches so graciously when I alluded to "Nasser's poodle," I decided to bring up something I had read in his autobiography, *In Search of Identity*. In a chapter that dealt with the Yom Kippur War, Sadat recalled a snag in the discussions to return the bodies of Israeli soldiers to their homeland. "Applying the Jewish principle of putting a price on everything," he wrote, "Israelis began to negotiate the price they expected to pay to recover their dead."

I quoted the sentence and said that after reading it, one could easily conclude, "Aha, Anwar Sadat! He is anti-Semitic, anti-Jewish!"

Sadat responded with another hearty laugh and adroitly replied, "Anti-Semite, this is something that has been invented to blackmail anyone and to scare anyone. No. I myself am a Semite. How could I be anti-Semite? They are my cousins."

Yet by then Sadat was losing patience with the "cousin" whose cooperation he needed most: the prime minister of Israel. The once promising peace initiative had run into serious obstacles, and by the spring of '78, the euphoric expectations of the previous November, after Sadat's trip to Jerusalem, had evaporated. The disagreements continued to harden over the summer until finally, in August, Carter intervened with the offer that brought Begin and Sadat to Camp David. Had it not been for Carter's invitation and his patient mediation during the difficult negotiations that followed, the peace agreement between Egypt and Israel almost surely never would have come to pass. Most historians agree that Carter's diplomacy at Camp David that summer was the high-water mark of his presidency.

The lion's share of the credit belongs to the leaders of the two countries that for the past three decades had been so belligerent toward each other. Each of them had to make major concessions. Sadat had pushed hard for a comprehensive peace plan that would have embraced the entire region, though he had to settle for the far more narrow treaty between Egypt and Israel. Begin yielded significant ground when he agreed to return the Sinai Peninsula to Egyptian control. But the adjoining Gaza Strip remained under Israeli occupation, as did the territories captured from Jordan and Syria in the Six-Day War: East Jerusalem, the West Bank, and the Golan Heights.

For all its limitations, the agreement was lavishly praised as a vital first step toward a durable peace that would extend throughout the Middle East. Hence, no one was surprised when, later that year, Menachem Begin and Anwar Sadat were jointly awarded the Nobel Peace Prize.

In the years since 1978, the Camp David accords have lost some of their luster, mainly because there has been no significant follow-up. Contrary to the more optimistic expectations, the treaty between Egypt and Israel did not provide the spark for other firm and lasting Arab-Israeli peace agreements. There were some encouraging moves in that direction, but they all were stymied by one thing or another. The chief stumbling block, of course, has been the Palestinian question, and at the heart of that complex and difficult issue loomed the flamboyant presence of the Arab leader whom Menachem Begin described as "the man called Arafat."

YASIR ARAFAT

YASIR ARAFAT WAS THE LEADER of a nation in exile. In one of the early *60 Minutes* pieces I did on the Middle East, I described the Palestinians as "the new Diaspora," and pointed out that most of those stateless refugees lived in the squalor of camps that were scattered throughout the Arab countries bordering Israel. Out of their misery had emerged the rebellious forces of the Palestine Liberation Organization. Arafat took over as chairman of the PLO in 1969, and with his scruffy beard, he came across as a Bedouin version of Fidel Castro. Yet when I finally met him in person, it was his warm and expressive eyes that caught my attention. They struck me as the eyes of a poet or a devout religious figure, and not at all what I expected to find in the face of a guerrilla leader who had dedicated his life to violence and revolution.

Our first meeting took place in March 1977 in Cairo. I'd gone there to do a story on Sadat, and when I heard that Arafat was in town, I was able to arrange an interview with him as well, even though his general policy in those days was to shun the U.S. media, which he dismissed as slavishly pro-Israel. I suspect the main reason Arafat granted my request was because he had been encouraged by recent news from Washington. In a major foreign-policy speech, Jimmy Carter had called for the creation of a Palestinian homeland, thereby becoming the first American president to adopt that position publicly, as I noted when I sat down with Menachem Begin later that year. In my interview with Arafat, he praised Carter's speech as "a progressive step, because for the first time, the president of America put his hand on the core of the whole crisis in the Middle East—the Palestinians."

Carter's speech was misleading, for it later became clear that a key ingredient in his proposal was Israel's ultimate approval of any blueprint for a Palestinian homeland. Which meant there was no real change in U.S. policy. To Yasir Arafat, Carter was just another American president under the thumb of the Jewish lobby. The Carter-driven Camp David accords only confirmed and deepened Arafat's resentment. The next time I interviewed him was in early 1979, and the dark brown eyes that greeted me at his PLO headquarters in Beirut were no longer soft and sensitive. Instead, they blazed with murderous fury because an Arab-Israeli peace agreement had been reached that did not include a plan for resolving the Palestinian problem. The chief target of his rage was his fellow Arab, Sadat, whom he reviled as "a quisling, a traitor," though his charges of betrayal also extended to President Carter. I asked him about that.

WALLACE: Why would Jimmy Carter want to betray the Palestinians? Because that's what you've said.

ARAFAT: I think he is a— He's looking for the votes.

WALLACE: So, he's just doing this for votes?

ARAFAT: I am sorry to say.

WALLACE: He will betray the Palestinians—

ARAFAT: I am sorry to say that what he is doing is only for some votes for the new election.

WALLACE: And you— By "some votes," you mean Jewish votes in the next election.

ARAFAT: Maybe. Votes—the Jewish votes or other votes.

WALLACE: Well, then, other votes?

ARAFAT: But mainly it is Jewish votes.

WALLACE: I see.

ARAFAT: I am sorry to say it.

In 1982, I returned to Beirut and interviewed him again, shortly before pressure from Israel's invading forces drove the PLO out of Lebanon. Following that expulsion, Arafat moved his command post to Tunis, and when I sat down with him there in 1989, he vigorously defended the intifada, the Palestinian uprising of riots, mayhem, and violence that engulfed the Israeli-occupied territories of Gaza, East Jerusalem, and the West Bank in 1987 and persisted over the next four years. We also talked about his more conciliatory positions, for Arafat had recently renounced terrorism and had formally acknowledged Israel's right to exist, a diplomatic step that reversed twenty-five years of PLO policy. That olive branch helped create the climate for direct negotiations with Israel, and in the aftermath of the 1993 Oslo Accords, he set up his headquarters in Gaza City, where I visited him twice. My seventh and last interview with him was in 2002 at yet another site, Ramallah on the West Bank.

Throughout most of the quarter century that had elapsed since I first met him in Cairo, Arafat's PLO guerrillas and Israel's armed forces were at each other's throats, and the depressing history they shared was mostly one of destruction and bloodshed. But on at least two occasions, Arafat came tantalizingly close to resolving the PLO's major disputes with Israel in a way that would have brought peace and stability to the region.

The first time was in 1993, when the two foes signed the Oslo Accords. The key elements in that historic agreement called for official recognition of the state of Israel, the withdrawal of Israeli troops from the Gaza Strip and West Bank, and a plan to implement Palestinian self-rule in those territories over a five-year period.

Arafat's counterpart in the agreement was Prime Minister Yitzhak Rabin, who had long been revered as one of Israel's great patriots. He had been a field commander in the 1948 War of Independence and the military chief of staff during the Six-Day War in 1967, and his towering reputation as a war hero gave him the stature and clout he needed to sell the Oslo Accords to skeptical Israelis. At the formal signing ceremony with President Bill Clinton on the White House lawn, Rabin shook hands with his longtime enemy, and although he did so with some hesitation, that gesture of goodwill signaled the dawn of a more tranquil era in the Middle East. Like Sadat and Begin fifteen years earlier, Arafat and Rabin were showered with praise for their diplomatic triumph. Like those previous leaders, they went on to receive the Nobel Peace Prize, an honor they shared with Israel's foreign minister, Shimon Peres, who had played a critical role in the long and difficult negotiations.

But the high hopes generated by the Oslo pact were abruptly shattered. In the fall of 1995, as plans were moving forward to implement the agreement, Yitzhak Rabin was assassinated by a right-wing Israeli fanatic, a terrorist who bitterly opposed the concessions that were being made to the Palestinians. His motive for killing Rabin had been to derail the peace process, and to a large extent, he succeeded. Moreover, that deadly assault was a sad reminder to all of us that acts of terrorism in the Middle East were not confined to Israel's Arab enemies.

The second golden opportunity came in 2000, when Israel's new prime minister, Ehud Barak, set out to revive the harmonious spirit of the Oslo Accords. This time around, President Clinton became an active participant in the negotiations. In July 2000 he summoned Barak and Arafat to meet with him at Camp David, where he hoped to pull off the kind of diplomatic coup that Carter had achieved there in 1978. Clinton was then in the final months of his presidency, and a Carteresque mediation of a long-standing Middle East dispute would have been an impressive capstone to his eight years in the White House.

Barak assured Arafat that he was committed to all the provisions that had been set down in the Oslo agreement, and with a sharp nudge from Clinton, he went even further. In addition to relinquishing all of the Gaza Strip and over 90 percent of the West Bank for the creation of an independent Palestinian state, Barak said Israel would be willing to give the Palestinians control over parts of East Jerusalem. That concession went well beyond any previous proposal to Arafat; never before had an Israeli leader offered to compromise on the status of Jerusalem, a city that both Jews and Arabs steadfastly claim as their capital.

Although it was a remarkably generous offer, Arafat rejected it. And in spite of intense pressure imposed on him by Clinton, he declined to make a counteroffer. The president was furious at Arafat and all but accused him of sabotaging the talks at Camp David, which he had convened with such high expectations and at which he had put his own reputation on the line.

For Arafat, pressure from Bill Clinton was not nearly as threatening as pressure from Hamas and other radical Islamic groups that were challenging his authority. Their growing influence within his own community was now so strong that Arafat did not dare to defy their unrealistic demands, which went far beyond anything the Israelis could accept. When I interviewed Arafat in Gaza City three months after the Camp David meeting, I asked why he had refused Barak's generous proposal. Arafat replied that if he had accepted, he would be "drinking tea in heaven with Yitzhak Rabin."

The collapse of the Camp David negotiations had a devastating effect on the peace process. When I visited Gaza in the fall of 2000, guerrilla attacks and similar uprisings were an almost daily occurrence there and on the West Bank. The new wave of violence had all the earmarks of the 1987 insurrection; indeed, it soon became known as "the second intifada." As for Ehud Barak, he had staked his career and reputation on being able to reach an agreement with Arafat, and his failure was political suicide. As the violence escalated that fall, he had to prepare for new elections, and in February 2001, Israeli voters veered sharply to the right and chose the notorious hard-liner Ariel Sharon as their next prime minister.

The last time I interviewed Arafat was in February 2002, in Ramallah, where he was a virtual prisoner in his own presidential compound. For the previous two months, Sharon had kept tanks positioned on the streets outside the compound and had vowed to confine Arafat to his quarters until he arrested a number of Palestinians the Israeli government had identified as terrorists. Among other things, the show of force underscored how much Sharon detested Arafat. I asked the PLO leader about that personal enmity, which stretched back over two decades or more.

WALLACE: Why does Ariel Sharon hate you so? He wanted you killed.

ARAFAT: He has tried to kill me thirteen times.

WALLACE: Right. Why does he hate you so?

ARAFAT: You have to ask him.

WALLACE: No, no, no, no. You have your own opinion. Why?

The only answer Arafat offered was that he was a man of peace, as he had demonstrated at the time of the Oslo Accords, and that Sharon had always been a staunch opponent of the peace process. Arafat then launched into his favorite litany about the Israeli occupation—which he called "the siege"—and how grievously the Palestinian people had suffered during the decades of Israel's military oppression. I had heard it all before, too many times before.

Throughout our last encounter, Arafat struck me as a rather pathetic figure, and not just because he was being subjected to the humiliation of virtual house arrest. He was seventy-two and looked considerably older, no doubt in part because of the Parkinson's disease he suffered from. Beyond advancing age and failing health, Arafat seemed to have lost the passion and fire I remembered from earlier visits. I saw him as a spent volcano, a lion in the depths of winter who had been declawed and could no longer roar.

Toward the end of our interview, I brought up a recent column by Thomas Friedman of *The New York Times*. Under the headline "Dead Man Walking," Friedman wrote that "few Americans, Israeli or Arab leaders believe anymore that he will ever lead his people into a peace deal with Israel. Everyone is just waiting for Mr. Arafat to pass away."

Arafat's reply was to remind me that he had been "elected from my people" and that he was still the leader of the Palestinian cause. I then quoted another comment that had come to my attention.

WALLACE: Ahmed Abdul Rahman, close friend, yes? He said
   recently, "At this moment, Arafat is the Christ of the Palestinian people." Christ died for his people. Correct? You've said
   fairly recently that you want to be a martyr for Jerusalem, for
   the Palestinian people.
ARAFAT: Yes, yes. I hope that I will die in Jerusalem. I had
   lived there when I was a boy, so I would like and I hope that I
   will have the opportunity to die there with my mother.

Arafat did not get his wish. His health continued to decline over
the next two years, and when he became mortally ill in the fall of
2004, he was still languishing in confinement at his compound in Ramallah. In a desperate attempt to stay alive, Arafat flew to a military
hospital outside of Paris, where he lapsed into a coma and died on
November 11. His body was flown back to Ramallah for burial the
next day. In accordance with his longtime desire, a request was made
for his burial in Jerusalem, but Prime Minister Sharon refused. When
the time came for his burial in Ramallah, thousands of Palestinians
swarmed through the compound in an outpouring of grief.

The emotional outbursts at Arafat's funeral were a strong reminder of how deeply he was revered by the Palestinian masses, who
had ample reason to regard him as a hero. His dynamic leadership
over the years had restored the Palestinians' sense of honor and pride
in their own identity. Largely because of him, they had come to believe in the promise of a brighter future, one that would lead eventually to independence and nationhood.

Arafat also had a reputation for being fearless, especially during
the early years, when he led the PLO in campaigns of guerrilla warfare. Those repeated attacks on Israelis made him a prime target for
assassination, and in my first interview with him in 1977, I asked if

he was concerned about that. "No," he replied, "my life is nonsense." That was his way of saying that he had become accustomed to living in constant peril and had reconciled himself to the likelihood of a violent death, no doubt sooner rather than later.

The valor of those early days did not extend to his role as peacemaker. When push came to shove in his negotiations with Israeli leaders, Arafat did not have the courage of his convictions. He allowed himself to be intimidated by terrorists within his own movement, and, cowed by their threats to dispatch him to an afterlife of "drinking tea with Yitzhak Rabin," he refused to take the bold steps necessary to achieve a firm accommodation with Israel. Time and again he squandered opportunities to lead the Palestinian people to the nationhood he had promised them, and that failure, I suspect, is apt to be Arafat's most enduring legacy.

Yet in an irony that Arafat would not have appreciated, his death had the effect of reviving prospects for a peace agreement. Mahmoud Abbas, the man elected to succeed him as president of the Palestinian Authority, was known to be a moderate who had long been committed to a peaceful resolution of the conflict with Israel. His election in early January 2005 by a clear-cut margin (he garnered 62 percent of the vote) was widely hailed as a strong and positive step in the right direction. Even Ariel Sharon praised Abbas as someone Israel could negotiate with in good faith, and Abbas responded in kind. Sharon, he said, was now "speaking a different language to the Palestinians," and that raised hopes for "a real peace."

Nor did it take long for the two leaders to confer in person. Just one month after Abbas's election, he and Sharon shook hands at a summit meeting in Egypt where each of them gave his pledge to a cease-fire that would bring an end to four years of violence in the region. Their agreement had all the earmarks of a fresh start down the road to a permanent peace, and as I write in the spring of 2005, there are signs that this latest initiative might possibly succeed where so many previous ones failed. An independent Palestinian state living in harmony with a secure Israel is, of course, a consummation devoutly to be wished, but as a longtime observer of the savage desert politics of the Middle East, I've learned to be prepared for the worst even as I fervently hope for the best.

THE SHAH OF IRAN
THE AYATOLLAH KHOMEINI

DURING THE 1970S, WHEN I was spending so much time in the Middle East that it seemed almost like my second home, the Arab-Israel conflict was not the only story from that region getting big play in the U.S. media. A far more urgent concern for most Americans was the sudden use of oil as a weapon against the United States and its allies. In late 1973 the world's largest oil producers drastically increased the price of their shipments to the West, and the Arab members of the oil cartel imposed an embargo on those shipments. These actions drove a spike of inflation into the U.S. economy and created a gasoline shortage at pumps from Maine to California. Motorists had to adjust to long lines at the filling stations, and to make matters worse, there were days when no stations had gas to sell at any price.

The world's two largest exporters of petroleum were Saudi Arabia and Iran, and in early 1974, I did *60 Minutes* stories on the leadership in both countries. That was when I had my first interview with the autocratic ruler of Iran, Shah Mohammad Reza Pahlavi. The shah was punctilious about his royal status, and before he would deign to be interviewed, my producer, Bill McClure, and I and the members of our camera crew had to line up in an appropriate pecking order and pay our respects to His Majesty, as though we were newly arrived diplomats presenting our credentials to the Peacock Throne.

In spite of his imperious manner, the shah turned out to be what we like to call "good copy." I was not given any ground rules or other advance restrictions as to questions, and as long as I observed the protocol and took care to address him periodically as "Your Majesty," I could ask him just about anything. In fact, he seemed to welcome questions that had an edge to them, and most of his answers were refreshingly frank. The more time I spent with him, the more I came to realize that he truly enjoyed the give-and-take of a spirited argument and would even go out of his way to instigate some friction. There was, for example, an exchange that took place early in our 1974 interview. The shah was aware that I had flown to Iran directly from Saudi Arabia, and when I alluded to that previous visit, he seized the opportunity to give me a little lesson in geographic nomenclature.

WALLACE: As you know, I have been across the gulf, the gulf that you call Persian and they call Arabian—

THE SHAH: Why do you call it that? You have been to school, haven't you?

WALLACE: Yes.

THE SHAH: What was the name that you have read during your school days?

WALLACE: Persian Gulf.

THE SHAH: All right. That's—

WALLACE: (Laughs) But they do call it the Arabian Gulf.

THE SHAH: Well, *they* can do many things.

We talked at length about the huge hike in oil prices, and he insisted that the major oil companies in the United States were profiting almost as much from the increases as were the countries that exported the petroleum. I challenged him on that assertion, but he stuck to his guns, and he may have been right. What I did know was that the shah had been a longtime critic of Western oil companies and their governments, and he had even chosen to couch his grievances against them in ethnic or genetic terms. I asked him about that.

WALLACE: You have said that the blue-eyed Europeans—the blue-eyed people of the United States—have plundered your country. Do you really believe that?

THE SHAH: I do, because just only take this oil thing, among others. For fifty years they were taking the oil and flaring the gas.

WALLACE: That is, burning it?

THE SHAH: Just burning it. What name would you give to this action?

WALLACE: Well, it was uneconomical, they said.

THE SHAH: Obviously, because they didn't care. . . .

WALLACE: And you do believe that we in the United States and the European nations—the blue-eyed ones—in a sense discriminated against brown-eyed oil?

THE SHAH: So far, yes.

That was the first of three interviews I had with the shah. I met with him again a year later, and on that occasion, I concentrated my queries on his secret police force, the SAVAK. Predictably, he indignantly denied the various accusations I quoted about SAVAK's methods of torture.

The next year, I returned to Iran, and when that piece was broadcast in October 1976, I noted in my on-camera open that "*60 Minutes* made its yearly pilgrimage to the shah's palace in Tehran to canvass the royal views of assorted topics." The topic that inspired his most provocative comments was the power of the Jewish lobby in the United States. As usual, the shah did not mince words. I questioned his claim that all American presidents were unduly influenced by that pressure group.

WALLACE: Surely, Your Majesty, you're not telling me that the Jewish lobby in the United States pulls the strings of the presidency?

THE SHAH: I think so. Sometimes they are disserving the interests of Israel.

WALLACE: Explain!

THE SHAH: Because they're pushing around too many people . . .

WALLACE: Why would the president of the United States pay attention to that lobby?

THE SHAH: They are strong.

WALLACE: Strong in what sense?

THE SHAH: They are controlling many things.

WALLACE: Controlling what?

THE SHAH: Newspapers, media—

WALLACE: Your Majesty!

THE SHAH: Banks, finances. And I am going to stop there.

WALLACE: Well, now, just a second. You really believe that the Jewish community in the United States is that powerful? They make the media reflect their view of foreign policy?

THE SHAH: Hm-hmm. Yes.

WALLACE: They do not report— *We* do not report honestly?

THE SHAH: Don't mix things, please! I don't say the media. I say *in* the media they have people, not the *entire* media. Some newspapers will only reflect their views, yes.

WALLACE: Well, *The New York Times,* for instance, is owned by the Sulzberger family, who are Jewish. Are you suggesting that *The New York Times* is biased in its treatment of the question of Zionism, Israel's existence, the United States' relationship with the Arab world?

THE SHAH: I will have to put all the articles of *The New York Times* written on this subject and draw the conclusion. You can put this through the computer and it will answer you.

WALLACE: What you're saying is that yes, you do believe.

THE SHAH: Well, let's wait for the answer of the computer.

WALLACE: *The Washington Post.*

THE SHAH: The same.

WALLACE: The networks.

THE SHAH: Less.

WALLACE: I must say, you're speaking with your characteristic candor.

THE SHAH: Yes, if you like. I try to be candid. I have always been.

I never saw the shah again, at least not in person. Over the next two years, Islamic fundamentalists who bitterly opposed his secular regime steadily gathered strength, and by the time I made my next trip to Iran in November 1978, they were in open rebellion. My assignment that fall was to cover the protests and riots that had broken out on the streets of Tehran. Two months later, those disorders escalated into a full-scale revolution, and the Peacock Throne was doomed. In fact, the shah and his family were fortunate to get out of Iran alive. Their escape in January 1979 infuriated the Muslim fundamentalists and especially their leader, the Ayatollah Ruhollah Khomeini, who had taken over as the spiritual head of the new Islamic government.

The royal family fled first to Egypt, and from there moved on to Mexico. To further complicate matters, the shah was stricken with cancer, and in October 1979, he formally asked permission to enter the United States for medical treatment. When his request was granted, Washington and President Carter became the targets of all the fury that had erupted in Iran. The mob protests in Tehran led to an assault that fall on the U.S. embassy and the seizure of its diplomatic corps. Thus began the long ordeal of captivity for fifty-two American hostages in a country that had been overwhelmed by the frenzy of religious fanaticism.

Even before the attack on our embassy, I had been making a strenuous effort to get back to Iran to interview the austere mystic who was the spiritual leader of the revolution. One of my producers, Barry Lando, was based in Paris and had built up contacts with anti-shah Iranian exiles who had lived there and were known to be close to the Ayatollah Khomeini. (In fact, they had been excellent sources for us when we were gathering information about SAVAK.) We reached out to them for help. But because I was perceived as having been sympathetic to the shah in our interviews, the word came back that 60 Minutes was—in the piquant phrase of one of Lando's contacts—"as welcome in Iran as bacon in a synagogue."

After the hostages were seized in early November, Lando renewed his pitch for an interview with the ayatollah. In light of the corrosive tirades he and his disciples had been directing at the U.S. government, I had serious doubts that Khomeini would agree to be questioned on American television. Besides, that wasn't the only story I had to deal with, so I flew to the West Coast to work on another assignment. Hence, I happened to be snooping around inside a toxic-waste dump in Stockton, California, when the call came through from Lando that the ayatollah had decided to grant our request. (I never did find out what suddenly made *60 Minutes* kosher in that synagogue.) There was a stipulation: We had to come to Iran "right away—instantly!"

I tore myself away from the charms of California's toxic-waste problem and hightailed it to the San Francisco airport. Unfortunately, I didn't have my passport with me, so, before boarding an over-the-North-Pole flight to London, I telephoned my New York secretary, Marikay Mead, and gave her a rather unusual assignment: to fly to London with my passport and the research material I had assembled on the hostage crisis. When I landed at Heathrow Airport, Marikay was there with the documents. (Such a maneuver could not be pulled off in today's climate of tighter security and much more stringent restraints on the CBS budget.)

I flew on to Tehran, where Lando and our camera crew were waiting for me, and the next morning we arrived in the holy city of Qum, where Khomeini had set up his headquarters. I was the first American reporter he had agreed to talk to since the hostages were seized two weeks earlier.

I soon discovered that when it came to interview protocol, the ayatollah was no shah. We had to submit our questions to his aides in advance, a condition we never would have agreed to if the circumstances had not been so extraordinary. Several of the questions were rejected as unacceptable, and even most of those that did pass muster did not elicit germane replies. He used the interview mainly as a forum for his simplistic platitudes and demands: "The shah is a criminal . . . Carter must return the shah . . . Unless he is returned, the hostages will not be freed . . . Islam protects the prisoners . . . Islam is humane . . ." That sort of thing.

Speaking through an interpreter, Khomeini uttered his pronouncements in a voice so toneless that it seemed almost robotic, and his manner was equally remote. Throughout our interview, which lasted over an hour, he generally avoided eye contact with me, preferring to stare straight ahead with his face locked in an impassive expression. Hardly ever did he glance in my direction or in any other way acknowledge my presence. Even though the interview was disappointing in many respects, it did give American viewers their first close-up look at the strange and forbidding enemy we were up against in Iran.

The one time the ayatollah *did* deign to observe me was when I brought up a remark that had been made about him by another Muslim leader. Here was how I put it to him:

"Imam, President Sadat of Egypt, a devoutly religious man, a Muslim, says that what you are doing now is—quote—'a disgrace to Islam.' And he calls you, Imam—forgive me, his words, not mine—'a lunatic.'"

I obviously had not included that among the questions we submitted for advance approval, and I'll never forget the look the interpreter gave me. It clearly said that if I expected him to translate that observation, then *I* had to be a lunatic. But I pressed him to do so, and he did after I pointed out that I had heard Sadat use those precise words on American television.

Khomeini looked straight at me, and I thought I detected a faint glint of curiosity in his eyes. He said in reply, "Sadat states he is a Muslim and we are not. He is not, for he compromises with the enemies of Islam. Sadat has united with our enemies."

After a pause, he added, "I demand that the Egyptian people try to overthrow him, just as we did with the shah."

The ayatollah was actually the second Muslim leader that year to call for Sadat's downfall—or worse—in an interview with me. Back in March, when Yasir Arafat had denounced Sadat as "a quisling, a traitor," I reminded Arafat that in many countries the penalty for treason is death, and I asked, "If the Egyptians want to kill Sadat for being a traitor, you say okay?"

"Yes," he replied.

Of course, that is what happened. In 1981 the world lost the most enlightened Arab leader of modern times when Anwar Sadat was shot and killed by Egyptian fundamentalists, who admitted they had been inspired by the Islamic uprising in Iran.

As tragic as Sadat's death was, the overthrow of the shah had a far more devastating effect on future events. Throughout his long reign, the shah was viewed by Washington as an important and reliable ally. We were aware that he was an autocrat and that his regime was in many ways a police state. But he was more responsive to Western values than most other leaders in the Middle East, and there was ample evidence to back up his claim that he was taking steps to modernize Iran. Best of all, from Washington's point of view, the shah was a militant anti-Communist, and that put him squarely on our side in the cold war. In a phrase used so often that it became a cliché, he was "our pillar of security in the Persian Gulf."

We didn't fully appreciate what a sturdy pillar he was until he was gone. The Muslim clerics who sparked the revolution in Iran transformed the country into an anti-Western theocracy, and a quarter century later, the fundamentalists were still in power and their Islamic regime was still a source of concern and anxiety to the United States and most of its allies. Iran was one of the menacing trio of nations that President George W. Bush denounced as an "axis of evil" in his State of the Union address in January 2002. (The other two were Iraq and North Korea.) The Bush administration was profoundly disturbed by growing evidence that Iran's new nuclear energy program included the development of nuclear weapons. Even those allies who did not share Washington's sense of alarm had to admit that an Iran armed with such weapons of mass destruction would pose a grave threat to international peace and stability. But the revolutionary changes within Iran were just part of the story, since the overthrow of the shah also set off an appalling chain of disruptions throughout the Persian Gulf region that have had dire and far-reaching consequences for the rest of the world.

In late 1979, just a few months after the shah was deposed, war broke out on Iran's eastern border when Soviet forces invaded Afghanistan. Russian officials who were working in the Kremlin at the time would later say it was unlikely that Moscow would have given the green light to that military action if Afghanistan's powerful neighbor had not been distracted by its internal upheaval. Among those who fought against the Soviet invaders (and were aided in their resistance by U.S. support) was a group of Muslim extremists known as the Taliban. The Russian occupation came to an end in 1989, and the Taliban eventually gained control of Afghanistan and set up a regime that was unusually cruel and despotic even by the harsh standards of the Middle East. In the mid-1990s, with the blessing of the Taliban, Afghanistan became a sanctuary for Al Qaeda, the Islamic terrorist group that had launched a jihad, or holy war, against the United States and its allies.

In the meantime, war had come into Iran from its western border. In 1980 the reigning tyrant in Iraq, Saddam Hussein, decided the time was ripe to exploit the post-shah turmoil in Iran, and thus began the eight-year war between those two Persian Gulf countries. Thanks to the hostage crisis, the U.S. government regarded Iran as its number one enemy in the region, so we generously contributed weapons and other forms of military assistance to Iraq. By the time the Iraqi-Iranian War ended in 1988, Hussein had managed, with considerable help from Washington, to build a military force that ranked as the fourth most powerful army in the world.

In 1990, Saddam Hussein ordered that army to invade Kuwait, which led to Desert Storm, the first American war against Iraq. The staging area for most of the offensive was Saudi Arabia, and that deployment infuriated Osama bin Laden, the fanatical leader of Al Qaeda. He would later proclaim that more than anything else, it was the presence of American infidels on the sacred soil of Saudi Arabia— the site of Mecca, the spiritual center of Islam—that transformed him and his followers into terrorists. Their apocalyptic rage propelled them on a path of destruction that led, in time, to the catastrophic attacks in New York and Washington on September 11, 2001.

Since then we have been engaged in a war on terrorism, a war that has been fought mainly on the battlegrounds of Afghanistan and Iraq, in the region where the dreadful chain of events began with the Islamic revolution in Iran.

FIVE

ICONS AND ARTISTS

MARGARET SANGER

AND NOW FOR A CHANGE of pace as we move away from political leaders at home and abroad and turn our attention to icons who touched our lives and emotions in less conventional ways. One such icon was Margaret Sanger, who was a guest on *The Mike Wallace Interview* in 1957. As the founding mother of the birth-control movement in America, she had a profound influence on the social and political forces that transformed the country in the twentieth century.

By the time I interviewed her, Sanger was seventy-eight and had been engaged in the cause that defined her life for over four decades. Yet in 1914, the year she launched the campaign for birth control—a term, incidentally, that Sanger herself coined—she was out of step not only with the power centers that governed America but also with most other feminists of that era, who felt that Sanger's issue was a distraction from their primary objective, which was to repeal laws that prevented their gender from voting. Although Sanger supported the suffragettes, the misery she encountered during the years she worked as a nurse and midwife in the slums of New York City convinced her that women had a more urgent need than the right to vote. "No woman," she wrote at the time, "can call herself free who does not have control over her own body." As it turned out, it was Sanger's crusade—more than any other—that led, in time, to the sexual revolution and the larger struggle for equality that became the women's movement.

It was an uphill battle. Sanger was jailed on eight separate occasions for her beliefs and acts of protest, and even after she succeeded in overturning laws that banned birth control, she still had to contend with her most implacable foe: the hierarchy of the Roman Catholic Church. Her public disputes with the Church's doctrinaire opposition to birth control were still raging when I interviewed her in the fall of '57.

WALLACE: You have said often that originally, the opposition to birth control was in law, and you had to fight against that. Today your opposition stems mainly from where—from what source?

SANGER: I think the opposition is mainly from the hierarchy of the Roman Catholic Church.

WALLACE: Of the hierarchy of the Church. You feel that the parishioners themselves, the laypeople of the Church, are not against it.

SANGER: They come to all of our clinics just the same as the non-Catholics do. Exactly the same.

WALLACE: Well, let's look at the official Catholic opposition to birth control. I read now from a Church publication called *The Question Box*. In forbidding birth control, it says the following: "The immediate purpose and primary end of marriage is the begetting of children. When the marital relation is used as to render the fulfillment of its purposes impossible (that is, by birth control) it is used unethically and unnaturally." Now, what's wrong with that position?

SANGER: It's very wrong. It's not normal, it's— It has a wrong attitude toward marriage, toward love, toward the normal relationships between men and women.

WALLACE: Your feeling is what, then?

SANGER: My feeling is that love and attraction between men and women, in many cases, is the very finest relationship. It has nothing to do with bearing a child. That's secondary many, many times. . . .

WALLACE: According to the tenets of Catholicism, they rule that birth control violates a natural law, therefore birth control is a sin no matter who practices it. Certainly, you can take no issue with the natural law—

SANGER: Oh, I certainly do take issue with it, and I think it's untrue and I think it's unnatural. It's an unnatural attitude to take. How do they know? I mean, after all, they're celibates. They don't know love, they don't know marriage, they know nothing about bringing up children nor any of the marriage problems of life, and yet they speak to people as if they were God.

It was most unusual in those days of social and political politesse to hear anyone attack the powerful hierarchy of the Catholic Church with Sanger's force and vigor. I shudder to think how scathing her comments would have been had she been alive in more recent years, when the stories surfaced about the heinous sexual abuses some American priests had inflicted on children and adolescents. At the same time, if she were alive today, she surely would applaud the dramatic changes in the lives of women; advances that were often the direct result of her pioneering efforts to give women control over their own bodies. Sanger did live long enough to witness the marketing of the contraceptive pill that she had helped develop, a major breakthrough that fueled the sexual revolution of the 1960s. And in 1965, the year before she died, the Supreme Court struck down a Connecticut law that banned the use of contraceptives, a decision that certified, once and for all, the legality of birth control.

It wasn't until after Sanger's death that the women's movement picked up steam and became the full-scale force that has had such a transforming effect on American society. One of its many triumphs was *Roe* v. *Wade,* the 1973 Supreme Court ruling that legalized abortion. The pro-choice campaign leading to that landmark decision was a logical and perhaps inevitable extension of Sanger's lifelong battle to make birth control legal and socially acceptable.

Because of the women's movement, Sanger now enjoys a historical stature that, I'm sure, she could not have anticipated when she was getting arrested for opening birth-control clinics and taking other steps to defy laws that banned contraception. I know I didn't anticipate it. When I interviewed her in 1957, her chief appeal to me was as a figure of controversy, an intrepid gadfly who had the temerity to challenge the moral authority of the Roman Catholic Church. Only in retrospect would I come to appreciate the depth of her influence. Over the past two decades or so, I have received more requests for quotes or excerpts from the broadcast Sanger appeared on than from any other interview I did in the 1950s. To me, at least, that is solid proof of her enduring relevance and her permanent place in the pantheon of the struggle for women's rights.

At the time of the millennium, when *Time* magazine and CBS News selected the hundred most influential men and women of the twentieth century, the luminaries were divided into five separate groups. One of them was labeled "Leaders and Revolutionaries." Among the twenty who made the final cut in that category were political giants who, for good or ill, had changed the course of world history (for example, Franklin D. Roosevelt, Winston Churchill, Vladimir Ilyich Lenin, and Adolf Hitler) and such outstanding moral crusaders as Gandhi and Martin Luther King, Jr. Only three women were included in that illustrious group. Two of them—Eleanor Roosevelt and Margaret Thatcher—were political leaders in the conventional sense, and the third was Margaret Sanger.

FRANK LLOYD WRIGHT
SALVADOR DALÍ
THOMAS HART BENTON

OF ALL THE INTERVIEWS I did in that long-ago era of black-and-white television, none was more stimulating for me than my conversations with the grand old man of architecture—Frank Lloyd Wright. At the age of ninety, Wright was in the deep twilight of a long life and brilliant career when I interviewed him in 1957. He had thoroughly earned his reputation as a maverick, an innovative genius who had rebelled against the formal constraints of conventional architecture. Moreover, his fiercely independent views were not confined to his own sphere of creativity, for Wright was also an astute and at times acerbic social critic. There's no doubt that he relished playing the curmudgeon, and he had a highly developed sense of his own worth, as I discovered early on in our interview.

WALLACE: You said many years ago that you would someday be the greatest architect of the twentieth century. Have you reached your goal?

WRIGHT: You know, I may not have said it, Mike. But I may have felt it.

WALLACE: You do feel it?

WRIGHT: But it's so unbecoming to say it that I should have been careful about it. I'm not as crude, as arrogant, as I'm generally reported to be.

WALLACE: What is arrogance?

WRIGHT: Arrogance is something a man possesses on the surface to defend the fact that he hasn't got the things he pretends to have. He's a bluff, in other words.

WALLACE: Let me ask you this: As an intellectual yourself, Mr. Wright, what do you think of President—

WRIGHT: I deny the allegation, and I refuse to marry that girl. I don't like intellectuals.

WALLACE: You don't like intellectuals? Why not?

WRIGHT: Because they're superficial. They're from the top down, not the ground up. I have always flattered myself that what I represented was from the ground up. Does that mean anything?

WALLACE: What do you think of President Eisenhower as an intellect?

WRIGHT: Well, now, don't ask me as an intellect, because how would I know? But he's a hell of a nice fellow, and one of the nicest things about him is that my wife voted for him, and I voted for Adlai Stevenson. . . .

WALLACE: What do you think of the American Legion, Mr. Wright?

WRIGHT: I never think of it if I can help it.

WALLACE: What do you mean by that?

WRIGHT: They're professional warriors, aren't they? I'm against war, always have been, always will be, and anything connected with it is anathema to me.

Elsewhere in our second conversation, we discussed his own field of endeavor, and on that subject, his opinions were even more pointed.

WALLACE: What do you think of church architecture in the United States?

WRIGHT: I think it's of course a great shame.

WALLACE: Because it improperly reflects the idea of religion?

WRIGHT: Because it's a paragon-monkey reflection and not a reflection of religion.

WALLACE: Well, when I walk into St. Patrick's Cathedral— and I'm not a Catholic—but when I walk into St. Patrick's Cathedral here in New York City, I am enveloped in a feeling of reverence.

WRIGHT: Sure it isn't an inferiority complex?

WALLACE: Just because the building is big and I'm small, you mean? Ah—I think not.

WRIGHT: I hope not.

WALLACE: You feel nothing when you go into St. Patrick's?

WRIGHT: Regret.

WALLACE: Because of what?

WRIGHT: Because it isn't the thing that really represents the spirit of independence and the sovereignty of the individual. Which I feel should be represented in our edifices devoted to culture.

At the time of our interview, Wright had recently completed his own highly original design for an edifice devoted to culture—the Guggenheim Museum in New York City. His vision of an open rotunda and a sloping circular ramp that ran from ground level to the top of the building was a radical departure from the norm in museum architecture, and like many of his other works, it provoked controversy. Even before construction began, there were complaints that Wright's design for the Guggenheim was so bold and dramatic that it was apt to overwhelm the art on display. Responding to that concern with his customary self-assurance, Wright wrote that "on the contrary, it was to make the building and the painting an uninterrupted, beautiful symphony such as never existed in the World of Art before."

Frank Lloyd Wright died in April 1959, a little over a year after our interview and just a few months before his last masterpiece opened its doors to the public. Overlooking Central Park, the Guggenheim soon took its place as a worthy neighbor of the Metropolitan and the other temples of fine art that are situated on the stretch of Fifth Avenue known as "Museum Mile."

A few years ago I was asked to name the weirdest person I've ever interviewed, and I replied without hesitation, "Salvador Dalí." In that category, nobody else came close to the flamboyant Spanish painter who had been in the forefront of surrealism, the avant-garde movement that shook up the art world in the 1920s and early '30s. Deeply influenced by Freud and the recent advances in psychoanalysis, Dalí's work explored the hallucinatory realm of the subconscious. It provided him with a fertile field of inspiration, and in his best and most celebrated paintings, like *The Persistence of Memory* (the one with the limp or melting watches), the imagery is intense and haunting.

Yet for all his talent—and he had many serious admirers—Dalí's work was all but overshadowed by his reputation as the reigning ec-

centric of the contemporary art world. With his over-the-top personality and his penchant for making outlandish statements, he seemed
intent on being perceived as a clown, a kind of high-culture cutup.
He tended to reserve his most extravagant comments for his favorite
subject—himself. Among other choice remarks, he once said, "Every
morning when I wake up, I experience an exquisite joy, the joy of being Salvador Dalí, and I ask myself in rapture, 'What wonderful
things is this Salvador Dalí going to accomplish today?'"

Although he had lived in the States for an eight-year stretch in
the 1940s, having fled Europe shortly after the outbreak of World
War II, he resettled in Spain in 1948. Through the years that followed, he made frequent trips to New York, which by then had become the thriving center of the international art scene. During his
sojourns in the city, he usually stayed at the fashionable St. Regis Hotel, where he spent a great deal of time sitting in the lobby. Even
those who knew Dalí well couldn't be sure why he did this. Was he
there to observe the hustle and bustle of all the goings-on in the
lobby, or was he merely putting himself on display in a prominent setting? He surely had no trouble drawing attention to himself with his
foppish manner of dress (theatrical cape, ornate walking stick, long
silk scarves, et cetera) and his signature mustache, a thin, neatly
trimmed handlebar, the tips of which curved so far upward that they
reached the top of his cheekbones.

Dalí popped up on my radar screen in the late fall of 1956, not
long after *Night Beat* went on the air. During one of his visits to New
York, he discovered our program and, I was told, became a fan of the
broadcast. So he passed the word, through his contacts in the city,
that he would like to be a guest on *Night Beat*, and both Ted Yates
and I heartily welcomed the overture.

Although I had an appreciation for fine art, I was no connoisseur.
If some of our viewers had the mistaken impression that I was

steeped in that culture, it may have been because they had seen me in a play that ran on Broadway in 1954. It was a light comedy called *Reclining Figure,* and I was cast in the role of an idealistic art dealer who knew his way around museums and galleries. I had been coaxed into the acting gig by my friend Abe Burrows, the author of *Guys and Dolls* and other hit musicals, who had been hired to direct *Reclining Figure.* I got through it okay, but I really didn't care much for the experience, and not once since then have I had the slightest desire to act onstage or on-screen. (Of course, I've often been accused over the years of indulging in all kinds of histrionics on *60 Minutes,* but that's a horse of an entirely different color.)

Even if I had some flair for acting, I would have been no match for a supremely gifted scene-stealer like Dalí. Since I was aware of his reputation, I fully expected him to come across as an outlandish bohemian. But I was not prepared for the sheer absurdity of most of his answers and comments, which were as surreal as the graphic fantasies he put on canvas. In his autobiography, Dalí had written that one of the few things he truly adored was old age, so I asked him about that.

WALLACE: Why do you adore old age?

DALÍ: Because the little young peoples completely stupid, you know.

WALLACE: Young people are stupid?

DALÍ: Dalí only believe geniuses are old people like Leonardo da Vinci who arrive at some real achievement.

At the time of our interview, I was a mere boy of thirty-eight (fourteen years younger than Dalí), so I didn't think his adoration of old age had much merit. Since then, with the passing years, I have gradually come to realize how profoundly wise he was on that subject.

In his book, Dalí had also asserted that "death is beautiful." I asked him, "What is beautiful about death? Why is death beautiful?"

He responded to that with some mumbo jumbo about how everything alive "is erotic, is ugly," but with the arrival of death, "everything becomes normal and sublime." That led to a bizarre claim of immortality.

WALLACE: Tell me this, what do you think will happen to you when you die?

DALÍ: Dalí not believe in my death.

WALLACE: You will not die?

DALÍ: No, no. Believe in general in death but not in the death of Dalí. Believe my death becoming very—almost impossible.

The conversation turned a little less loopy when I brought up his critics. I reminded him that his fellow artist Max Ernst, who had painted in the same avant-garde style, had described him as "the racketeer of surrealism." From an article in *Time* magazine, I quoted this assessment: "Most of his fellow artists regard Dalí as a practical joker who will do anything for a laugh, even if it means creating bad art."

"Is one very simple question of jealousy," Dalí replied with a sly smile. "Myself attracts one tremendous quantity of money for my genius. The thermometer of my success is the jealousy of the people around me."

Finally, in an effort to elicit his views on the competition, I asked him, "Which contemporary painters, if any, do you admire?"

"First Dalí. After Dalí, Picasso."

And that was it: The list stopped at two. Still, it was considerate of him to include Pablo Picasso, who, after all, was almost universally regarded as the greatest artist of the twentieth century. It's difficult to imagine any conversation about modern art without some reference to Picasso, so it's hardly surprising that his name came up—though in a disparaging way—when I interviewed another famous painter, Thomas Hart Benton, on *60 Minutes* in 1973.

In so many ways, Benton was the polar opposite of Dalí and all the other modernists who broke away from traditional painting. Both his life and his art were deeply rooted in America's heartland. His forebears were hardy pioneers who had helped to shape the political landscape in Missouri when it was a frontier outpost on the western edge of the United States. He was named after his great-uncle, the Thomas Hart Benton who was elected to the U.S. Senate in 1821—the year Missouri became a state—and served there for three decades. His own father later served as a congressman from the Show-Me State.

The spirit and values that Benton inherited from that frontier culture were reflected in his work. Best known for his large and vivid murals, his art was firmly grounded in history and the lives of real people. He was an ardent regionalist who drew his strength and inspiration from the traditions of the rural South and Midwest and the down-to-earth folks who lived there. That approach to painting brought Benton considerable success, but it also put him sharply at odds with surrealism and all the other major innovations that transformed art in the twentieth century. In the early 1930s, when he was living in New York, he taught at the Art Students League, and one of his prize pupils was a young man from Cody, Wyoming, named Jackson Pollock. The two artists became close friends, but a few years later, Pollock made his move in a radical new direction and became a leading exponent of abstract expressionism, a style that has to be viewed as the antithesis of Benton's realistic oeuvre.

Over the years, Benton acquired a reputation for being a hard-drinking, intellectual brawler who seized every opportunity to rail against abstract painting and most other avant-garde styles. In his view, modern art had been contaminated by forces that were effete, sterile, and elitist, and his cantankerous assaults included gay-bashing comments about the pernicious influence of homosexuals on the art world. In return, he was roundly scorned as a reactionary, a relic from a rustic past.

By the time I caught up with him in 1973, Benton was nearing the end of his long and combative life. When I interviewed him at his summer home on Martha's Vineyard shortly before his eighty-fourth birthday, I asked him about his advancing age.

WALLACE: Do you hate getting old?

BENTON: No. I feel good. I feel fine. I don't hate getting old.

WALLACE: You still work.

BENTON: I don't even hate to die. I don't give a damn.

WALLACE: What do you mean?

BENTON: I don't care.

WALLACE: You mean when your toes turn up?

BENTON: That's it. That don't ever bother me. People say
    when you get old, you get to thinking about death—as the
    lawyers put it, in contemplation of death—that you make a
    move. I make no moves in contemplation of death.

We then talked about his work and his many quarrels with the modern art establishment, which led to an exchange about one of the more influential members of that clique.

WALLACE: John Canaday of *The New York Times*, I think
    you'll agree, is one of the most prominent critics of the art
    scene.

BENTON: One of the mouthiest, anyhow.

WALLACE: Well, you know what he calls you?

BENTON: No.

WALLACE: A patriarchal cornball.

BENTON: Well, very good.

WALLACE: What do you think of that assessment?

BENTON: I don't care anything about that. (Laughs) He's a simpleminded art critic. Well, it's all right. If he likes to see it that way, all right. I call him an arty critic. Canaday's only one example of a whole pack of them.

WALLACE: So—but this does not really sting you? You don't take it—

BENTON: When I was young, it did. Yes, I used to get angry. Today I just laugh.

WALLACE: Are you a cornball?

BENTON: Probably. What of it?

In 1935, when he was at the height of his success (his self-portrait had recently adorned the cover of *Time* magazine), Benton became so fed up with the art scene in New York that he left the city where he had lived for many years and returned to his roots in Missouri to get back to what he called "human contact with real people." He later described New York and other big cities as "coffins for living and thinking," and when I asked him why he was so aggressively anti-urban, Benton replied, "I just feel that life within them is simply not good enough anymore. You don't get enough out of it. The pressures are too great, the dirt's too much, the stinks are too much, and the intellectual world stinks, too, when it's shut in and doesn't get out into the world. I think that the intellectual world of New York is even worse than the Congress of the United States."

I also reminded him about his controversial criticism of Picasso, whose works he had disdained as "artistic decadence." He elaborated on that indictment: "What I meant to say there, that when art comes to be made out of art rather than out of the meanings that are in life, it is entering into a period of decadence. Now, from this I would say that Picasso represents, more than any artist, that peculiar state because he makes pictures out of pictures all the time."

In the *60 Minutes* profile, I noted that Benton and his wife, Rita, spent half the year on Martha's Vineyard and the other half at their home in Kansas City. What I did not mention was that my wife and I were among their summer neighbors on the Vineyard. Before I did the story on him, Benton and I had, at best, a nodding acquaintance. That was mainly because his family lived up-island, near Chilmark, the site of a lively art colony; our digs were in Vineyard Haven, where distinguished authors (like my friend Bill Styron) and stellar journalists (like my friend Art Buchwald) preferred to estivate.

One day in the summer of 1974, a little over a year after my piece on Benton was broadcast, he called me to request a favor. He had been asked to take part in a lecture series at the Methodist Church in Edgartown, the purpose of which was to raise money for the Martha's Vineyard Arts Association. The problem was that Tom Benton had no stomach for making speeches of any kind in any forum, so he had agreed to participate only on the condition that he could bring along Mike Wallace and the *60 Minutes* profile to serve as props or helpmates. I readily gave my consent to that arrangement. Even under those circumstances, when the fateful evening arrived, Tom showed up at the church with a case of the jitters. Fortunately, I had anticipated his outbreak of last-minute stage fright, and I had the perfect remedy. Fully aware of his lifelong fondness for the sauce, I had come equipped with a flask that contained his favorite libation—cold and very dry gin martinis—and for the next half hour or so, we stood outside the church and gulped them down with the fervor of parched Bedouins quaffing at an oasis. Thus fortified, we entered the church fully prepared to be as loquacious and provocative as the occasion required.

In his remarks to the audience, Tom alluded to our hearty imbibing. He said that "before performing, one should drink gin and not bourbon, because bourbon sneaks up on you, while gin arrives with a punch, letting you know exactly where you stand, or fall." He did not fall, and after showing the *60 Minutes* profile, I had the happy experience of interviewing him all over again. In its story on the event, our local paper, the *Vineyard Gazette,* said that Benton and I "held the audience in a spell," and the reporter went on to praise Tom for his "deliberate and delightful orneryness."

Thomas Hart Benton died at the age of eighty-five just five months after that special evening, and all I can say now about that is how grateful I am that he waited until after I got a chance to know him and become his friend.

ITZHAK PERLMAN
VLADIMIR HOROWITZ

AS I'VE INDICATED, I HAVE never tried my own hand at painting or sculpture or any of the other fine arts. (My longtime colleague, Morley Safer, is the painter-in-residence at *60 Minutes.*) But classical music is another story. As a boy growing up in Brookline, I began taking violin lessons when I was ten and kept at it until I was seventeen. My violin teacher would later claim in interviews that I was not an especially diligent pupil; he said I talked too much during the lessons and that I had a knack for coming up with all kinds of implausible excuses to explain why I hadn't been able to practice. I'm sorry, but that is not how I remember it. I mainly recall the times when I was so pleased with my playing that during practice sessions, I would open all the windows in my room so that neighbors and passersby could catch an earful and be impressed by my musical prowess.

My teacher, Harry Ellis Dickson, was such a gifted violinist that he played in the first section of the Boston Symphony, and at a time when my sister's husband, Alfred Krips, was the concertmaster of that orchestra. Harry went on to become a conductor of the Boston Pops Orchestra, filling in for Arthur Fiedler and, later, John Williams. His daughter, incidentally, was also a close friend of our family. Her name was Kitty Dickson, but she is known to most Americans by the name she acquired when she married a Brookline neighbor, Michael Dukakis, who has the distinction of being the only governor of Massachusetts ever to run for president.

As for my own progress as a violinist, I was good enough to be given the honored role of concertmaster of our orchestra at Brookline High School. That turned out to be the high-water mark of my musical career. When the time came for me to go off to the University of Michigan in 1935, I didn't take my violin to Ann Arbor. In the end, I suppose Harry Dickson was right about me. Although I had been blessed with some talent, I did not have the drive or the discipline to become a first-rate fiddle player. As the famous virtuoso Jascha Heifetz once put it, to become an accomplished concert violinist, one "must have the nerves of a bullfighter, the vitality of a woman who runs a nightclub, and the concentration of a Buddhist monk."

I quoted that comment by Heifetz when I introduced a *60 Min-*

utes profile I did in 1980 on another brilliant violinist, Itzhak Perl-man. Born in Israel, Perlman had his first big success on an American stage at the age of thirteen, when he played his fiddle on *The Ed Sullivan Show*. He was given his first violin when he was a child of three, and the following year he was stricken with polio. As much as audiences over the years have been dazzled by Perlman's musical skill, they have been even more impressed by the courage and strong will it took to overcome his severe disability. I asked him about that.

WALLACE: I would think there might be a tendency, forgive me, to feel sorry for this crippled fiddle player.

PERLMAN: (Laughs) Well, I think that in the beginning there may have been, and I think that—

WALLACE: Were you aware of it?

PERLMAN: Oh boy, was I aware of it! I could show you reviews when I first came to the United States: "Handicapped violinist pretty good, despite disability." Or "Crippled blah, blah, blah, dah, dah, dah . . ." And "As he went on the stage hobbling on his shining aluminum crutches and very heavily sat down, but afterwards we forgot all about it and it was just music." And so on. And every, every single review had to mention that.

WALLACE: Got to you?

PERLMAN: And that the— Oh yes, it got to me, because it was just taking away from the matters at hand.

Recalling the intense focus and hard work that had gone into my teenage exercises with the violin, I was struck by something I had heard about Perlman's casual approach to practice sessions.

WALLACE: Who was it—André Previn who said that he came
in one day to watch you practice, and you were practicing and
watching *I Love Lucy* on television simultaneously?

PERLMAN: (Laughs) Well, it depends on what you practice.
Actually, the best show to practice on is baseball.

WALLACE: You can turn off the sound.

PERLMAN: You turn off the sound, you see what's going on,
and you practice your technique. I'm not talking about practicing thinking or anything like this. That's a totally different
thing. I did some of my greatest practicing when I was in London watching cricket. I mean, cricket, you know, cricket . . . is
a very, very slow game.

Perlman had an impish sense of humor, and once he became an
established virtuoso, he would often regale audiences with his banter
from the concert stage. There was, for example, the silly joke he
sometimes told about how Beethoven's death left some of his admirers so bereaved that, on a group visit to his grave, they decided they
had to have one last look at their beloved Ludwig. So they dug up his
grave, and when they pried open his coffin, they were severely
scolded by Beethoven. "Please, please, leave me alone," he demanded. "Can't you see that I'm de-composing?"

Shamelessly corny, perhaps, but it invariably got a big laugh,
probably because that kind of nonsensical remark seemed so deli-
ciously out of place at a serious classical concert.

During our interview, Perlman's mischievous streak surfaced on
several occasions, and there was one response in particular that I've
always treasured. He had referred to the violin as a Jewish instrument, so I rattled off the names of some past and present masters—
Heifetz, Yehudi Menuhin, Isaac Stern, and Perlman himself—and

then asked him why so many world-class fiddle players happened to be Jewish. With a broad grin and appropriate manual gestures, he replied, "You see, our fingers are circumcised and, you see, which gives it a very good dexterity, you know, particularly in the pinky."

When we aired that 60 Minutes piece, Perlman was thirty-five and was already being hailed as the finest violinist of his generation; since then his stature has only increased. In recent years, he has devoted much of his time and energy to nurturing the talents of future virtuosos. He and his wife, Toby, run the Perlman Music Program, which provides intensive instruction in five instruments—violin, viola, cello, bass, and piano—for students between the ages of twelve and eighteen. Every summer, gifted youngsters from all over the world spend six weeks at the Perlman music camp on Shelter Island, a picturesque retreat off the eastern coast of Long Island, and Perlman himself often conducts and/or performs at their concerts.

Itzhak Perlman wasn't the only world-class musician I interviewed on 60 Minutes. Three years earlier, in 1977, I had the thrill (and there's no other word for it) of doing a story on a towering genius, a man esteemed by most of his peers as the greatest pianist of the twentieth century—Vladimir Horowitz.

Gaining access to Horowitz was a rare privilege. He was notorious for having an aloof, even reclusive personality, and he almost never consented to requests for interviews. But in the late fall of '77, he was approaching a special occasion—the fiftieth anniversary of his American debut, a spectacular performance with the New York Philharmonic that had become the stuff of legend—and he agreed that such a milestone was worth the fuss of some media attention.

This assignment was one of the very few that made me nervous. I have seldom been intimidated by the people I've interviewed, no matter how important or powerful or brilliant they were reputed to be. But the prospect of going one-on-one with Horowitz did get to me a little. The way I saw it, discussing music with Vladimir Horowitz was like having a chat about the theory of relativity with Albert Einstein. No matter how much homework I did, there was no way I could measure up.

My concerns proved groundless. When we began working on the Horowitz story, he was in Chicago, where he was preparing to give a concert, a kind of tune-up for the golden-anniversary celebration two months later. Since we wanted to include footage from that concert in our profile, the *60 Minutes* crew and I flew to Chicago and, on the day before the performance, paid a visit to Orchestra Hall to look things over, decide on camera positions, and otherwise get our bearings. While we were doing that, Horowitz suddenly showed up. Without knowing that we were there, he had come to the hall to check out the piano, test the acoustics, and otherwise get *his* bearings. So I walked up to him, and just as I was about to introduce myself, he looked at me and said, "Mike Wallace. I watch you every Sunday night."

I could hardly believe that this musical titan, a man I regarded with so much awe, was presenting himself to me as a regular viewer of *60 Minutes*. Needless to say, that chance encounter was just what I needed to dispel the anxiety that had been gnawing at me, and when the time came for our interview at his town house in New York, I felt completely relaxed and comfortable in his presence. So much so that I even resorted to some playful needling, as I often did when I interviewed people I admired a great deal and whose company I enjoyed. For example, when Horowitz insisted that it didn't bother him if some other pianist received more money for a concert, I was quick to point out how unlikely that was.

WALLACE: If somebody gets more money? You tell me one other solo performer in classical music who gets eighty percent of the gross, which is what Vladimir Horowitz gets.

HOROWITZ: Well, I didn't do it my whole life. After fifty years of playing, I got this.

WALLACE: You get three times as much as any other classical performer today, I am told. And you smile when I tell you this because you know it's the truth, and you're proud.

HOROWITZ: I'm not proud, but this—it is so.

It was obvious that the irreverent tone I had adopted was a rare experience for Horowitz, who was accustomed to being treated with a punctilious deference usually reserved for royalty. Instead of taking offense, he seemed to be stimulated and even amused by my rather flippant approach, and so did his wife, who sat in on the interview. As the daughter of the renowned conductor Arturo Toscanini, Wanda Horowitz had grown up in a musical aristocracy. She and Horowitz were married in 1933, and since then she had devoted her life to being his constant companion (he never traveled anywhere without her) and most trusted adviser. She was also his most demanding listener, as I discovered when I brought her into the conversation.

WALLACE: Do you talk frankly when he plays well, and when he plays not so well?

MRS. HOROWITZ: Oh, absolutely.

HOROWITZ: Unfortunately, yes.

WALLACE: She does?

HOROWITZ: She's not always right, but she talks.

MRS. HOROWITZ: But most of the time I'm right. . . .

WALLACE: And you pay attention, maestro?

MRS. HOROWITZ: Don't say no. (Laughs)

HOROWITZ: I will say—I will say sometimes.

MRS. HOROWITZ: Well, sometimes.

WALLACE: No, I'm quite serious about this.

HOROWITZ: You know, I take her ears because she knows my ups and downs. . . . She knows my playing, you know, so she can judge.

We also talked about the difficult times he had been through, notably the period when he didn't play at all in public. In 1953, when he was forty-nine and very much in his prime, Horowitz suddenly announced that he was tired of the pressures of touring and was going to stop doing concerts for a while. Twelve years passed before he played in public again, and during this long hiatus, he lived mainly as a recluse. In fact, there was a two-year stretch when he never once left his town house.

HOROWITZ: I was in this room, very happy.

WALLACE: You were in this room, very happy?

HOROWITZ: Very happy.

WALLACE: And you, madame?

MRS. HOROWITZ: Not so happy.

In spite of what he told me, Horowitz himself was not so happy during this period of withdrawal. The truth of the matter was that he spent much of that time coping with depression, and I didn't fully appreciate what an ordeal that must have been for him until I had my own bout with the disease a few years after our interview. He eventually came out of it, and in 1965 he finally resumed playing in public. His much-heralded return to the stage took place at the same site where, as a young man, he had made his triumphant American debut. Wanda Horowitz had her own special memory of that comeback event. "He came out, and there was a big line of people on both sides of Carnegie Hall," she recalled. "And somebody said, 'Oh, Mr. Horowitz, we stood in line all night.' And I said, 'You know what? I stood in line for twelve years.'"

Horowitz was born in Kiev, but he left the Soviet Union in 1926 and did not return until sixty years later. He eventually settled in the United States and became an American citizen in 1942. He gave many benefit performances during World War II, the most famous of them in 1945, when he played "The Stars and Stripes Forever" at an event in Central Park celebrating the Allied victory that brought an end to the war. At one point in our interview, Horowitz told me how proud he was to be an American and how much he loved the United States. That made me think of the patriotic occasion in the summer of '45, so I began trying to goad him into playing the Sousa march again for our *60 Minutes* audience.

WALLACE: Do you love this country enough, maestro, to respond to a request for you to play something that you haven't played in many, many years in public?

HOROWITZ: Yeah, but I don't know it.

WALLACE: You know what I'm going to ask you?

HOROWITZ: Yes, I know because they ask me all the time. . . .

WALLACE: Are you enough of a patriot?

HOROWITZ: No, I forgot that. I didn't play—

WALLACE: Come on. You haven't forgotten it.

HOROWITZ: I didn't play— I tell you, I don't know it. But I have to remember. It's too difficult.

WALLACE: I'm sure that it's difficult.

His wife now joined in the prodding. "Go ahead, go on," she urged, and her encouragement must have made the difference, because he launched into a rousing rendition of "The Stars and Stripes Forever," thus giving me (and later, our viewers) the sublime pleasure of hearing the Sousa warhorse played as it had never been played in public—or at least not since that memorable day in Central Park thirty-two years earlier. That impromptu recital at his town house inevitably became the highlight of our story on Vladimir Horowitz.

During these years, the 1970s and early '80s, I did pieces on other eminent "longhairs," as classical musicians were often called back in the days before Americans of the hippie generation adopted the shaggy look as their badge of identity. The seventieth birthday of composer-conductor Aaron Copland was celebrated on *60 Minutes,* and I later did a story on Leonard Bernstein, whom I had known since childhood. We were both born in 1918, and we grew up in the same community. In fact, when I was working on the Bernstein profile, one of the wags in our office suggested that we call it "Two Boys from Brookline." I also did a piece on Mikhail Baryshnikov not long after he defected from the Soviet Union; I introduced that one with the rather bold assertion that "never before has one extraordinary dancer so captured our imagination."

Because I grew up in a musical family (my sister, Helen, was a gifted pianist), and because of my own teenage adventures with the violin, I felt comfortable in and conversant with the world of concerts and ballet. But I regret to say that my enthusiasm for classical music did not extend to opera, the dubious charms of which have always eluded me. Still, exceptional talent must be recognized wherever it is found, so I made occasional visits to that hybrid arena of robust arias and florid librettos. In the mid-1970s, I did stories on two of the world's finest sopranos, who could not have been less alike in background or temperament. One was Maria Callas, the fiery Greek diva who had a stormy romance with Aristotle Onassis and lost him to

Jacqueline Kennedy. (That love triangle had all the passion and histrionics of a grand opera.) The other was the gracious Beverly Sills, who was born in Brooklyn and who, in her younger days, was known as "Bubbles" Silverman. Finally, I did a story on the most celebrated tenor of his generation, Luciano Pavarotti, in 1993, the year he sang in front of a half million fans at a special concert in Central Park, a gala event that was transmitted on television to forty-seven countries.

Nor was I the only member of our team who dabbled in high culture. Morley Safer, Ed Bradley, Harry Reasoner, and all the other correspondents who have worked on *60 Minutes* over the years have done their own periodic pieces on artists of one stripe or another. Call it a diversion, if you wish, for there is no denying that our magazine show is perceived primarily as a broadcast that focuses on scandals and corruption and other stories that provoke controversy, and scandal, corruption, and controversy is what's just ahead.

SIX

CON MEN AND
OTHER CROOKS

MICKEY COHEN

IN THE ASPHALT JUNGLE, JOHN Huston's classic film noir about a gang that plans and carries out an elaborate jewel heist, one of the characters with a flair for expression describes criminal pursuits as "a left-handed form of human endeavor." In the spirit of that felicitous phrase, let me say that over the years, I've had dealings with more than a few moral southpaws. The first one to make an appearance in my particular rogues' gallery was a mobster named Mickey Cohen, who was one of our first guests on *The Mike Wallace Interview* after we made the jump to ABC in the spring of 1957. Of all the interviews I've done during the past half century, that's the one I've regretted the most because what happened with Cohen in our studio that night seriously undermined our position at ABC and, for a while at least, damaged my credibility as a reporter.

Reaching out to a shady character like Cohen was part of our overall effort to light a fire under the new network program. Both Ted Yates and I realized that the vast majority of our interviewees would come from the ranks of conventional celebrities: Hollywood stars, ambitious politicians, literary lions, and others of that ilk. But we figured that if we spiced up the roster from time to time with offbeat, cutting-edge guests who were not from the glittering mainstream, we would have a better chance of igniting the kind of buzz that had made *Night Beat* such a success during its six-month run on Channel 5 in New York.

In his heyday, Mickey Cohen had been a crook of some repute, especially on the West Coast, where he worked closely with his long-time partner in crime, Bugsy Siegel. Although Cohen's principal activities were gambling and bootlegging, he was well acquainted with other, rougher games. He was known to have killed some people who had crossed him in one way or another. But when we contacted him in the spring of '57, Cohen insisted that his criminal pursuits were all in the past. He had gone legit and was now making a modest living as a florist, an improbable line of work for someone who had long been accustomed to the high-roller action of bookmaking and peddling illegal booze.

We made it clear to Cohen that we weren't interested in talking to him about floral arrangements or tropical plants. What we wanted from him were stories about the Bad Old Days. We were hoping that recollections of his life in the underworld would give our audience some understanding of what a mobster did and what organized crime was like on the inside. After hearing what we had in mind, Cohen said he would be happy to give us "the lowdown."

Cohen flew into New York from Los Angeles, and our writer and researcher Al Ramrus was dispatched to the airport to meet him. There Al discovered that our guest had not traveled alone; arriving with him were two companions whom he introduced only as Arlene and Itchy. In keeping with our agreement, Al checked them into a suite at the Hampshire House on Central Park South, not far from our studio, but Cohen did not find the accommodations acceptable. It was then that we learned the former gangster had an obsession about hygiene and was so fastidious that he refused to share a bathroom with anyone else. We approved their move into a larger suite, one that offered more plumbing facilities, thereby assuring his pristine privacy.

All the trouble and expense seemed to be worth it, or at least that was my first impression once we began the interview. For the most part, Cohen did talk freely about his life on the wrong side of the law, even though some of his remarks were more than a little self-serving. At one point, for example, he piously boasted that he had never been involved in narcotics or prostitution, as if that abstention were enough to make him a model citizen. I wasn't about to let him get away with it.

WALLACE: Well, wait just a second. You say you've never mixed with prostitution, never mixed with narcotics.

COHEN: That's right.

WALLACE: Yet you've made book, you have bootlegged. Most important of all, you've broken one of the commandments— you've killed, Mickey. How can you be proud of not dealing in prostitution and narcotics when you've killed at least one man, or how many more? *How* many more, Mickey?

COHEN: I have killed no men that in the first place didn't deserve killing.

WALLACE: By whose standards?

COHEN: By the standards of our way of life. And I actually, in

all of these killings—in all of these what you would call
killings—I had no alternative. It was either my life or their life.

As he rambled on in this vein about how he had killed certain
people because he had no choice, I couldn't have been more pleased.
These were exactly the kinds of unsavory comments I'd hoped to
draw out of him. Then the conversation turned to his highly lucrative
but illegal gambling empire, and that was when we got into trouble—
serious trouble. Cohen claimed that in order to keep that racket running smoothly over the years, he had to shell out vast sums of money
in bribes to politicians and law-enforcement officials. That led me to
ask him: "Now, Mick, without naming names, how far up in the
brass do you have to bribe the cops to carry on a big-time bookmaking operation?"

Cohen neglected to answer the question, but unfortunately, he
did name names, and one in particular: William Parker, the chief of
police in Los Angeles. I never did find out what set Cohen off on
such a tirade, but he suddenly filled the air with an outburst of vi-
cious slander. Parker, he said, was "nothing but a thief. This man is as
dishonest politically as the worst thief that accepts money for pay-
offs. . . . He's a known alcoholic. He's been disgusting and he's a
known degenerate. In other words, he's a sadistic degenerate of the
worst type."

If this torrent of invective had been unleashed in a story I was
doing for 60 Minutes, there would have been no problem. By then the
standard practice in TV journalism was to film or tape an interview in
advance, and such loose-cannon comments would have been
checked for accuracy and weighed for discretion before being put on
the air. In this case, once it became clear that Cohen had no evidence to back up his abusive remarks, they would not have been in-

cluded in the broadcast. But *The Mike Wallace Interview* was broadcast live, and therein lay the peril. Cohen's libelous charges were heard by our viewers in real time, at the precise moment they were uttered. Still, that was no excuse for my lapse in judgment, for I had been doing live interviews long enough to recognize the danger signs. As soon as Cohen finished his diatribe, I should have said something like: "Now, wait a minute, you're calling the police chief of Los Angeles a sadistic degenerate, and that's undoubtedly actionable. I want to disassociate myself from all such accusations unless you can prove to me right now, at this instant, that what you're saying is true. Give me book, chapter, and verse. Otherwise, let's move on to something else."

Instead, I was so caught up in the heat of the moment that I proceeded to talk my way more deeply into hot water. Referring to his target as "the apparently respectable Chief William Parker," I urged Cohen to elaborate on his charges, and he was only too happy to oblige. In fact, he extended his allegations to other law-enforcement officials in Los Angeles.

As soon as we were off the air and I saw the expression on Yates's face, I knew we had a problem. Yet even after we had reviewed the broadcast and discussed it at some length, I still clung to the belief that even an ex-mobster would not have made such accusations unless he had the goods to nail the man he was talking about. To get reassurance on that point, Yates and I hustled over to Cohen's suite at the Hampshire House. Mr. Clean had just taken a shower, an ablutionary rite he apparently performed several times a day, and he greeted us wearing nothing more than a towel draped around his ample midriff. We moved directly to the point and told him how concerned we were.

"Mike, Ted, forget it," Cohen replied in a tone of serene confidence. "Parker knows that I know so much about him, he wouldn't dare sue."

Unfortunately, Police Chief Parker did not agree. At a news conference the next day, he threatened legal action and severely took us to task. "I am not concerned about the specific comments of such a person," he said, dismissing Cohen. "However, I am concerned about the authority of a television station to use that type of slander. A slanderous magazine story must be picked up at a newsstand, but TV enables slander to be brought into the living room."

That was enough to set off alarm bells at ABC. Prior to my next interview, our viewers were addressed by Oliver Treyz, the president of ABC Television. This was the same Oliver Treyz who, six months later, issued a formal on-air apology for the statement Drew Pearson made on *The Mike Wallace Interview* about the authorship of *Profiles in Courage*. I vigorously objected to that mea culpa, but in the aftermath of the Cohen interview, I fully agreed with the network's attempt to make amends. I was standing next to Treyz when we went on the air and he solemnly intoned:

"Last Sunday night something most unfortunate, unexpected, and profoundly regrettable occurred while Mr. Wallace was questioning Mickey Cohen. Leonard Goldenson, our president, joins me most earnestly in stating that the American Broadcasting Company retracts and withdraws in full all statements made on last Sunday's program concerning the Los Angeles city government, and specifically, Police Chief William H. Parker. . . ."

Treyz added a few more lines of remorse and ended by saying that ABC "deeply regrets the matter and offers its sincere apologies." He then turned to me. I said, "I join sincerely and earnestly in the statement of retraction and apology."

The humble pie we gulped down on national television was not enough to mollify Parker. He proceeded to sue ABC for two million dollars. Although the suit never came to trial (Parker eventually settled out of court for forty-five thousand dollars), the legal squabble and the adverse publicity it engendered took a heavy toll on us.

Among other things, the unfortunate encounter with Mickey Cohen undermined our self-assurance. We had come to ABC with a confidence that bordered on hubris. We were convinced that we had the moxie to turn our local hit show into a big winner on the national stage. Moreover, we had the trust and support of our new bosses, who encouraged us to pursue the probing interviews and controversial subjects that had been our stock-in-trade on *Night Beat*. Shortly before we had closed the deal with the network that spring, I was invited to break bread with Leonard Goldenson in his private dining room. He said to me, "Mike, you will not be doing your job properly unless you make this building shake every couple of weeks." With more than a little help from the loquacious Mr. Cohen, we had set off a tremor of earthquake force and intensity, but for some reason, Goldenson neglected to compliment us on the terrific job we had done. I didn't hear from him at all for several months after the Cohen interview.

However, our chief nemesis at ABC was neither Goldenson nor his second in command, Treyz, but the head of the network's news department, John Daly—or John *Charles* Daly, as he preferred to be called. Daly had been opposed to the whole idea of *The Mike Wallace Interview*. He made it clear that he did not consider me to be a "real" journalist but merely an interviewer, and an irresponsible one at that. I learned from some people who were close to Daly that when our *Night Beat* team was hired, he had told Goldenson and Treyz that bringing us into ABC was a serious mistake because we were bound to cause trouble for the network. In the wake of the Cohen broadcast, he was able to crow "I told you so"—and he did.

In other words, we were put squarely on the defensive, and once we lost our swagger, we also lost a lot of the driving force that had fueled the success of *Night Beat*. I even had to endure the indignity of a legal watchdog during our broadcasts. Not long after the Cohen interview, ABC's insurer, Lloyd's of London, insisted on the following new policy: Each night we went on the air, a lawyer would sit in the studio just outside of camera range, and there, facing me, he would hold up cue cards at sensitive moments warning me to BE CAREFUL or STOP or RETREAT. It was so demeaning that I routinely referred to the lawyer as "my nanny," but under the circumstances, I was in no position to object to his presence.

Still, we didn't exactly fold up our tent and slink off into oblivion. We continued to soldier on through the rest of 1957 and deep into 1958, during which time I did a number of interviews that were very well received, like the ones with Orval Faubus and Frank Lloyd Wright and Margaret Sanger, as well as several others I have not cited in this narrative. But we were never able to escape entirely from the shadow cast by the Cohen episode, and the subsequent flap over the Drew Pearson interview didn't help matters. Hence, when our contract with Philip Morris expired in the spring of '58, we were hardly surprised by the tobacco company's decision not to renew it. That naturally made our situation at ABC even more precarious, and though we managed to keep the show afloat for a few more months, it was obvious that our days there were numbered. So, rather than wait for the ax to fall, we arranged for safe passage back to the more congenial sphere of local television.

It still took a while to recover from the damage. The lingering fallout from the Cohen and Pearson broadcasts continued to dog me. Even some reviewers who had previously praised my candid style of interviewing now turned on me. I had come to be regarded in many circles as a reckless hip-shooter whose lust for sensationalism had plunged my network into legal jeopardy. It was during this period that I learned a vital and valuable lesson: If you choose to court controversy, then you better understand that it's a two-edged sword and you're likely to get cut up a bit in the process.

I don't want to overstate the difficulty of the post-ABC years. I had no trouble finding work, and I made a very nice living in a variety of jobs during the late 1950s and early '60s. But I couldn't help noticing that no offers came my way from any of the three networks. In their eyes, I apparently had become a pariah, and I pretty much remained one until early 1963, when I launched a vigorous effort to get hired by one of the networks, and the president of CBS News, Dick Salant, decided to take a chance on me. That marked my return to network journalism, and this time it was for keeps.

JIMMY "THE WEASEL" FRATIANNO
JOE BONANNO

I WON'T GO SO FAR as to say that my distressing experience with Mickey Cohen made me gun-shy (as it were), but twenty-four years passed before I interviewed another bona fide mobster. And I do mean bona fide, because they didn't come any more authentic than Jimmy "The Weasel" Fratianno, who for years had been one of the Mafia's most ruthless hit men. Fratianno agreed to appear on *60 Minutes* in 1981, since his life of crime and violence was the subject of a forthcoming book called *The Last Mafioso*. When I say he appeared on our broadcast, I should point out that the man viewers saw that night did not bear much resemblance to how Fratianno really looked. He was in the federal government's Witness Protection Program and was being kept under very tight wraps. I have only a vague idea of where our interview took place. In accordance with the terms of our arrangement, U.S. marshals picked us up at Washington's National Airport and took us on a meandering ride through the Virginia countryside. We eventually arrived at a government safe house on the Potomac River, and there Fratianno was waiting for us. As soon as he was disguised to everyone's satisfaction and we had our camera set up, I got down to brass knuckles.

WALLACE: Jimmy, who was the first person you killed?

FRATIANNO: Frankie Nicoli.

WALLACE: Where did you kill him?

FRATIANNO: In my house.

WALLACE: How did you kill him?

FRATIANNO: We strangled him.

WALLACE: In your own living room?

FRATIANNO: Right.

WALLACE: And then he dirtied your living room?

FRATIANNO: A little blood.

WALLACE: Yeah. A little blood and a little, er—discharge.

FRATIANNO: Yeah. (Laughs) How did you know that? A little urine, yeah.

WALLACE: You smile when you think back about it?

FRATIANNO: Well, what are you going to do?

He then talked about some of his other victims in the same tone of casual self-assurance. It was obvious that Fratianno looked back on his accomplishments with a strong sense of professional satisfaction.

WALLACE: You were a good killer?

FRATIANNO: I just had the talent to do things like that. I never made any mistakes.

WALLACE: A matter of some pride?

FRATIANNO: No. I just— Some people are a little better than others. But I think it would bother me if I killed an innocent person.

WALLACE: What do you mean by "an innocent person"?

FRATIANNO: Well, you're an innocent person. (Laughs)

WALLACE: I'm glad to hear you—you don't have designs—

FRATIANNO: I mean somebody innocent, you know, that is not involved in criminal activities.

Fratianno's own criminal activities began on the streets of the Italian ghetto in Cleveland where almost all his friends were hoodlums. By the time he was a teenager, he was regularly getting into trouble with the law. He served seven years in prison for armed robbery, and would go on to spend a total of almost twenty years behind bars. It was a Cleveland policeman who dubbed him "a weasel," and the nickname became his badge of identity. In our interview, he recalled with palpable pride the day he became a "made" member of the Mafia in a ceremony that included pricking his finger to draw blood from it and kissing other Mafiosi on their cheeks. I asked him what was so special about becoming a made member of that criminal empire.

FRATIANNO: Well, most people get made because they want respect.

WALLACE: Respect from whom?

FRATIANNO: Well, respect when you go to another town.

They send you to the boss and they take you around. They take care of your hotel and you meet a nice class of people.

WALLACE: You meet a nice class of people! You meet some other mobsters?

FRATIANNO: Well, you also meet some nice people. I met George Raft. . . . I know many a times I went to Vegas where nobody could get a seat. I got a front seat because I was Jimmy Fratianno.

I was amused by the example he chose to make the point that he met a nice class of people. In his heyday as a Hollywood actor, George Raft achieved some measure of stardom, but he invariably played gangsters and others who were engaged in "a left-handed form of human endeavor." I had the feeling that Fratianno's high regard for Raft had more to do with the characters he had portrayed than with the man himself.

One of Fratianno's best friends in the *real* underworld was Chicago mobster John Roselli, who originally proposed Jimmy the Weasel for membership in the Mafia. According to Fratianno, Roselli was involved in a plot that could have had a serious effect on the cold war.

WALLACE: Did the Mob actually have a contract with the CIA to assassinate Fidel Castro?

FRATIANNO: John Roselli did, yeah.

WALLACE: Johnny Roselli, your friend, the fellow who proposed you for the Mob, had a contract to do what, for whom, under what circumstances, with whom?

FRATIANNO: Well, to kill Castro for the CIA.

WALLACE: Tell me what you know.

FRATIANNO: Well, all I know is that Johnny told me that they were going to kill Castro for the government. And he says, "Geez, if we do this, we'll get all the favors that we want."

The assassination obviously did not pan out, and the Mafia had to find other ways to elicit favors from the U.S. government.

For all his proud boasting about being a made member of the Mafia, Fratianno was still just a hit man, a foot soldier in the army of thugs who served in the trenches of organized crime. Two years later, I interviewed one of the generals of that army—Joe Bonanno. He, too, had agreed to abandon the sacred policy of *omertà*—the Mafia code of silence—by appearing on *60 Minutes* because he, too, had an autobiography he wanted to promote. That book was called *A Man of Honor,* and when it was published in 1983, Bonanno was seventy-eight and living in retirement in Arizona. Long before his own book was written, he had achieved a kind of indirect literary fame, for it was widely believed that Bonanno was the model for the title character in *The Godfather,* the Mario Puzo novel that became the source for three blockbuster movies. Whatever the case, there's no doubt that he had been a capo don, one of the most powerful of all the Mafia bosses, and since his long criminal career dated back to the 1920s, I asked him about the legendary Mob king of that era.

WALLACE: You knew Al Capone?

BONANNO: I happened to know him, yeah.

WALLACE: What kind of a man?

BONANNO: Al Capone was a very jolly guy.

WALLACE: Al Capone was a jolly guy?

BONANNO: Very jolly . . . I like him.

WALLACE: Why did you like him?

BONANNO: For his character, for his approach, for his—the way he handle himself, and the way—the external appearance. But I never know Capone from inside.

I met with Bonanno at his home in Tucson, and sitting in on our interview was his son, Bill, who was so amused by my startled expression when his father described the mastermind of the St. Valentine's Day Massacre and other criminal excesses as "a very jolly guy" that he burst out laughing. The conversation then turned to a longtime rival for power within the Mafia hierarchy—Lucky Luciano— and the Bonannos, father and son, enlightened me on the primary difference between the two Mob leaders.

BILL BONANNO: Here you have two young fellas coming up in the—in the world, in their own world, seemingly from the same background.

WALLACE: Bonanno and Luciano.

BILL BONANNO: And Luciano, and instantly having a conflict of philosophy, a philosophical conflict.

WALLACE: And what, basically, was the conflict in philosophy?

JOE BONANNO: Luciano was an American product.

BILL BONANNO: An American product.

JOE BONANNO: And I was a Sicilian product.

BILL BONANNO: Right. That is the conflict, and the conflict boiled down to the Americans wanted everything to revolve around money, making money.

WALLACE: And your father wasn't?

BILL BONANNO: His whole life has been one of trying to live up to his own principles and his own traditions, which have come in conflict with the new traditions of this country.

Some of their remarks had a familiar ring they would not have had if my interview with the Bonannos had taken place before 1972, the year *The Godfather* appeared on movie screens throughout the world. The enormous success of that film about another immigrant family from Sicily—the Corleones—and its two sequels elevated the Mafia to the stature of romantic myth, almost on par with that long-time staple of popular legend, the Hollywood western. And so, as Joe and Bill Bonanno expounded on their loyalty to family values and ethnic traditions, there were moments when I had the feeling that I was listening in on a conversation between Don Vito Corleone (Marlon Brando) and his son Michael (Al Pacino).

The sense of identification with *The Godfather* was even more acute when we looked at pictures of Bill's marriage to Rosalie Profaci. The lavish reception his father had hosted on that occasion bore a striking resemblance to the opening scenes in *The Godfather,* which many consider to be the most festive wedding celebration ever portrayed in a movie. Included on the VIP guest list at the Bonanno nuptials were all the major Mafia chieftains. I commented on their attendance.

WALLACE: Every—forgive me—mobster in the world, it
   seemed, in the United States, was at that hotel in New York.
   Detroit was there. Cleveland was there. Buffalo was there. Los
   Angeles was there.

JOE BONANNO: All United States was there.

WALLACE: All United States was there.

JOE BONANNO: Yeah. Like congressmen was there. Judges
   was there.

BILL BONANNO: Frank.

JOE BONANNO: Frank Sinatra got— He couldn't come and

sing . . . Bennett—Tony Bennett sang all night with a nice
voice.

BILL BONANNO: The Four Lads were entertaining.

JOE BONANNO: Yeah, yeah.

BILL BONANNO: Some opera singer was there.

JOE BONANNO: Opera singers was there.

BILL BONANNO: There were three thousand people there,
and I venture to say, according to FBI statistics, that there are
not more than four thousand, quote, "Mafia members," unquote, in the whole United States.

Mingling with all the Mafiosi were the congressmen and the
judges and the lawyers and the bankers and all the others who, for one
reason or another, felt obliged to attend Bill Bonanno's wedding out of
respect for his father. Moreover, it's a safe bet that, over the years, Joe
Bonanno benefited from having such influential connections in the legal and political arenas. For all his high-profile reputation as a Mafia
boss, the only crimes for which he was convicted were obstruction of
justice and contempt of court. And for those rather modest white-
collar offenses, he spent only twenty-six months behind bars.

Following our interview, he lived for another two decades, until
2002, when, at the ripe old age of ninety-seven, Joe Bonanno finally
passed on to his eternal reward, or whatever.

CON MEN

MOBSTERS LIKE JIMMY FRATIANNO AND Joe Bonanno represented, each in his own way, the hard-core domain of organized

crime, where murder and other acts of violence came with the territory. But before I turned my attention to those Mafiosi, I had already done quite a few stories on swindlers and other rogues who specialized in soft-core crime. All things considered, it was better to fall into the clutches of one of those white-collar criminals than to incur the displeasure of the Mafia. Victims of con men might get fleeced out of their hard-earned life savings, but they ran little risk of getting their kneecaps broken or "sleeping with the fishes."

By the early 1980s, I'd done so many pieces on nefarious scams of one kind or another that investigative journalism was regarded by many to be my principal métier. Oh, I was commended every now and then for my reporting from the Middle East and for my interviews with political leaders in Washington and such cultural icons as Itzhak Perlman and Vladimir Horowitz. But those assignments rarely provoked the kind of visceral response from viewers that some of my investigative stories did. And what was true of my work was, to a large extent, true of *60 Minutes* in general.

That was not what we had in mind when we started out in the fall of 1968. At the time of our debut, Don Hewitt openly acknowledged that insofar as he was influenced by print journalism, his model for *60 Minutes* had been *Life* magazine. Like *Life,* we were picture-oriented, tightly edited, and we sent cameras all over the world to cover major events. At the same time, we kept an alert eye for lively features and human-interest stories so that we could offer the kind of balance that had made *Life* such a huge success. That formula was our guiding light during our first few years on the air.

The event that thrust us into the investigative realm was the Watergate scandal. Like so many other journalists, we were drawn into that deluge when it battered the White House in 1973, and for the next year or so, we did several pieces on the stunning disclosures that eventually destroyed Richard Nixon's presidency. But that was just part of its impact. The scandal also had a profound effect on American journalism.

Watergate sparked a wave of enthusiasm for investigative reporting, and as the infectious fever spread through newsrooms across America, we were among those who caught the bug. For us, there was a special challenge, because the prevailing view at the time was that television could not deal with that kind of journalism. The assumption was that because the camera was such an intrusive presence, TV reporters could not engage in the stealthy tactics that were so often needed in order to expose corruption and other misdeeds. (No one had to be reminded that the best reporting on the Watergate cover-up was the gumshoe work done by print journalists, most notably Bob Woodward and Carl Bernstein at *The Washington Post*.) We set out to demonstrate that not only could we do such stories on *60 Minutes,* we could do them as well as our brethren in print.

Over a two-year period, from the winter of 1976 to the spring of 1978, I focused most of my attention on investigative reports, some that struck nerves with our viewers, many of whom responded with expressions of outrage toward the miscreants and/or gratitude to us for having exposed the scoundrels.

The subject of a story we did in Chicago was corruption within the Medicaid program. On that one we worked closely with a nonpartisan reform group called the Better Government Association. According to the BGA and other sources, several clinical laboratories in the Chicago area were offering lucrative kickbacks on their Medicaid transactions. In league with the BGA, we set up a bogus medical clinic and invited a number of the suspect labs to come in and discuss using their services for our Medicaid business. Since we had a hidden camera installed behind a one-way mirror on the wall, and I was listening to the conversations from an out-of-sight position in an adjoining room, it did not take us long to gather damaging evidence on all the kickbacks we were offered. "The Clinic on Morse Avenue" was broadcast in February 1976; not long thereafter, nine labs in the Chicago area were permanently cut off from the Medicaid program, and eleven others were temporarily suspended.

The key figure in another story we did on corruption in Chicago was an accountant named Philip Barasch, who served as a middle-man in a scheme whereby certain city inspectors were accepting bribes to overlook serious building-code violations. We learned about him from Pam Zekman, an investigative reporter for the *Chicago Sun-Times,* who had joined forces with our friends from the BGA. Zekman and a BGA investigator had come up with their own version of our phony clinic, in this case a neighborhood bar called (appropriately) the Mirage Tavern. Identifying themselves as the husband-and-wife owners of the tavern, they soon became clients of Barasch, who schooled them in the discreet niceties of bribe bestowal. His counsel was not confined to bribery: He also advised them on how to reduce their tax bite by shaving 40 percent off their income reports.

For me, the high point of the assignment came when I interviewed Phil Barasch in a hotel suite we had rented. After asking him a few leading questions, which he parried, I summoned Zekman and her "husband," the BGA watchdog, from an adjoining room. Once Barasch realized he had been set up, he reluctantly acknowledged that he had given the couple advice on how to pay off the city inspectors. But he vigorously denied that he had shown them how to falsify their income reports. Shifting to a sympathetic tone (and a more subtle ploy), I suggested there was no reason for him to be so uptight about it, because it was my understanding that people who ran small cash-oriented businesses like the Mirage Tavern routinely received pointers from their accountants on how to conceal part of their income. I should also mention that even though our CBS camera was quietly rolling, we were in a private hotel suite where there was a strong sense of being cut off from the rest of the world. Which helps to explain what happened next. When Barasch agreed that the widespread practice of tax fraud was "common knowledge," I gently moved in for the payoff, using a phrase that I would later adopt as the title of this book.

WALLACE: I know it's common knowledge, and apparently, you are among the people who do it. That's all that we're trying to— I mean, look, *between you and me*—
BARASCH: Yeah.
WALLACE: —you do it, everybody does it.
BARASCH: I presume everybody does it to an extent . . .
WALLACE: You mean, if they wanted to put every tax accountant in jail who did that kind of thing—
BARASCH: They'd all be in.

Between you and me! Poor Phil Barasch had allowed himself to forget that our interview was being recorded on-camera, and when we broadcast the piece a few weeks later, his statement that "everybody does it" (including him) was made "between you and me" and the millions of viewers who were watching *60 Minutes* that night. In large part because of that admission, a federal grand jury subpoenaed Barasch's records and those of five other accountants who had been hired by the Mirage Tavern.

A California story that caught our attention had to do with a clinic at a spa called Murrieta Hot Springs. It promised to provide "miracle cures" to victims of cancer and other serious diseases.

From various sources, we heard about complaints that the man who ran the place, R. J. Rudd, went out of his way to court wealthy patients who, once enrolled in the cure program, were pressured into making large financial contributions to the clinic. Acting on the theory that it takes a con game to catch a con man, the producer of the story, Marion Goldin, and her film crew—cameraman Greg Cook and soundman James Camery—enrolled at Murrieta under false pretenses. Camery identified himself as a wealthy investment counselor who was suffering from an illness that had recently been diagnosed as leukemia. Cook claimed to be Camery's concerned nephew, and to justify the camera equipment he had brought with him, he said he was a professional photographer, which actually was not that far from the truth. As for Goldin, she pretended to be the ailing man's longtime secretary. To enhance the impression of affluence, our *60 Minutes* trio arrived at the clinic in a rented Rolls-Royce.

During their weeklong stay at Murrieta, our three poseurs were able to obtain enough information to prove that the clinic was an utterly fraudulent enterprise that had indeed been established for the sole purpose of prying donations out of wealthy patients, most of whom were elderly as well as ill. With their hidden camera and microphone, Goldin, Cook, and Camery were able to film and record most of that evidence. When the time came for me to appear on the scene, I had all the ammunition I needed to confront Rudd with a flurry of incriminating practices, from bogus diagnoses (Camery, who in truth was in fine health, was told by the doctor who examined him that his illness was not leukemia but a "leaky lung" that required treatment) to phony medications that were nothing more than placebos. But when I accused him directly of running "a con-game operation," he piously denied it.

When we probed into Rudd's shady past, we learned that Murrieta had been preceded by several other fraudulent schemes he had concocted over the years, and in other states besides California. In a spin-off of the title from an avant-garde French film, *Last Year at Marienbad,* we called our report "This Year at Murrieta," and a few months after we broadcast it in January 1978, Rudd was convicted in Florida of bilking an elderly woman stricken with leukemia out of twenty-five thousand dollars in a land-investment swindle. The Murrieta Hot Springs health spa was declared bankrupt with liabilities of nearly thirty-seven million dollars.

Early on in my interview with R. J. Rudd—before I revealed that the wealthy folks who had arrived at his clinic in a Rolls-Royce were, in reality, members of the *60 Minutes* team—he tried to impress me with his academic credentials. He boasted that he had a Ph.D. each in economics and philosophy, and to back up those claims, he showed me his diplomas from Christian Tennessee University and Trinity Christian College in Florida. I had never heard of either school, and with good reason; when we did some checking, we learned that Rudd's diplomas were nothing more than mail-order degrees from fictitious universities. We naturally included his phony education in "This Year at Murrieta," and in the flood of mail that came our way after we aired the piece, we read about numerous other people who had acquired sham diplomas. Our curiosity aroused, we went to work on an investigative story called "A Matter of Degrees."

We soon discovered that diploma mills were a thriving industry from coast to coast. After looking over the crowded field, we decided to concentrate on California Pacifica University in Los Angeles. We were drawn to that college by its promotional brochure, which characterized California Pacifica as "the custodian of the intellectual capital of mankind." Our next move was to provide a "student" worthy of that academic bastion. We arranged for a *60 Minutes* cameraman, Wade Bingham, to meet with the president of California Pacifica, Ernest Sinclair.

Bingham, who was in his early fifties, had attended college as a young man for just one year. But Sinclair assured Bingham that his thirty years as a cameraman were all the credits he needed for a master's degree in business administration. Bingham paid $2,150 for tuition, and although he never went to class, never read a textbook, and never took an exam, he received his degree from California Pacifica. Not long after Bingham's "graduation," a film crew and I visited the California Pacifica "campus," which was located in a Hollywood building just above a wig shop. I'll never forget the expression on Ernest Sinclair's face when we walked into his office. Even though he was talking on the phone at the time, he promptly acknowledged our arrival.

SINCLAIR: (On phone) Hey, wait a minute. Hey, *60 Minutes* is in here. Can you believe it?

WALLACE: How are you?

SINCLAIR: *60 Minutes* here! Hold the phone.

WALLACE: Nice to see you.

SINCLAIR: (Still on phone) I'm trying to tell you his name. Let's see . . . Hey, this is my favorite. Gosh! What's your What's your last name?

WALLACE: Wallace. Mike Wallace.

SINCLAIR: Mike Wallace!

The effusive greeting was typical of Sinclair, who turned out to be one of the most engaging rogues I've ever encountered. His flaky exuberance was a large part of his charm, and when I questioned him, he cheerfully admitted that his fake-diploma operation was a lucrative racket. I complimented him on the slick brochure for California Pacifica and the impressive array of faculty members featured in it. I then asked him about some of them, starting with a man named Mario Ugarte, who was identified as the dean of the college of education.

> WALLACE: Is he here now?
>
> SINCLAIR: He's not here.
>
> WALLACE: Rosalba Riano, the administrative assistant?
>
> SINCLAIR: Right. We did make communication with her by telephone, and she is alive and well, and she's in New York in the garment district.
>
> WALLACE: But she's no longer your administrative assistant?
>
> SINCLAIR: No. I know I'm— No, she never did come to our school.
>
> WALLACE: Terrel Harvey, is he still dean of your college of law?
>
> SINCLAIR: I could— I could probably say yes, and I could probably say no.

Although his glib patter was entertaining, Sinclair was talking himself into serious trouble, and he must have understood that, because he was no stranger to legal difficulty. He already had served time in three states for mail fraud, and a few days after we broadcast "A Matter of Degrees" in April 1978, he was arrested and once again charged with that crime. Ingratiating to the end, Sinclair later wrote from prison to let me know that he intended, finally, to go straight and to thank me for helping put him on the road to reform.

And so it went through the late 1970s and beyond as we steadily built up our investigative credentials and infused *60 Minutes* with a bold new spirit and identity. It was around this time that someone came up with the line "You know it's going to be a tough week when you show up at your office on a Monday morning and a *60 Minutes* camera crew is waiting there." The remark soon became a kind of defining mantra that we heartily embraced. In the eyes of our admirers, our show had become a television descendant of the muckrakers, that vigorous breed of reformers whose moral passion and diligent reporting did so much to strengthen the craft of journalism back in the early 1900s.

We also had more than a few detractors. For the most part, the criticisms that came our way had to do with the various deceptions we employed to get the goods on our quarries. By the early 1980s, the complaints had become so frequent that almost every time we aired an investigative story, our tactics were called into question. So we decided to confront the accusations directly in the open forum of our own broadcast, and in September 1981 we launched the new season with a special edition of *60 Minutes*, a program devoted entirely to the subject of our alleged transgressions.

We invited three distinguished print journalists to appear on the show: Eugene Patterson, the crusty veteran editor of the *St. Petersburg Times* (and before that, *The Atlanta Constitution* and *The Washington Post*); Ellen Goodman, the syndicated columnist from *The Boston Globe*; and Bob Greene of *Newsday*, who had won a Pulitzer Prize for his work as an investigative reporter. In one of his rare on-camera appearances, Hewitt sat in on behalf of *60 Minutes*, and so, in my humble, self-effacing way, did I.

To provide stimulus for our panel discussion, we looked at excerpts from some of our more flamboyant investigative pieces, including "The Clinic on Morse Avenue" and "This Year at Murrieta." Most of the criticisms were voiced by Patterson and Goodman, and they centered on our use of hidden cameras and other furtive techniques. The phrases used most frequently in the objections were "ambush journalism" and "entrapment." To no one's surprise, Hewitt and I did not agree with those assessments, especially when it came to the charge of entrapment. We noted, for example, that although the two men who had presented themselves as comanagers of our mock clinic in Chicago were, in reality, staff members of the Better Government Association, at no time and in no way did they suggest the clinic was seeking kickbacks of any kind. In every case, it was the visitors from the laboratories who initiated those offers, and all we did was document their proposals.

It was altogether fitting that I was the correspondent on the hot seat when we faced our critics that night. There's no denying that, for better or for worse, I was the on-air reporter who was most closely associated with our adventures in investigative journalism. One reason for that was because the producers I worked with were especially eager to explore that challenging terrain, and let me take a moment here to doff my cap to two of them in particular: Barry Lando and Marion Goldin. Lando produced the Chicago stories on our bogus clinic and Mirage Tavern, as well as some others of that nature before he moved on to Paris, where he became my main producer on the assignments that took me to the Middle East and other overseas locations. The many stories I did with Goldin included the California pieces on Murrieta and Ernest Sinclair's diploma mill.

Even though I did not agree with the charges leveled against us on that special edition of *60 Minutes* (a broadcast that, by the way, was Goldin's idea), I didn't think we were entirely blameless. In my opinion, our major fault was an excess of zeal. There were times when we got so caught up in the investigative fever that we adopted a sort of crusade mentality and wound up doing reports that projected more heat than light. One day in 1980 another member of my producing team, Norman Gorin (who also did some first-rate work in the investigative sphere), received a call from a friend who said he had a story proposal. Gorin had a keen sense of humor, and his first response was: "Yes, but is it a national disgrace? It has to be a national disgrace. That's the only kind of story I'm allowed to work on these days."

As we moved into the 1980s, we trimmed our sails a bit, in terms of both the tactics we used and the number of pieces we did. When I say "we," I'm referring to *all* the correspondents who worked on *60 Minutes*. Just because I was more heavily involved in investigative reporting than my on-air colleagues were doesn't mean that they steered clear of the genre. All of them had delved into scams of one kind or another, and even though we cut back on the volume, all of us continued through the years that followed to take on periodic assignments that enabled us to add fresh portraits to our respective rogues' galleries.

Twenty-one of those portraits were selected for publication in a 2003 book called *Con Men*. Compiled by a freelance editor named Ian Jackman, *Con Men* is (in the clarion boast of the subtitle) an omnibus of "fascinating profiles of swindlers and rogues from the files of the most successful broadcast in television history." The opening chapter is an account of my 1978 story on R. J. Rudd and his contemptible clinic at Murrieta Hot Springs, followed by other pieces we did over the next two decades, various stories by each of the show's correspondents.

I was asked to write an introduction to the book, and I began it by recalling a comment that Morley Safer made back in 1981 or thereabouts. "A crook," he said, "doesn't feel he's really made it as a crook until we've told his story on *60 Minutes*." Over the years we've done our best to give more than a few crooks the recognition they deserved.

SEVEN

THE GENERAL AND THE
WHISTLE-BLOWER

GENERAL WILLIAM C. WESTMORELAND

OF ALL THE CONTROVERSIES I'VE been caught up in over the years, none was as traumatic as the firestorm that erupted in 1982 after we broadcast a *CBS Reports* documentary called "The Uncounted Enemy: A Vietnam Deception." That furor was one for the ages, and before it finally ran its course over three years later, my CBS colleagues and I had to go through the ordeal of a $120 million libel suit. In addition, I was stricken with a severe case of clinical depression. The irony is that until we did that documentary, I had a fairly cordial relationship with the principal figure in our story, General William C. Westmoreland. I certainly did not agree with all his military assessments and optimistic predictions when he was in command of our forces in Vietnam, but I had no reason to question his honor or integrity. And Westmoreland had indicated that he had some respect for my work as a reporter.

I first met the general in March 1967, when I began a two-month assignment in Vietnam. This was over a year before the birth of *60 Minutes,* and I had been working as a field correspondent since the summer of '66, when I relinquished my anchor post on the *CBS Morning News.* Most of my reporting during this period dealt with domestic politics and civil rights, which was just fine, except I wanted to take a break from that drill and spend some time overseas. By the mid-1960s, no foreign story was bigger than the war in Vietnam, so I asked my bosses to send me to Saigon.

I was told in advance that Westmoreland welcomed the arrival of older reporters in Vietnam, in large part because he believed that those of us who had served in World War II (I was a junior naval officer in the Pacific theater) were more likely to be in tune with the values and judgments of senior officers like him. I don't know how much that mattered, but I will say that, like millions of other Americans, I was an early supporter of our military mission in Vietnam. As time went on, I began to question the decisions that gradually transformed the conflict into a full-scale American war, and by 1967, I shared in the growing concern over the fact that even after all those escalations, we'd been unable to achieve the victory we'd been led to expect.

Concern was not the mood I encountered at the headquarters of the U.S. combat mission in Saigon, where I was ushered into the commanding presence of General Westmoreland. With his ramrod posture and firmly set jaw, "Westy" struck me as the very model of military assurance, and that initial reaction was reinforced when I was given the opportunity to spend some time with him. Not long after I arrived in Saigon, I was invited to accompany the general on a daylong air tour of firebases and field briefings across the length and breadth of South Vietnam. At one of our stops, we walked through the military hospital at Cam Ranh Bay, where wounded soldiers gazed up at their commander with admiration. It was an impressive performance, in keeping with the calm and steady optimism he exuded.

Westmoreland and his top aides kept insisting over and over that although the U.S. mission had gone through some rough patches, we had finally gained the upper hand in the war. (In hindsight, my main regret is that he refrained from uttering in my presence the phrase that would later cause him so much grief, his confident boast that there was "light at the end of the tunnel.")

From my own observations and conversations I had with reporters who had spent the past several years in Vietnam—especially R. W. Apple of *The New York Times* and William Touhy of the *Los Angeles Times*—I came to the sad conclusion that our troops were bogged down in a quagmire. By the time I returned to the States that spring, I was more convinced than ever that our intervention in Vietnam had been a terrible mistake, a tragic waste of lives and resources.

In spite of my disillusion, my reporting on Vietnam was even-handed (as, of course, it should have been), so Westmoreland had no reason to believe that I had turned against the war. If he had been privy to my personal feelings, he probably would not have written the letter he sent me in 1972 after *60 Minutes* aired an update of a story I had done a few years earlier on three wounded veterans who had been shipped home from Vietnam without their legs. "Dear Mike," the general wrote in response to that broadcast, "I just want to tell you that it was a first-class piece of reporting. I have never seen better." I wrote back to thank him, and that was the last contact I had with

Westmoreland until May 1981, when I interviewed him for the documentary that brought our cordial relationship to a shattering end.

The catalyst who brought the two of us together for what proved to be a momentous encounter was the producer of the documentary, George Crile. A former editor at *Harper's* magazine, Crile had been hired in 1976 to produce broadcasts for the documentary unit we called *CBS Reports*. Over the next five years, he put together a number of excellent, award-winning documentaries. I was well aware of his sterling reputation when he came to me one day in early 1981 and proposed that we work together on a new project he was developing for *CBS Reports*.

Crile said he was pursuing a story about an elaborate deception that had been carried out by senior officers in Vietnam over a period of several months in 1967. According to the primary source, a former CIA analyst in Vietnam, General Westmoreland's intelligence apparatus had deliberately underreported the size and strength of enemy forces in South Vietnam. The motive was to give credence to all the optimistic claims that the U.S. military was in control of the war and moving toward an inevitable and decisive victory. But as a result of those doctored estimates, U.S. troops in the field, political leaders in Washington, and the American people were unprepared for the scope and intensity of the Tet offensive the enemy launched in January 1968, a full-scale assault that had a devastating impact on the course of the war.

Although I was fascinated by what Crile told me, I felt I had to decline the offer. I explained that because of my *60 Minutes* obligations, there was no way I could find time to get involved in such an ambitious undertaking. Crile persisted, assuring me that he would do all the time-consuming spadework and even most of the interviews. He went on to say that, given the documentary's explosive nature, the main correspondent had to be a seasoned reporter who had clout and authority, especially when it came to interviewing. Elaborating on that point, Crile said that much of the broadcast would be structured around interviews with Westmoreland and other high-ranking officials; Crile needed a correspondent who wouldn't hesitate to press them for answers to tough and challenging questions. I found his argument persuasive, so I changed my mind and told Crile he could count on me, as long as he understood that my work for *60 Minutes* had to remain my top priority.

Over the next several months, Crile diligently tracked down the information he needed to build his case, and true to his word, he kept my participation to a minimum. He did check in from time to time to let me know how he was progressing, and the more he told me, the more I came to realize how damaging the evidence was about the military intelligence operation in Saigon. Among the more startling revelations were those made by some of Westmoreland's own top deputies, who acknowledged—for the first time in public—that there had been a conspiracy to "cook the books" and prevent the full strength of enemy forces from being disclosed in intelligence reports. No indictment was more damning than one made by General Joseph McChristian, who had been the chief intelligence officer in Saigon. He told Crile that when he had submitted accurate estimates of enemy troop strength, they were suppressed by Westmoreland. He described that and similar decisions to provide misleading numbers as "falsification of the facts." Crile then asked if such deceptions violated any statutes in the Uniform Code of Military Justice, and McChristian replied, "Not that I'm aware of. But there's something on a ring that I wear from West Point that the motto is: 'Duty, Honor, Country.' It's dishonorable."

That was the kind of stuff I had in my arsenal of notes when the time came for my interview with Westmoreland. Although Crile had sent a letter spelling out the topics I'd be focusing on, Westy greeted me warmly and evinced no sense of foreboding. He seemed to regard me as a kindred spirit, and I could understand that. During my brief assignment in Vietnam, I had always treated him with the utmost respect, even after I became highly skeptical of the war and his assessment of it. But once our interview began, it did not take long for his mood to darken.

I brought up the critical moment in the spring of 1967 when General McChristian and his chief deputy, Colonel Gains Hawkins, came across information that enemy forces were much larger than previous intelligence reports had indicated. They presented that new information to Westmoreland along with a proposal that the official reports be revised to reflect the dramatic increase in the estimates of enemy strength. Westmoreland refused to accept their recommendation, and when I asked him why, he replied, "I didn't accept it because of political reasons."

"What's the political reason?" I asked. "Why would it have been a political bombshell?"

"Because the people in Washington were not sophisticated enough to understand and evaluate this thing, and neither was the media."

This was a stunning admission that cut straight to the heart of the matter. By the spring of 1967, both Westmoreland and his commander in chief, Lyndon Johnson, knew that neither Congress nor the American public would tolerate another major escalation in Vietnam, especially one on a scale necessary to defeat an enemy nearly twice as large as previous intelligence estimates had indicated. They also knew that such an escalation would have fanned the flames of the growing antiwar movement and touched off a fresh round of critical blasts from an increasingly hostile press. Those concerns were the main "political reasons" why Westmoreland chose to reject the new and more accurate intelligence figures.

The official military term for the estimates of enemy troop strength is "order of battle," and later in our interview, I asked Westmoreland about a decision in the summer of 1967 to drop an entire category of the Vietcong army—the self-defense militia—from the order of battle. He was, by then, acutely irritated with the whole tenor of our discussion, so instead of answering my question, the general decided that the time had come to put me in my place with a verbal reprimand. "This is a nonissue, Mike," he snapped. "I made the decision. I don't regret making it. I stand by it. And the facts prove that I was right. Now, let's stop it!"

"All right, sir," I said, and paused briefly to give him a chance to simmer down. But I had no intention of obeying his command. Instead, I rephrased the question in a more direct and detailed way.

WALLACE: Isn't it a possibility that the real reason for suddenly deciding in the summer of 1967 to remove an entire category of the enemy from the order of battle—a category that had been in the order of battle since 1961—was based on political considerations?

WESTMORELAND: No, decidedly not. That—

WALLACE: Didn't you make this clear in your August twentieth cable?

WESTMORELAND: No, no. Yeah. No.

WALLACE: I have a copy of your August twentieth cable—

WESTMORELAND: Well, sure. Okay, okay . . .

I then quoted from the cable in question: "We have been projecting an image of success over the recent months. The self-defense militia must be removed or the newsmen will immediately seize on the point that the enemy force has increased. . . . No explanation could then prevent the press from drawing an erroneous and gloomy conclusion." Confronted with that solid evidence, Westmoreland had no choice but to admit that the major reason for the decision was, in effect, to conceal the true strength of the enemy forces from the media and their readers and viewers back in the States.

But time was running out for the U.S. command in Saigon. Just five months after that deception was put into effect, the Vietcong launched the Tet offensive, and we all learned, to our dismay, that the enemy we were up against in Vietnam was much larger and stronger than we had been led to believe.

Crile went on to explore other aspects of the story during the late spring and summer of 1981, and I conducted a few more interviews that were included in our report. When the editing was completed in the fall, everyone who screened the final cut agreed that it was a very strong documentary, and one bound to provoke some controversy, even though our focus was on events that had occurred fourteen years earlier during a war that Americans had not fought in since 1972.

"The Uncounted Enemy: A Vietnam Deception" aired on January 23, 1982, and three days later, General Westmoreland held a news conference at which he denounced the documentary as "a preposterous hoax" and accused me of subjecting him to a "star-chamber" inquisition. In spite of the general's objections and a few other grumbles of dissatisfaction, the initial press reaction was overwhelmingly favorable, and the kudos did not come from just the usual suspects, the so-called liberal media. Among those who praised our report was the conservative columnist William F. Buckley, who had long been a staunch defender of the U.S. intervention in Vietnam. But four months after we broadcast "The Uncounted Enemy," *TV*

Guide published a strident attack on the program, and that was when the real controversy began.

The magazine article, coauthored by Don Kowet and Sally Bedell, certainly had an eye-catching title: "Anatomy of a Smear—How CBS Broke the Rules and 'Got' Gen. Westmoreland." The problem was that the text did not live up to the sensationalistic come-on. All the criticisms made in the piece dealt with Crile's reporting and editing procedures, and while a couple of those complaints had some merit, the others were either specious or irrelevant. Far more significant was the fact that Kowet and Bedell stopped short of challenging the substance of the broadcast, the solid evidence we presented to back up our allegations about the deception in Vietnam. After all their huffing and puffing about process, they ended the article with the following conclusion: "We do not know whether Crile and his colleagues were right about General Westmoreland and his military intelligence operation." At which point, a dispassionate reader might rise to inquire, "Well, if you're not prepared to refute the CBS charges against the general, then where is the 'smear'?"

Unfortunately, that was not the position the new president of CBS News, Van Gordon Sauter, chose to adopt. Rather than taking the criticisms in stride and pointing out that the substance of the documentary was in no way discredited by the article, Sauter announced, with considerable fanfare, that he had ordered an in-house investigation of the magazine's allegations. Crile and I were not happy about that decision, and we made no attempt to conceal our displeasure.

Crile, in particular, had more to worry about than the internal report Sauter had ordered. Throughout the spring and early summer of '82, pressures were building within CBS News to isolate him as the culprit in the controversy. In fact, rumors began to spread that he was on the verge of being fired. When I got wind of them, I forcefully passed the word to Sauter (through intermediaries) that if Crile was sacked, I would have no choice but to resign. I pointed out that I was inextricably linked to the broadcast, and if Crile was guilty of the kind of grievous errors that warranted dismissal, then so was I. After all, I noted, the headline accusation in the *TV Guide* piece was that we had "smeared" General Westmoreland, and I was the one who had interviewed him.

Beyond that, there was a moral principle at stake that went to the heart of broadcast journalism. I strongly believe that a correspondent must bear major responsibility for what he reports on the air. This is especially true when the story in question is the kind of investigative piece that is apt to stir up controversy. After all, we reporters rarely hesitate to accept the plaudits that come our way when a story is well received, even though much of the time, it's our off-camera producers who deserve most of the credit. So it seems to me we should shoulder our share of the blame when things go wrong.

Getting back to the summer of 1982, the in-house probe of the allegations leveled against "The Uncounted Enemy" was completed in July, two months after the *TV Guide* piece was published, and its findings only exacerbated the tensions within CBS News. On one side of the dispute were colleagues who embraced the internal report in all its particulars, and on the other side were those who agreed with Crile and me that it was seriously flawed. Our faction believed that, among other misjudgments, the report gave far too much credence and legitimacy to charges in the article that, in our view, were too trivial or extraneous to warrant a serious response.

So the arguments raged on within our shop, and that discord put

Van Gordon Sauter in a bind of his own making. Because he had made such a big public brouhaha about the internal investigation, there was no way he could keep the conclusions under wraps. He had to acknowledge them, and he did. However, in the statement he released to the press about the official CBS report on the documentary, he also cited the various in-house objections to its findings. More than anything else, Sauter's attempt to reconcile the opposing views was an exercise in equivocation, and as such, it resolved nothing and satisfied no one. That point was clearly grasped by Tom Shales, the television critic for *The Washington Post*. In his column about the ambiguous tenor of Sauter's statement, Shales wrote that "instead of dispelling the cloud that had formed over the program, CBS News all but seeded it for rain." And the cloudburst was not long in coming.

Ever since we broadcast our documentary, General Westmoreland had explored the prospect of a libel suit against CBS. The first few lawyers he contacted discouraged him from taking that legal action. All of them stressed how difficult it was for a public figure like the general to build a case for libel, and their judgments may also have been influenced by the initial public reaction to the program, which ran strongly in our favor. But the publication of "Anatomy of a Smear" in May—and CBS's ill-advised reaction to it—ignited a storm of controversy that raged across most of the summer. By the early fall of 1982, the climate of public opinion had undergone a significant change. By then many Americans had come to believe that we had indeed perpetrated a "smear" in order to "get" General Westmoreland, and that was enough to persuade a Washington lawyer named Dan Burt to represent Westmoreland in a $120 million libel suit against CBS.

Burt was the president of the Capital Legal Foundation, a conservative public-interest firm, and in taking on the case, he was no doubt driven by a political agenda. Perhaps the same could be said about our esteemed defender, David Boies, a partner in the New York firm of Cravath, Swaine & Moore. (This was the same David Boies who later fought so vigorously on behalf of Al Gore and the Democrats in the epic recount battle that took place in Florida during the weeks after the 2000 presidential election.) For the next two years, Burt and Boies were pitted against each other in the elaborate pretrial maneuvers, a kind of bloodless trench warfare fought with depositions and sundry legal strategies (a discovery motion here, a change-of-venue motion there) as well as in the media, where (ironically) Burt had the upper hand. He was adept at public relations, and he saw to it that in one forum after another, Westmoreland was portrayed as a maligned hero. Burt was so confident his PR manipulations would lead to legal victory that in an interview with *USA Today* in the spring of 1983, he proclaimed that "we are about to see the dismantling of a major news network."

In his quiet way, Boies was just as confident. While Burt was scoring flashy points in the media, Boies was building his defense around what he called "a fortress of depositions" that either reaffirmed our broadcast's disclosures or corroborated them. "Our case could not be stronger," he assured us at one point during the pretrial phase. Boies also kept reminding us that the official verdict would be delivered not in the court of public opinion, where Burt and his team were playing to the grandstand, but in a federal courtroom in lower Manhattan, where the trial in the case of *Westmoreland* v. *CBS* finally began in October 1984.

In spite of Boies's optimism, the early weeks of the trial did not go well for us. As the attorney for the plaintiff, Burt had the first shot at the jury, and the witnesses he called took turns denouncing "The

Uncounted Enemy" and the network that had put it on the air. We were accused of using "lies" and "fakery" to achieve our goal, which (according to their testimony) was to destroy the reputation of a great American military hero. The hero himself was on the witness stand for nine days. At the age of seventy, Westmoreland still cut an imposing figure, one that projected all the patriotic virtues of a West Point man who had devoted his life to serving his country in uniform. That gave weight to his repeated denials of the charges we had leveled against him and to his countercharges that CBS had been one of the media culprits whose "negative reporting" had helped to bring about the failure of the U.S. mission in Vietnam.

The trial dragged on for four months, and through it all, the only personal contact I had with Westmoreland took place on the very first day of the proceedings, when I went to a men's room in the courthouse and found myself standing at a urinal next to him. The general and I exchanged curt nods and proceeded to go about our business at our respective urinals—at swords' point, so to speak.

I attended most of those early sessions that fall, which was not a pleasant experience. It was no fun sitting in a courtroom day after day and hearing yourself and your colleagues vilified as liars and frauds and even traitors. I knew most of what was being said about us was nonsense, but that was small consolation. My reputation as a fair and credible reporter was being torn asunder by the calumnies coming out of that courtroom, and I thought that even an eventual verdict in our favor would not be enough to repair the damage.

The more I heard, the more dejected I became. The trial was upsetting me so much that I couldn't go to sleep at night, and when I took sleeping pills to overcome the insomnia, I woke up in the morning so groggy that I didn't want to get out of bed. I lost my appetite and no longer had any interest in doing things I normally enjoyed doing. Like most people, I'd been down in the dumps on other occasions for one reason or another, but never before had I experienced this kind of constant, mind-racking despondency. I felt as low as a snake's belly, yet when I sought help from a doctor I'd been going to for years, he assured me that I had nothing serious to worry about. "You're just going through a difficult period," he said. "But you're a tough guy, Mike, and you'll snap out of it in no time."

Putting aside the "tough guy" compliment (if that's what it was), he was dead wrong about my snapping out of the black mood in no time. What my doctor failed to recognize was that I was sliding down the slope into a clinical depression. As fall gave way to winter, I sank ever more deeply into that dark and devastating malaise, which was crushing my spirit and even sapping my will to live. Shortly before the New Year, I came perilously close to committing suicide. I probably would have taken the plunge into that abyss had it not been for the love and caring support I received from the woman in my life, who was both an old friend and a new romance.

That last comment, I realize, requires a few words of explanation. The woman I'm referring to was Mary Yates, the widow of Ted Yates, my dear friend and colleague from the early years of *Night Beat* and *The Mike Wallace Interview*. After working together on those programs for several years, we went our separate ways—he to NBC and I to CBS—and even though we were now at rival networks, our friendship continued to flourish. One of the saddest days of my life came in June 1967, when I heard that Ted had been shot and killed in East Jerusalem while covering the Six-Day War between Israel and its Arab neighbors.

Through the years that followed, my wife, Lorraine, and I remained friends with Mary and her family. (She and Ted had three sons—Ted Jr., Eames, and Angus.) Lorraine and I had been married since 1955, the year before Yates came up with the idea for *Night Beat,* which did so much to change all our lives. But after many years of happiness together, we began to drift apart. By the early 1980s, it had become painfully clear to both of us that we somehow had lost the magic that once had made us so close, so in 1984, Lorraine and I agreed, with deep regret, to get divorced. As I struggled that year to adjust to the challenge of living alone at the age of sixty-six, I reached out to close friends for support, and one of them was Mary. The more time we spent together, the more we came to realize that our long friendship was blossoming into something deeper, and by the fall of '84 we had become what the gossip columnists used to call "an item." Mary and I formally tied the marital knot in 1986, and we've been together ever since.

I bring up this personal background to introduce Mary, who played such a critical role in my survival that December in 1984 when I felt I was on my last legs. Recognizing that I was completely losing my grip, she got me to a hospital, where I came under the care of a psychiatrist named Marvin Kaplan; along with Mary, he deserves the credit for saving my life. Thanks to Dr. Kaplan's wise counsel in our therapy sessions and the medication he prescribed, I was soon on the road to recovery.

I was in the hospital for ten days, and at my request, the public announcement about my confinement said I was being treated for "nervous exhaustion." That was an absurdly bland term for the mental and emotional anguish I was going through, but I preferred to conceal the true nature of my illness, and for a long time I clung to that position. As I mentioned in Chapter Two, it took me several years to work up the courage to talk publicly about my depression. But once I crossed that emotional Rubicon, I became involved in fund-raisers and similar events aimed at shedding light on the problems of mental illness and the various misconceptions that often deter victims from getting the help they need.

One of the insidious aspects of depression is that it has a tendency to recur, and since that initial attack in the winter of 1984–85, I've had two relapses. The last one occurred in 1993, and the remedy Dr. Kaplan prescribed then was a new drug called Zoloft. That medication produced the desired effect, and since then, I'm happy to say, I've been the jovial, easygoing chap you've seen on television over the years.

While I was in the hospital in January 1985, I received flowers from General Westmoreland and his wife, Kitsy. I was touched by that olive-branch gesture, especially since the Westmorelands, by then, had ample reason to be displeased with the way the trial was going. By the time I was released from the hospital, all the momentum had shifted and was flowing in our direction. Boies had begun his case for the defense, and true to his word, his impressive stockpile of depositions was being converted into strong and convincing testimony on our behalf. George Crile proved an excellent witness with his lucid and insightful comments on the documentary, the tape of which was shown as evidence. But the most lethal blows to Westmoreland's case were delivered by General Joseph McChristian and Colonel Gains Hawkins, the two high-ranking intelligence officers from the U.S. command in Saigon. In their testimony, they not only reiterated the stunning revelations they had made on our broadcast, they went into even more detail about the deceptions that Westmoreland had sanctioned in 1967.

It was almost time for me to take the witness stand, and I viewed that prospect with considerable anxiety. I was concerned not about what I might say in my testimony—I was fairly confident on that score—but about how I might appear. The medication I had been taking at that time—an antidepressant called Ludiomil—had some side effects, and one of them caused my hands to shake involuntarily. The last thing I needed was for jurors to wonder why my hands were trembling; I could vividly imagine the questions that might form in their minds: Is he that nervous because he has something to hide? Is he afraid of being exposed as a libelous scoundrel who truly did set out to "smear" General Westmoreland? Fortunately, it never came to that, because just two days before I was scheduled to testify, Westmoreland withdrew his libel suit. Just like that, it was all over.

Westmoreland's abrupt decision to throw in the towel did not sit well with many of his conservative supporters, who had been pulling for him to win "revenge" against the network that had besmirched his reputation. Some of them grumbled that the general had wilted under the pressure and had deserted the cause. But Westmoreland knew what he was doing. There was no point in drawing out the trial to its official and all but inevitable verdict. Westmoreland's big mistake was not withdrawing when he did but his decision to initiate the costly libel suit in the first place. In that respect, his legal action stands as a parable of the U.S. involvement in Vietnam. The mistake was not pulling out of Vietnam when we did, but the succession of tragic blunders that led us into the quagmire.

At the same time, I believe that the management of CBS News had only itself to blame for the libel suit. If Van Gordon Sauter had not overreacted to the piece in *TV Guide,* the resulting uproar would have petered out in a week or two. It was Sauter's public call for an in-house investigation—and the deeply flawed report that came out of that probe—that kept the controversy boiling and created a climate that could be viewed as conducive to a libel suit against us.

But for all the disappointment and frustration I felt toward my superiors on that occasion in 1982, it was nothing compared to my feelings of outrage and betrayal thirteen years later, when—for the first time—the corporate management of CBS emasculated a *60 Minutes* story I had done just as we were preparing to put it on the air.

JEFFREY WIGAND

THE ANTI-SMOKING CRUSADE THAT SWEPT across the country in the latter part of the twentieth century had such a profound and powerful impact on our social habits that it is startling to look back to a time when cigarettes permeated almost every aspect of American culture. Nowhere was their presence more pervasive than on our airwaves. In writing about my interview programs in that distant era of black-and-white television, I've made occasional mention of the fact that our sponsor was Philip Morris. Ours was just one voice in a cacophony of sales pitches to entice viewers to smoke a particular brand, for we had plenty of competition from other tobacco companies.

Throughout most of the 1950s, NBC's evening news show was the *Camel News Caravan,* with its recurring vow of commitment: "I'd walk a mile for a Camel." Its chief rival for the dinner-hour audience was *Douglas Edwards with the News* on CBS, which was sponsored by Pall Mall. ("Outstanding, and they are mild!") And the millions of Americans who tuned in to Jack Benny's popular comedy show every week were acutely familiar with this brisk assertion: "L S M F T—Lucky Strike Means Fine Tobacco." Another catchy slogan was the ungrammatical "Winston tastes good like [*sic*] a cigarette should." For several years my sponsor's favorite gimmick had been a diminutive bellhop who cried out the name of the brand as if it—or he—were an important hotel guest who had to be paged: "Call for Philip Morris . . ." But the Philip Morris people didn't need the bellhop and his hearty shout on *The Mike Wallace Interview*. That was because they had me.

The show's format called for me to open with a commercial spiel on behalf of the cigarette. After the interview was over, I would turn to the camera and do some more selling. On one occasion, I opened the broadcast with a few remarks about a recent trip I had made to Europe and what a good ambassador Philip Morris had been during that overseas visit.

"Wherever I went, whenever I offered someone one of these Philip Morrises, I made a friend—or [holding up the cigarette pack] we did. . . . It happens wherever I go. So I'm more convinced than ever that today's Philip Morris is something special. After all, where else can you find a man's kind of mildness except in today's Philip Morris? Here is natural mildness, genuine mildness. No filter, no foolin'. You see, no filter is needed, because the mildness comes from the tobacco itself. . . ."

That riff was, I'm afraid, all too typical. To further enhance the aura of my devotion to the product, I generally smoked when I was on the air, even during the interviews. I was under no obligation to do so, but since I happened to be a heavy smoker at the time, I thought of it as a natural indulgence. The main reason I smoked on camera was not to please our sponsor but because both Yates and I believed it helped to sharpen the visual effect we were trying to achieve. Our stark set, with its klieg lights stabbing into the faces of the interviewees, gave our broadcast the austere look of a verbal prize ring, and the plumes of smoke curling from my cigarette fit in perfectly with that image. Besides, I was in very good company. The most celebrated television journalist of that era—Edward R. Murrow—almost never appeared on the air without a burning cigarette clutched between his fingers.

Even after *The Mike Wallace Interview* went off the air, I continued to do commercials for Philip Morris because, frankly, they were a lucrative source of income during a period when I was bouncing from one job to another. When I finally extricated myself from them in the fall of 1962, my decision had nothing to do with cancer or any other health concern. That was the year I made up my mind to go straight and work exclusively in news, and I knew no network would hire me as a correspondent if I was still appearing in commercials, regardless of the product. As it was, the residual stigma from my fling with sales pitches proved to be an obstacle that was not easy to overcome. But thanks to Dick Salant, the president of CBS News, I was given an opportunity to build a new career in network journalism.

In 1964 the surgeon general, Luther Terry, issued his famous report that established an unmistakable link between cigarettes and lung cancer. Seven years later, cigarette commercials were banned from the nation's airwaves, and not long after that, I joined the growing horde of Americans who quit smoking. The social revolution to eradicate smoking was well under way by then, and it persisted, with ever increasing force and intensity, over the next two decades. In the 1990s, I did a couple of *60 Minutes* stories on the life-and-death struggle that had come to be known as the Tobacco War.

The producer I worked with on those pieces was Lowell Bergman, whose forte was investigative reporting. Among the stories we had already done together were a look at accusations of child abuse at a preschool in Los Angeles and a 1992 probe into the so-called Iraq-Gate banking scandal. In early 1994 we fixed our gaze on the tobacco industry and the inflammatory dangers posed by cigarettes. We called that story "Up in Smoke," and in it, we reported that fires ignited by cigarettes were the number one cause of fire deaths in America, with most of them occurring in bed after a smoker has drifted off to sleep with a lit cigarette. Our story revolved around some confidential documents about a top-secret project that had been carried out by my old sponsor, Philip Morris. According to the documents, which were leaked to Bergman by an anonymous source, the purpose of the undertaking was to develop a fire-safe cigarette that smokers would find acceptable. It was called Project Hamlet, because the pet phrase within the company for the question it explored was "To burn or not to burn."

The documents were quite technical, so to help us decipher them (as well as authenticate them), we hired a highly skilled analyst as an off-camera consultant. He was a chemist named Jeffrey Wigand, and until recently, he had been director of research at another tobacco firm, Brown & Williamson. After making a detailed study of the documents, Wigand told Bergman they contained solid evidence that Project Hamlet had been a success: The research scientists at Philip Morris had come up with a way to produce a fire-safe cigarette that would also be consumer-friendly. Wigand went on to say that what made him angry was the fact that Philip Morris had declined to move on to the next step and had kept its discovery under a thick veil of secrecy.

By the time "Up in Smoke" was broadcast in March 1994, Bergman had spent enough time with our consultant to know that Wigand's anger was not confined to Philip Morris's lack of follow-through in the quest for a fire-safe cigarette. The two of them had talked about how embittered Wigand was over what had happened to him at Brown & Williamson. When he was hired in 1989 as head of B&W's research-and-development operation, he was encouraged to focus his scientific skills on reducing the health hazards in cigarettes. This was at a time when executives at all the tobacco companies were insisting there was no firm evidence that smoking was a prime cause of cancer and other serious diseases. But according to Wigand, they were fully aware of how harmful cigarettes were.

Even though his conversations with Bergman were off the record, Wigand still had to be circumspect, because when he was fired by B&W in 1993, the terms of his severance package included a stringent confidentiality agreement. So he did not go into specifics about what he had learned during his four years there. Nevertheless, Bergman felt certain from what Wigand did say, and from his overall manner, that he had the kind of explosive information that had never before been divulged by someone who had been part of the inner workings of a major tobacco firm. The challenge for Bergman was to get Wigand to go on the record, to blow the whistle on B&W in a *60 Minutes* interview with me.

That was no easy task. Wigand had been warned that if he violated his confidentiality agreement with B&W, he would be sued for breach of contract. Yet Bergman could sense that in spite of the powerful legal deterrent, Wigand wanted to spill the beans on his former employer. For one thing, he was still smoldering with resentment over the way he had been treated at B&W. For another—and this was a far stronger motive—he was outraged by the policies of deception that made it possible for B&W (as well as other tobacco companies) to produce and sell cigarettes that imperiled the health of millions of smokers. As he put it in one of his conversations with Bergman, he was struggling to resolve his "moral crisis."

So Bergman decided to stay in touch with Wigand, to phone him fairly often and to make periodic visits to his home in Louisville. The purpose was to build a relationship based on the deep concern they shared about the harmful effects of smoking and to develop a bond of trust that would encourage Wigand to defy the confidentiality agreement and appear on *60 Minutes*. Thus began a long campaign of earnest pep talks and hand-holding that lasted through the rest of 1994 and deep into the following year. Bergman's patience and perseverance paid off, even though it wasn't until the summer of 1995 that Wigand finally gave Bergman the green light to set up the interview with me.

Wigand's on-camera indictment of his former employer proved as strong and compelling as Bergman had predicted. One of his first disclosures was the flat assertion that tobacco executives had long known nicotine was an addictive drug. That flew in the face of a memorable scene at a 1994 congressional hearing on the health hazards of smoking, at which CEOs from the nation's seven largest tobacco firms stood in a row elbow to elbow, raised their right hands, and swore that they believed nicotine was not addictive. Among those who joined in that chorus of denial was Wigand's former boss at B&W, Thomas Sandefur, whom Wigand accused of having "perjured himself." I asked him to elaborate on that charge.

> WIGAND: Part of the reason I'm here is I felt that their representation, clearly—at least within Brown & Williamson's representation—clearly misstated what they commonly knew as language within the company: that we're in a nicotine-delivery business.
> WALLACE: And that's what cigarettes are for?
> WIGAND: Most certainly. It's a delivery device for nicotine.
> WALLACE: A delivery device for nicotine. . . . Put it in your mouth, light it up, and you're going to get your fix.
> WIGAND: You'll get your fix.

Wigand went on to reveal that the policy at B&W was to manipulate and adjust the fix by enhancing the effect of the nicotine through the use of chemical additives, a process known throughout the tobacco industry as "impact boosting." What was more, when he came up with evidence that some of those additives increased the danger of serious disease, his concerns were largely dismissed. We then talked about his research project to develop a safer cigarette, and how all his efforts in that direction had been thwarted at every turn. At one point, he said, he became so frustrated that he took his complaints directly to the head man, Thomas Sandefur.

WALLACE: What did he say to you?

WIGAND: "I don't want to hear any more discussion about a safer cigarette."

WALLACE: (Voice-over) And he says Thomas Sandefur went on to tell him:

WIGAND: "We pursue a safer cigarette, it would put us at extreme exposure with every other product. I don't want to hear about it anymore."

WALLACE: All the people who were dying from cigarettes.

WIGAND: Essentially, yes.

WALLACE: Cancer.

WIGAND: Cancer.

WALLACE: Heart disease, things of that nature.

WIGAND: Emphysema.

After listening to some more of Wigand's allegations, I said to him, "In other words, what you're charging Sandefur with, and Brown & Williamson with, is 'ignoring health considerations consciously.'"

"Most certainly," he replied.

I could well understand why the honchos at B&W came to regard Wigand as an alien presence in their midst, and why, after he was fired, they were so determined to keep him clammed up. His portrait of the cynical deceptions that shaped the policies at his former company—and, by implication, at other tobacco firms—could hardly have been more scathing. It was very strong stuff. As we were about to discover, it was too strong for the collective stomach of the CBS brass.

One day in mid-September, about a month after I interviewed Wigand, I was summoned to a meeting with Ellen Kaden, the CBS general counsel. Also present were Lowell Bergman, Don Hewitt, and Eric Ober, the president of CBS News. At the time, we still had some loose ends to tie up on the story we were building around the Wigand interview, and it was not yet scheduled for broadcast. But Kaden knew all about the interview, and that was what she wanted to talk about. "I think we have a problem," she said, and then she used the phrase "tortious interference." Translated from the legal jargon, that meant persuading someone to break a contract with another party. Because Wigand had a firm confidentiality agreement with B&W, she said, CBS could be "at grave risk." My initial reaction was to assume that Kaden was merely raising a lawyerly flag of caution, a stern warning that we should be extremely careful in the way we edited the interview. Only later would I come to understand how determined the corporate management of CBS was to prevent Jeffrey Wigand from appearing on *60 Minutes*.

Over the years, our program and other CBS News shows had done stories that displeased and even alarmed the so-called suits who presided over the network. That came with the territory, for there was a natural, built-in conflict between the news culture and the corporate culture. But never before, in the long history of CBS, had the top brass pushed so hard to undermine a story that hadn't even been edited for broadcast. Even more disheartening was the fact that neither

Ober nor Hewitt put up any serious resistance to the corporate pressure. When it came to that, I was especially sore at Hewitt, who, after all, had long been our staunch champion and protector at 60 Minutes. He and I had several spirited arguments that fall. He kept insisting that we were not "crusaders" for the commonweal (a rather odd view of a program that, under his leadership, had become renowned for its bold investigative journalism). I kept lashing back that there were important First Amendment issues at stake that he should be defending.

My distress was nothing compared to Bergman's. He was furious at all his bosses, and I couldn't blame him. He had pursued this tobacco scandal for the past year and a half, and he knew that bagging the Wigand interview elevated our story to a level of major consequence, on par with the best pieces ever done on 60 Minutes. Nor did Bergman believe that the tortious-interference concern had much merit. He cited the top-secret documents from Brown & Williamson that had been leaked over the past year to various media outlets. Since those documents corroborated Wigand's main allegations, they undercut the whole point of the confidentiality agreement. Furthermore, Bergman argued, even if B&W's clamps on Wigand were binding, it had to be an implausible stretch to extend them to him and CBS.

My own view of the legal threat was not so cavalier. Inasmuch as both sides in the tobacco war were driven by a passion for litigation, I thought we should at least consider the prospect of a lawsuit against us. At the same time, I shared Bergman's suspicion that CBS's objections to the Wigand interview had more to do with family and corporate considerations than with legal fears per se. For example, one of the tobacco executives who had sworn under oath that he believed nicotine was not addictive was Andrew Tisch, the CEO of Lorillard and the son of CBS chairman Laurence Tisch. In our interview, Wigand had labeled such testimony as perjury, and so, quite aside from the legal implications, airing that assessment on 60 *Minutes* would not have been good for the Tisch family's image or financial interests. In addition (although neither Bergman nor I knew this at the time), Lorillard was in negotiations that fall to buy six brands of discount cigarettes from Brown & Williamson, a purchase that was announced in late November. To complicate matters still further, Larry Tisch and his top deputies were putting the final touches on a deal to sell CBS to Westinghouse for $5.4 billion. So, given all the givens, the last thing the Tisch family wanted that autumn was a tobacco-company lawsuit against CBS.

In the weeks following our September meeting with Tisch's general counsel, Ellen Kaden, she steadily strengthened her tortious-interference argument until it became a virtual demand that the Wigand interview be killed. I suspect she did so because she and her corporate colleagues perceived weakness and acquiescence on the part of Hewitt and Ober. In early November, Hewitt came up with what I'm sure he regarded as a Solomonic solution. He decided to broadcast a sanitized version of our tobacco story without the Wigand interview.

My first impulse was to endorse that compromise, on the time-honored theory that half a loaf is better than you-know-what. But the more I thought about it, the more I came to believe that Hewitt's decision was a terrible mistake. Among other things, it would set a dangerous precedent; I could easily imagine it becoming the foundation for a change in network policy whereby management would claim the right to cut segments from any story that incurred its displeasure. Hewitt was clearly trying to have it both ways. He apparently thought that airing the piece without Wigand would provide a cover for his capitulation to the CBS brass. I remember how disgusted I was when a *New York Times* reporter quoted Hewitt as saying that the castrated version was "better, I think, than what we had before."

Two days before the revised story was scheduled to air, I called Peter Lund, who, as the president and CEO of the network, ranked just under Tisch in the corporate hierarchy. I told him that the only way I could go along with the sanitized version was if I could close the program with some on-camera remarks that would be critical of the suppression that management had imposed on us. And, I said, I wanted his permission to do so. Lund's first response was a heavy sigh; he obviously didn't like what he was hearing. Nevertheless, he said that if I truly felt that strongly about it, then I should go ahead and have my say. I think he sensed from my icy tone that if he didn't grant my request, I might resign in protest and raise an even bigger public howl. (As Lyndon Johnson once said about his FBI director, J. Edgar Hoover, "Better to have him inside the tent pissing out than outside the tent pissing in.")

The truth is, I had given serious consideration to quitting on principle. The main reason I didn't was because I was not yet ready to retire from a career that had given me so much satisfaction, and at the age of seventy-seven, I felt I was much too old to make a fresh start somewhere else. Moreover, I had a strong hunch that if we stayed the course and steeled our way through this crisis, we would find a way to broadcast the Wigand interview on *60 Minutes*.

The reedited version of our story was built around the stockpile of leaked documents that Bergman had assembled, and we aired it on November 12, 1995. Even in its emasculated form, it was a powerful indictment of the tobacco industry. But in my on-camera open, I pointed out that the story would have been far more powerful if we had been able to include my interview with the first whistle-blower to come forth from the executive suite of a major tobacco firm. I then reported the legal concern that prevented us from airing the Wigand interview, and noted that "we are not allowed even to mention his name or the name of the company he worked for." At the end of the program, I came back on-camera and made the following statement:

"A footnote to the controversy about the tobacco piece you saw at the beginning of the hour tonight. We at *60 Minutes*—and that's about a hundred of us who turn out this broadcast each week—are proud of working here and at CBS News, and so we were dismayed that the management at CBS had seen fit to give in to perceived threats of legal action against us by a tobacco-industry giant. We've broadcast many such investigative pieces down the years, and we want to be able to continue. We lost out, only to some degree, on this one, but we haven't the slightest doubt that we'll be able to continue the *60 Minutes* tradition of reporting such pieces in the future without fear or favor."

Although the expression of dismay was measured and restrained, I thought it was forceful enough to make the point that we were seriously at odds with our corporate superiors. However, it wasn't forceful enough to satisfy Bergman, who had turned on me as well. He felt my presence on the revised version gave it a legitimacy it did not deserve, and that by agreeing to take part in the broadcast, I was betraying him and Wigand and the story we had done. In his eyes, I was lumped in with Hewitt and the others who had caved in to the CBS management.

Unfortunately, Bergman was running out of colleagues to alienate. Although I sympathized with his frustration and anger, he went way overboard in his caustic criticisms of Hewitt and others, including me. Hewitt spread the word around the shop that because of his disloyalty, Bergman could no longer be entrusted with important assignments, and several *60 Minutes* staffers, taking their cue from the boss, began to distance themselves from him. Acutely aware that he was being consigned to limbo (at least for the time being), Bergman concluded that as long as Hewitt was running the show, he would be treated as a pariah at *60 Minutes*. Hence, no one was surprised by his decision two months later to leave the broadcast.

Another casualty of that internal quarrel was my close relationship with Hewitt. There is no doubt that the two producers who had the most positive and enduring impact on my career were Ted Yates, during the early years, and Don Hewitt, during his long reign at *60 Minutes*. I am eternally indebted to him for the way he reached out to me back in 1968 when he was preparing to launch his innovative magazine program. Over the years he and I shared a special bond, in large part because I have the happy distinction of being the only correspondent who has worked on *60 Minutes* every year since its inception. (In the spring of 2005, I completed my thirty-sixth season on the show.) Nor can it be denied that we've had our share of scraps and squabbles. Some of the memos we exchanged from time to time bristled with sharply worded complaints, and rejoinders no less pungent. But none of our disagreements was serious enough to cause permanent damage until the rift over the Wigand interview. That dispute ruptured our long-standing bond in ways that could not be repaired. I could never forgive Hewitt for not standing up to the corporate muzzling that had trashed the First Amendment and dishonored the strong tradition of fearless reporting that had long been our trademark at *60 Minutes*. Although we patched things up on the surface and continued to work together with some degree of harmony, I could no longer view him with the respect, much less the affection, that I once had felt so profoundly.

My public criticism of CBS management was not confined to the remarks I made at the end of the broadcast that Sunday night. The next day I accepted an invitation to appear on *The Charlie Rose Show*. Joining me was my on-air colleague Morley Safer, who has been a member of the *60 Minutes* family almost as long as I have. He and I were in basic agreement on the Wigand issue, and conspicuous by their absence were three key CBS people who did not agree with us: Ellen Kaden, Eric Ober, and Don Hewitt all declined invitations to join us on Rose's show. The main point I made was that by caving in to the dictates of CBS management, "we were simply dead wrong." Taking a shot directly at Larry Tisch, I accused him of having "tarnished" a great network.

Others added their voices to the chorus of disapproval. In an editorial that ran under the headline "Self-Censorship at CBS," *The New York Times* had this to say: "The most troubling part of CBS's decision is that it was made not by news executives but by corporate officers who may have their minds on money rather than public service these days." It then referred specifically to the imminent $5.4 billion sale of CBS to Westinghouse. The editorial also accused us of betraying the legacy of Edward R. Murrow, and you can imagine how much we enjoyed reading that.

A few days later, the New York *Daily News* ran a story on the controversy in which Jeffrey Wigand was outed by name as the whistle-blower whose identity we were not allowed to reveal. (To this day, I have no idea where that leak came from.) In late November, Wigand provided a deposition to lawyers who were involved in a Mississippi civil action against tobacco manufacturers, and that led the way to the payoff on my hunch that at some point, my interview with Wigand would be aired on *60 Minutes*. Thanks to a large assist from *The Wall Street Journal*, we were able to open our broadcast in early February 1996 with the full story on Wigand. After running through the necessary background in my on-camera introduction, I told our viewers:

"But now things have changed. Last week *The Wall Street Journal* got hold of and published a confidential deposition Wigand gave in a Mississippi case, a November deposition that repeated many of the charges he made to us last August. And while a lawsuit is still a possibility, not putting Jeffrey Wigand's story on *60 Minutes* no longer is."

And that, by any decent law of logic, should have been that, except this was a controversy that refused to die. In the spring of 1996, *Vanity Fair* published a lengthy article by Marie Brenner on the Wigand saga that was called "The Man Who Knew Too Much." Three years later, Hollywood released a film called *The Insider,* based on the magazine piece. In both the article and the movie, the most appropriate title for the CBS portion of the story would have been "The Gospel According to Lowell Bergman."

In both the print and film versions, Bergman was portrayed as the lone CBS knight in shining armor who was not intimidated by the fire-breathing dragons who ruled the evil corporate empire. As for the rest of us at CBS News who had been involved in the story, we were depicted, for the most part, as venal or craven wretches who had no business calling ourselves journalists. Yes, I'm exaggerating, but I truly believe that the movie, in particular, was seriously skewed in that direction. No one should have been surprised by those distortions, because the primary CBS source for both the magazine piece and the film was Bergman.

For all its inaccuracies, *The Insider* had its compelling moments, in large part because of the performances by the actors in the three principal parts. For what it's worth, I thought Russell Crowe was superb in the role of Jeffrey Wigand. But even though Al Pacino played a very good Al Pacino, I didn't recognize much of Lowell Bergman in his rendition. As for Christopher Plummer's performance, let me just say that it's not the worst thing in the world to see yourself portrayed on the silver screen by a handsome and urbane Canadian who has been hailed as the most gifted classical actor in North America. I may not know that much about how they make movies in Hollywood, but I do know enough to recognize typecasting when I see it.

Jeffrey Wigand paid a heavy price for his defiance of his former bosses at Brown & Williamson. Even before he made the decision to blow the whistle on them, he and his family were subjected to all kinds of harassment, including telephone calls threatening physical harm. "Leave tobacco alone or else you'll find your kids hurt" was the message of one such call. After Wigand was publicly identified as the primary source for the tobacco story we broadcast in November 1995, B&W retained a high-octane PR firm that promptly launched a nasty smear campaign to besmirch both Wigand's professional reputation and his personal character. One of the casualties of all these pressure tactics was his marriage, which ended in divorce in 1996. And, following through on its threat, B&W did sue Wigand for violating the confidentiality agreement.

Then the tide began to turn in Wigand's favor. For one thing, the lawsuit against him was dismissed as part of a sweeping multistate settlement that grew out of the Mississippi civil action against the tobacco industry. Thus liberated from those legal restraints, Wigand became—in the best sense—a poster boy for the anti-smoking movement. The brave stand he took against his former employer encouraged other tobacco insiders to come forward and blow their own whistles. Each new revelation bolstered the already vigorous campaign being waged against the industry in courtrooms and state legislatures throughout the country.

In recent years, Wigand has focused most of his energies on "Smoke-Free Kids," a nonprofit organization he founded to counter the industry's longtime strategy to "hook them young and hook them for life," as he put it. As a certified expert on the addictive power of cigarettes, he understands better than most that working to establish a generation of smoke-free teenagers is the best hope for achieving the goal of a smoke-free society.

EIGHT

VALENTINES

SHIRLEY MACLAINE

A ND NOW WE GO TO the back of the book, to mostly less serious matters, stuff that's intended to be entertaining, even gos-
sipy, the kind of interview I've done down the years with some
regularity—more, perhaps, with women than with men—people the
television audience flocks to, the spice of life. And I cannot think of
a better way to introduce these valentines than to shine a spotlight on
an actress I truly adore, Shirley MacLaine.

I identify her as an actress, and properly so, but when I first saw
Shirley on the Broadway stage back in 1954, it was her dancing more
than her acting that I was drawn to. She began that year as a nineteen-

year-old chorus gypsy who bounced around from one musical to another. She was in the chorus line of *The Pajama Game* when it opened in May 1954 and, in addition, was understudy to Carol Haney, the dancing star of the show, which became one of that season's biggest hits. What happened next was like something out of a Damon Runyon fable about the Great White Way. When Haney fractured her ankle, MacLaine stepped into the role and made the leap from obscurity to instant stardom. Soon, she was on her way to Hollywood.

Over the next several years, she became a familiar figure on our movie screens, where she displayed a special knack for playing young women with "loose" morals. In *Some Came Running,* she was a pathetic floozy who had a hopeless crush on a war hero played by Frank Sinatra. In *The Apartment,* she was an elevator operator in a Manhattan office building who had an affair with a married insurance executive. And in *Irma la Douce,* she was a Parisian prostitute who enjoyed her work far too much to suit her jealous boyfriend. For each of these performances, MacLaine received an Academy Award nomination. Also by this time, the early 1960s, her younger brother, Warren Beatty, had followed her to Hollywood and was building his own brilliant career as an actor and director. (The family surname was Beaty, with one T, when they were growing up in Richmond, Virginia.)

Working in *Some Came Running* brought MacLaine into Frank Sinatra's raucous orbit, and she had the distinction of becoming the only female member of his notorious Rat Pack. "I was sort of their mascot," she would later recall. Partly because of her close association with that exuberant frat-boy clique, whose members included such Sinatra cronies as Dean Martin, Sammy Davis, Jr., and Peter Lawford, she acquired a reputation for being a carefree spirit, even a bit of a "kook," a term very much in vogue in those days. Although MacLaine was married at the time, she rarely saw her husband, a businessman who preferred to live and work in Tokyo, and she didn't let her marital status cramp her frolicsome lifestyle. According to those who knew her well, she loved to party on the fast tracks that ran through Hollywood and Vegas, and she had no qualms about burning her candles at all available ends.

In the late 1960s, MacLaine brought her movie-star clout into the political arena, where she became a crusader for various liberal causes. She worked on Senator Robert Kennedy's insurgent campaign for the presidency in 1968, and was a delegate at that year's Democratic convention, the one that sparked the bloody confrontations on the streets of Chicago between antiwar demonstrators and the police. Four years later, she was once again a Democratic delegate, this time as an ardent supporter of the party's nominee, Senator George McGovern.

I didn't catch up with her until early 1984, when she was basking in the acclaim that had greeted her latest movie, *Terms of Endearment*. In that film, she played an eccentric widow and possessive mother whose daughter is dying of cancer, and many critics hailed her performance as the greatest triumph of her career. But that wasn't the only milestone in her life when I interviewed her shortly before that year's Academy Awards ceremony. She was a few weeks shy of her fiftieth birthday, and had recently published a controversial book called *Out on a Limb*, in which she wrote about her belief in reincarnation and extraterrestrial beings. Although I talked to her about *Terms of Endearment*, I confess I was far more curious about her wacky metaphysics.

WALLACE: I'm told that good friends said, "Shirley, for Pete's sake, don't write about your karmic destinies."

MACLAINE: It wasn't for Pete's sake, it was for Christ's sake, it was for God's sake, I mean, on your mother and your friends and everything that is sacred, don't do this.

WALLACE: Yeah, I mean that—that my daughter was my mother in a prior life and my karmic destinies probably indicate that I used to be a prostitute before, and—and you were a man at one time, and you believe in extraterrestrial beings. And forgive me for being an old-fashioned—

MACLAINE: No, that's easy, your attitude is easy. It's very easy to be cynical like you are just now.

WALLACE: Skeptical. I reject the word—

MACLAINE: Well, it had a panache [*sic*] of sarcasm in it.

WALLACE: Okay, okay.

MACLAINE: A large dash of it.

WALLACE: Yeah. You really believe that you've lived lives before and—

MACLAINE: Oh yes, Mike. I don't— There is no doubt in my mind about it.

WALLACE: Uh-huh. And you really believe in extraterrestrials. Have they— Do they come visit you on the porch? (Reacting to MacLaine's grimace) "Now you're being unpleasant, Wallace," is what you're saying.

MACLAINE: Yes. This is what I was a little afraid of.

WALLACE: Hold it!

MACLAINE: Now, you don't have to be that unpleasant. It doesn't become you, you know? I mean, I'm just speaking of my own experiences and my own desires, and it's a kind of childlike wonder that could really possibly speculate on other dimensions. What's wrong with that? Some of I— I mean, we speculate on that dimension every time we pray to God or cross ourselves or kneel down and say, "Help me."

Our interview ran on *60 Minutes* the night before the Hollywood glitterati assembled for their annual gala, at which—as had been predicted—MacLaine won her first Oscar. In *Terms of Endearment*, the feisty widow she portrayed has an affair with her next-door neighbor, a former astronaut played by Jack Nicholson, and she talked about that with her customary candor in her acceptance speech. Directing her gaze at Nicholson, who was seated in the audience, MacLaine thanked him for guiding her through the joys of middle-aged sex.

My relationships with the people I've interviewed have varied from one person to another. Much of the time, they didn't go beyond the interviews. We had our conversations, the pieces built around them were broadcast, and that was it. I never saw them again, or ran into them rarely, and then only by happenstance. On other occasions, the interviews led to more contact that at times evolved into friendships. And that was what happened with Shirley MacLaine.

Yet the chummier we became, the more I intuited that what she had in mind was something more than friendship and her intentions became transparent when she began sending me thoughtful gifts of one kind or another. I remember, in particular, a wonderful cable-knit tennis sweater she bestowed on me. And after I casually mentioned to her that I was fond of ice-cream floats, she began arranging for those confections to be delivered to my office with some regularity. I probably shouldn't have been surprised by all this attention, because I knew Shirley had a reputation for being attracted to journalists. Back in the days when she was a political activist, she was romantically linked with the columnist Pete Hamill, and before that, she had an affair with Sander Vanocur, who was then a top correspondent for NBC News. But it soon became clear that the design she had for me went beyond a mere fling. She was very close to her mother, who, as a young woman, had given up her dream of becoming a star actress to raise a family, and who then encouraged both Shirley and Warren to pursue careers in show business. Now, these many years later, Shirley told me that her mother firmly believed part of her daughter's karmic destiny was to become the next Mrs. Mike Wallace.

Well!!—as Jack Benny would have put it. Yet I must point out that there was nothing unseemly in any of this. Our flirtation, such as it was, took place in the spring and early summer of 1984. By then Shirley had divorced the businessman who lived in Japan, and my twenty-nine-year marriage to Lorraine had recently come to an end, so each of us was unattached and therefore fair game. Even though we went out a few times, Shirley and I never became intimate. In fact, one of our first dates became a triple date of sorts when we were joined by Mary Yates, who, it turned out, *was* destined to become the next Mrs. Wallace.

I'm happy to say that my friendship with Shirley has continued to flourish, and to this day she and I remain pals. I also had the pleasure of interviewing her again in 2000, when we did a *60 Minutes* update of the story we'd broadcast sixteen years earlier. She had just finished another book about her bizarre reincarnations called *The Camino: A Journey of the Spirit,* and we talked about some of the men who had been lovers in her current life and in previous existences.

WALLACE: You wrote that you had an affair in this life with Olaf Palme.

MACLAINE: With—this lifetime, yeah.

WALLACE: Yeah. Who was at the time—

MACLAINE: Swedish prime minister.

WALLACE: Prime minister of Sweden. Who, in a past life, Olaf Palme, was Charlemagne.

MACLAINE: Yeah. Well, that's what it said in my vision.

WALLACE: With whom you also had an affair.

MACLAINE: Yes, but one of many.

WALLACE: Back when you were a Moorish girl.

MACLAINE: That's right.

WALLACE: And you witnessed androgynous people giving birth to androgynous children.

MACLAINE: Yes.

WALLACE: And you were androgynous.

MACLAINE: Yes.

I pointed out that many people, myself included, found her "recollections" preposterous. I asked if it bothered her to be regarded as a "nutcase."

"Listen," she declared, "they said that about Christopher Columbus. They certainly said it about Jesus Christ. Ho-ho, they killed him for it. I mean, they say it about everybody who's innovative. I think I'm innovative. I'm old enough to have earned the right to be innovative and get a big kick out of the people who think I'm a nutcase."

Just the sort of answer I should have expected from a lady who insists that she had carnal relations with (among others) the first ruler of that vast and ambitious enterprise known as the Holy Roman Empire.

VANESSA REDGRAVE

BACK IN THE 1960S, WHEN she became vigorously engaged in politics, Shirley MacLaine embraced strong liberal positions on most of the hot-button issues that blazed across that turbulent decade and beyond, well into the 1970s. But her left-wing convictions were downright moderate compared to those of a British actress I interviewed in 1979. Even "radical" is probably too mild a term to describe the inflammatory Marxist views of Vanessa Redgrave. In that respect, the American movie star she most closely resembled was not MacLaine but Jane Fonda, and I made the comparison in our *60 Minutes* profile of her. Like Fonda, I said in my on-camera open to the story, Redgrave is "an actress who puts her political beliefs up front, before her acting career, and her money where her mouth is."

In addition to their passionate commitment to left-wing causes, the two actresses had similar pedigrees: Both of them were daughters of renowned actors. In fact, on the night Vanessa was born in 1937, her father, Michael Redgrave, was playing Laertes in a London production of *Hamlet* that starred Laurence Olivier in the title role. At the curtain call that evening, Olivier proclaimed to the audience, "Ladies and gentlemen, tonight a great actress has been born. Laertes has a daughter!"

The daughter of "Laertes" had no trouble fulfilling that prophecy. Her initial success was on the stage, where, thanks mainly to her work with the prestigious Royal Shakespeare Company in the early 1960s, she became known as one of England's leading classical actresses. Redgrave then brought her distinctive elegance to a number of movie roles. Her first major film was the 1966 cult classic *Morgan,* in which she earned an Academy Award nomination for her performance as the ex-wife of a demented artist who goes to extreme lengths to prevent her from marrying another man. Two more Oscar nominations rapidly followed, one for her portrayal of the avant-garde dancer Isadora Duncan in 1968 and the second three years later, when she was cast in the title role of *Mary, Queen of Scots.*

Along with her growing stature as an actress, Redgrave had acquired a reputation as a political firebrand. One of her first moves in that direction came in 1962, when she made a controversial visit to Cuba, where, according to rumors at the time, she had an affair with Fidel Castro. By the mid-1970s she had become a fervent Marxist and was devoting more time to public protests than to her acting career.

Still, she managed to keep her politics and artistic life separate until 1977, when the two forces converged in a stormy collision. That was the year she produced and narrated a documentary film called *The Palestinian*, which was severely critical of Israel and its policies. That was also the year she played the title role in *Julia*, in which she costarred with her American soul mate, Jane Fonda. The movie was adapted from an episode in a memoir by Lillian Hellman—the part played by Fonda—and much of it dealt with Hellman's early struggles to become a writer and her romance with author Dashiell Hammett. The main focus was on Hellman's longtime friendship with the radiant and mysterious Julia, who, as a member of an anti-Nazi underground group in the years leading up to World War II, persuades Hellman to take a perilous train trip from Vienna to Berlin to deliver large sums of money desperately needed to buy freedom for Jews and other victims of Hitler's oppression.

Redgrave's performance in *Julia* earned her a fourth Oscar nomination, but because of her polemical documentary in support of Yasir Arafat and the Palestine Liberation Organization, the Jewish Defense League launched a campaign to deny her the Academy Award. To its considerable credit, the Hollywood community resisted that pressure, and on the night of the big Oscar bash, she received the statuette for Best Supporting Actress. Instead of taking the high road in her acceptance speech, Redgrave lashed out at her antagonists within the Jewish lobby. After thanking her "dear colleagues" in the Academy, she told them, "You should be very proud that in the last few weeks you have stood firm and you have refused to be intimidated by the threats of a small bunch of Zionist hoodlums. . . ."

Her intemperate remarks shifted the controversy into a more explosive gear, and fueled my interest in doing a *60 Minutes* story on this combative actress. At first she rejected our overtures, but eventually she agreed to be interviewed, and when I talked to her at her home in London in early 1979, Redgrave made it clear that she had no regrets about what she had said at the Oscar ceremony a few months earlier.

REDGRAVE: Zionism is a brutal, racist ideology, and it is a brutal, racist regime, and it wasn't built to protect anybody at all except private profit.

WALLACE: Is the fact of Israel a conspiracy of Germany and France and the United States and Great Britain and—

REDGRAVE: Yes.

WALLACE: It is?

REDGRAVE: In a word, yes. It was and is, yes. . . .

WALLACE: Why are the Palestinians so interesting to you as a cause, Vanessa? Why not the Cambodians? Why not the Ugandans?

REDGRAVE: Well, it's not a case of why not anybody else, but the situation with the Palestinians is unique. They are the only people who have been turned into exile, who don't have any country at all.

WALLACE: The point would be made by Israelis that, first of all, they aren't the first in history, that, after all, the Jews, who had been there two thousand years before, were Palestinians, too.

REDGRAVE: And why shouldn't they have a home? But why

does that mean depriving a whole people of their homes and their land and their rights?

I went on to report that Redgrave's commitment to the Palestinian cause was just a small part of a grandiose crusade that encompassed the whole world. She was a leading member of something called the Workers' Revolutionary Party, which, at the time, was the most militant left-wing group in Britain. When I did the story on her, she was one of her party's candidates for a seat in Parliament, a campaign she had no hope of winning or of even coming close to victory. (When the election returns were counted, the winning Labour candidate had 12,556 votes compared to 394 for Redgrave.) But running for public office in a democratic election was merely a sideshow for the Workers' Revolutionary Party; its ultimate goal was to destroy capitalism throughout the world and transfer all political power to the working class. When asked how Redgrave and her fellow revolutionaries hoped to achieve that objective, she acknowledged that the road to their utopia would not be a peaceful journey. "The working class is going to have to take power through armed insurrection," she told me.

Later on, after observing her in action on the campaign trail and at various protest demonstrations, I asked her, "Do you never stop? I mean it, do you never stop politics?"

"No," she replied, "I never do."

Yet as I happily discovered, there was another, warmer side to Vanessa Redgrave. When she wasn't preaching from her soapbox about the need for a Marxist revolution, she came across as kind and thoughtful and quite charming. Somewhat to my surprise, I truly liked her.

As the years passed, her career continued to flourish. Among other achievements, she received two more Oscar nominations for her work in films that, like *Julia,* had strong literary origins: one in 1984 for *The Bostonians,* adapted from a Henry James novel; and the other in 1992 for *Howards End,* based on a novel by E. M. Forster. What many Redgrave aficionados regard as her crowning triumph came in the spring of 2003, when she conquered Broadway with her portrayal of Mary Tyrone in a revival of Eugene O'Neill's masterpiece *Long Day's Journey into Night.* For that performance, she won a Tony to go along with her other laurels.

The casting of Redgrave in that production of *Long Day's Journey* provoked a lively buzz of anticipation in New York's cultural circles. Partly in response to that, I suggested that we do an update of our 1979 profile of her, in much the same way we had done an update of the story on Shirley MacLaine. Redgrave was still deeply engaged in left-wing politics (her primary passion in 2003 was Chechnya and its struggle for independence from Russia), and I thought the combination made her a worthy subject to revisit. But the proposal was nixed by my superiors at *60 Minutes* on the grounds that an update on Redgrave "wasn't right" for our audience. I replied, with some irritation, that I found it hard to imagine an audience that would not be interested in seeing a story on how one of the most accomplished actresses of our time chose to play a classic role in what is widely considered to be the greatest play ever written by an American dramatist.

My earnest pitch fell on deaf ears. I soon realized that there was nothing I could say that would persuade my betters to give their stamp of approval to another story on Vanessa Redgrave. I thought their negative reaction was wrong at the time, and for whatever it's worth, I still think it was a mistake.

BARBRA STREISAND

ANOTHER MOVIE STAR WHO HAS used her glamour and power to advance political causes dear to her liberal heart is Barbra Streisand, who was the subject of a profile I did in 1991. Unlike MacLaine and Redgrave, whom I met for the first time in the context of assignments for *60 Minutes,* Streisand was someone I had known for many years. You could even say that I knew her before she became Barbra Streisand; or, to put it more accurately, I knew her when she was an obscure nineteen-year-old bohemian from Brooklyn who was just making her start in show business.

I'm talking here about the early 1960s, a time when my own career was going through an uncertain period of transition. In the interval between *The Mike Wallace Interview* and CBS News, one of my chores was to host a show for Westinghouse called *PM East,* a combination talk-and-entertainment program similar in format to what Jack Paar was doing on *The Tonight Show* at NBC.

Streisand was one of our guests on *PM East.* At the time—the summer of 1961—she was known only to a small coterie of fans who were plugged into the cabaret scene in New York and had seen her perform at a small club in Greenwich Village called Bon Soir. Among them, happily, was a member of our *PM East* staff, and on his recommendation, we invited her in for an audition. The moment she opened her mouth and we heard that magnificent voice, we all recognized she was something special.

The number Streisand chose to perform was "A Sleepin' Bee" from the Broadway show *House of Flowers,* a song that became one of her early hits. The reaction to her debut on *PM East* was so enthusiastic that she became one of our regular guests, appearing on the show more than a dozen times over the next several months. I recall a night in November 1961 when she sang a duet with Mickey Rooney ("I Wish I Were in Love Again") and another later that fall, when she sang "A Taste of Honey," another early hit. Even more memorable was the time in early 1962 when she sang "Moon River," "Lover, Come Back to Me," and "Cry Me a River," all on the same night.

I described Streisand as a bohemian a few paragraphs back because that was how I thought of her in those days. She always played it straight when she was singing, but when she joined me and our other guests for the "talk" portion of the show, the more quirky side of her nature bubbled to the surface. She strove to be unconventional in word and deed, and enjoyed being perceived as an eccentric. In at least one respect, she did live like a gypsy. One night, when I happened to notice that she was carrying a large key ring with lots of keys, I asked what they were all for. "Oh," she replied with a shrug, "I sleep around."

I thought such a comment required some explanation. She proceeded to tell me and our viewers that she didn't like to go home to Brooklyn every night, so she had keys to the apartments of various friends in Manhattan who let her crash on their sofas or whatever. "They trust me and I trust them, and that's what the keys are for," she said. She also made a point of insisting that the manifold sleeping arrangements were all quite innocent.

Streisand often came across as feisty and argumentative. In particular, she seemed to get a kick out of provoking me, and in ways that I did not always find amusing. There was, for example, her reaction to an embarrassing incident I had to endure on the night when Burt Lancaster was one of our guests.

From time to time, I would veer away from the upbeat patter that set the general tone on *PM East* and revert to the more confrontational style that had defined my presence on *Night Beat* and *The Mike Wallace Interview*. My exchange with Lancaster was one such occasion. I had read somewhere that he had a ferocious temper, so I asked him if that was true and, if so, what made him prone to such angry outbursts. Lancaster didn't care for that line of questioning; he had come on the show to plug his latest movie, *Birdman of Alcatraz*, and that was all he wanted to talk about. When I continued to press him about his temper, he accused me of being "self-consciously sensational." I thoroughly enjoyed his testy response; it was fun to be back in my natural element. Then I made a tactical mistake that left me wide open for a cutting rejoinder. After noting that I had a reputation for asking direct questions in television interviews, I capped the point with this smug remark: "I daresay that you have a certain familiarity with my work."

"Very little," Lancaster replied with a steely grin. That was bad enough, but the put-down became even more humiliating a few moments later, when he stood up and walked off the show, the only time that has ever happened to me.

After he left, other guests on the set were kind enough to offer me commiseration, but Streisand took a different tack. "Well, I don't blame him," she said. "You kept asking him about his temper, and he showed it." She refrained from adding "so there," but the point of her comment was clearly that I had gotten my comeuppance or just deserts.

What I found so striking about Streisand in those days (aside from her singing) was her attitude of supreme self-assurance. I had to keep reminding myself that she was still a kid, a teenager, for she projected the aura of a woman who knew for certain that she was on her way toward becoming not just a star but the kind of superstar who becomes a legend. In some ways, she already had the demeanor of a diva who believes it's only fitting that the rest of the world revolve around her. I couldn't fault Streisand for having such self-esteem, because I figured that given her extraordinary talent, it was probably impossible for her *not* to foresee a glorious career.

Nor did it take long for her to arrive there. In 1962 she made her Broadway debut in a musical called *I Can Get It for You Wholesale*. The leap to stardom came two years later, when, at the age of twenty-two, she created the part of Fanny Brice in *Funny Girl*. To this day it remains her signature role. Then it was off to Hollywood to make the film version of *Funny Girl,* for which she won an Oscar for Best Actress. She went on to star in two more movie adaptations of Broadway musicals, *Hello, Dolly!* and *On a Clear Day You Can See Forever.*

Streisand then set out to prove that she was not just a singing actress, and she did so with her work in the 1970 nonmusical comedy *The Owl and the Pussycat*, and with her portrayal of a left-wing activist in *The Way We Were*. Through it all, she kept on singing. Over a span of four decades, starting with her first album in 1963, she put together a string of hit recordings.

Streisand had long been on my A list of entertainers I wanted to profile on *60 Minutes*. But after all her success, she became rather reclusive and generally avoided direct contact with the media. Once she achieved superstardom, she felt she no longer needed the aggravation of being questioned by reporters. So I patiently waited for the right opportunity, and it finally came in 1991, a year when there were two major events in her career. One was a musical retrospective called *Just for the Record . . . ,* a four-album boxed set that looked back over thirty years of her singing career. The other was

The Prince of Tides, a movie in which she not only starred but directed. (It was the second time she took on the role behind the camera as well as in front of it. She had made her directorial debut in 1983 with *Yentl.*) As I had hoped, Streisand's desire to generate buzz for the new movie and album overcame her reluctance to have her privacy invaded, and so she agreed, at last, to be interviewed by me for *60 Minutes.*

Since I hadn't forgotten what an irritant she had been on occasion back in the *PM East* days, I was hardly surprised to learn that Streisand had not been popular with some of the people she had worked with over the years. She had often been accused of being a control freak who always had to have her own way. In our interview, I put it to her, point-blank.

WALLACE: Why are you so attackable?

STREISAND: You tell me.

WALLACE: Because you're so versatile, so successful, and you have the reputation for bitchery. You know that.

STREISAND: No, for being difficult, I would say. . . .

WALLACE: You would love to control this piece.

STREISAND: Absolutely. What, are you kidding? Of course. I don't trust you.

WALLACE: When are you going to be fifty?

STREISAND: Uugghh!

Her response made me laugh, and I confessed that the only reason I had asked her the question was because I was curious to see how she'd answer. After informing our viewers that Streisand would turn fifty in about five months, I gallantly averred that she still looked almost as young as she did in her television appearances from the early 1960s, some clips of which we included in the 1991 profile. In fact, much of the *60 Minutes* piece dealt with our shared recollections of the years when we first knew each other. Our trip down memory lane included a visit to her old apartment, a third-floor walk-up above a popular seafood restaurant on Third Avenue, which she rented for sixty bucks a month. (Moving into that apartment presumably brought an end to her "sleeping around" habit.) As we stood on Third Avenue and looked up at the digs she had inhabited in those days, I asked her a question that had come to mind during our nostalgic stroll through her old neighborhood.

WALLACE: Did you believe thirty years ago, when you slept there, that you were going to be Barbra Streisand?

STREISAND: I knew that ever since I was seven years old.

WALLACE: You really did?

STREISAND: It just had to be. Yeah, there was no other way for me to be.

Later, when the conversation turned to *PM East,* we talked about our early impressions of each other.

WALLACE: You know something? I really didn't like you back thirty years ago.

STREISAND: How come?

WALLACE: And I don't think you liked me, either.

STREISAND: I thought you were mean. I thought you were very mean.

WALLACE: I didn't— I didn't think that you paid much attention to me, because you were totally self-absorbed back thirty years ago, when we worked together.

STREISAND: I resent this. You invite me as a guest on your show, and you liked— We would talk about all kinds of subjects that interested me, right?

WALLACE: Right.

STREISAND: So you were using me as a guest on your show to talk.

WALLACE: Yeah.

STREISAND: Now, how do you dare call me self-involved?

WALLACE: Self-involved is one thing. Self-absorbed is— You know something? Twenty or thirty years of psychoanalysis, I say to myself, "What is it that she's trying to find out that takes twenty to thirty years?"

STREISAND: I'm a slow learner.

WALLACE: How many years have you been in psychotherapy, off and on?

STREISAND: How about in the— Why do you sound so accusatory?

WALLACE: I'm not accusing—

STREISAND: Are you against psychotherapy?

Talking about psychotherapy could not have been more relevant, because in *The Prince of Tides,* she played a psychiatrist who helped the character played by her costar, Nick Nolte, cope with deep-seated problems that stemmed from his traumatic childhood. That was a subject—an unhappy childhood—with which Streisand was all too familiar. Her father died when she was just an infant, and the man her mother married six years later turned out to be a stepfather out of Dickens. According to Barbra, he once told her she couldn't have any ice cream because she was too ugly. And when he wasn't insulting her, he treated her with almost total neglect.

STREISAND: The man never talked to me.

WALLACE: Why?

STREISAND: Why. You know, at the time that I was a child, I mean, I just thought that I was awful, I must be awful. I remember he . . . was a man who couldn't give affection.

WALLACE: Yeah, but he must have been nuts about your mother.

STREISAND: He was—he was mean to my mother. I saw him mean to her. This was not—this was not a nice man.

Yet she was the first to admit that her own relationship with her mother was marked by discord. "My mother," she recalled, "never said to me, 'You're smart, you're pretty, you're anything. You could do what you want.' She never told me anything like that. My mother was— I would say to my mother now, 'Why didn't you ever give me any compliments?' She said, 'I didn't want you to get a swelled head.'"

Before my interview with Streisand, I had an on-camera conversation with her mother, during which I asked her, "Are you very proud of Barbra?"

"Who would not be? Who would not be proud of this girl?"

"Are you close?" I asked.

This was her reply: "She hasn't got time to be close to anyone."

I thought that remark spoke volumes, so I quoted it to Streisand during our interview. And this was *her* response: "She said 'to anyone'? Or did she say to her?"

"To anyone," I clarified. "That's your own mom."

Streisand began to cry, and as she wiped the tears from her eyes, she said, "You like this, that forty million people have to see me, like, do this."

Since I knew that she had a troubled childhood and that there were serious frictions in her relationship with her mother, I thought there was a germane link between the skeletons in her family closet and the ones that her therapeutic character unearthed in *The Prince of Tides*. Why promote a movie celebrating psychotherapy if you don't want to talk about your own demons?

But that wasn't how Streisand chose to view it, and when we approached her a few years later with a proposal to do an update of the 1991 profile, she made it clear that she was totally uninterested.

TINA TURNER

I MANAGED TO MAKE IT through the first seventy-eight years of my life without ever attending a rock concert, and I was serenely confident that I could continue to avoid that dubious pleasure. But thanks to an unexpected twist in my karmic destiny, I was obliged to go to a rock concert in the summer of 1996 as part of a *60 Minutes* story I did that year on Tina Turner. It wasn't even supposed to be my assignment. The proposal for the profile of Turner had been submitted by one of the producers who worked with Ed Bradley, whose taste in music was (and still is) far more adventurous than mine. But when word came back that Turner had opened a brief window in her busy schedule to accommodate a *60 Minutes* interview, Bradley was off on another assignment halfway around the world, in Burma, as I recall. Since it would have been discourteous to ask Turner and her people to cool their heels until Ed returned from Asia, I was asked to pinch-hit for him, and thus soon found myself in her magnetic presence.

Although I was not that conversant with Turner's music, I did know a few things about her personal life, especially her stormy relationship with her former husband and mentor, Ike Turner. That had been the subject of a 1993 movie in which Angela Bassett and Laurence Fishburne played the Turners. From that film and other sources, I learned that Tina was born Annie Mae Bullock in Nutbush, Tennessee. The daughter of sharecroppers, she spent much of her childhood picking cotton and dreaming of ways to break free from the bonds of rural poverty. She moved to St. Louis in 1956, when she was sixteen, and it was there that she met Ike Turner, who was the leader of a rhythm-and-blues band that had enjoyed some success in local clubs. Turner had a keen eye and ear for talent, and when he heard Annie Mae sing in an informal audition, he promptly brought her under his wing, and she soon became his lead vocalist. He eventually married her and changed her name, and his band was rechristened the Ike & Tina Turner Revue.

With her exuberant and earthy singing style, and her fast-paced dancing on legs hailed as the shapeliest ever to stomp and strut across a concert stage, Tina Turner became one of the most dynamic performers in the history of rock music. But behind the scenes of her public triumphs, she was severely and repeatedly abused by her husband. Over the course of their sixteen years together, Ike Turner bashed and bruised Tina's face so many times that she later needed corrective surgery to repair her nose and damaged sinuses. Finally she broke away from him in 1976, but for the next few years, her career languished while she struggled to reshape her identity as a solo performer. The big breakthrough for Tina Turner without Ike came in 1984, when her comeback album *Private Dancer* sold ten million copies and won three Grammy Awards. She then published a brutally candid autobiography called *I, Tina,* which chronicled the years of physical abuse inflicted by Ike, and that book provided the source material for the 1993 movie. (The title of the film, *What's Love Got to Do with It,* was drawn from one of her biggest hits.) When I interviewed Turner in the summer of '96, I asked if she regretted revealing so many wretched details about her life with Ike.

TURNER: Now, I would have to say no, I don't regret it. What I regretted is that it was ugly to me, and I—and I—and the people found it out.

WALLACE: Hmm.

TURNER: How can I explain that to you? I never would have let the people know. But as long as I kept that under the rug, it might have held me back as well.

WALLACE: You had to bring it to closure, so to speak?

TURNER: That's right. Absolutely. And it— People won't leave it alone. I'm constantly reminded. It's been nearly twenty years. Ike has married twice since then.

At the time of our interview, Turner had been living in Europe for over a decade. I talked to her at her home in the south of France, which she shared with the current man in her life, a German-born record-company executive named Erwin Bach. He was sixteen years younger than Turner, and I asked him what it was like to be involved with an older woman who was also a world-famous rock star.

BACH: I'm not in love with the rock act.

WALLACE: Yeah.

BACH: I'm in love with the human being.

WALLACE: Yeah. You proposed to her, and she turned you down. Why?

BACH: Well, I proposed to her before her fiftieth birthday because I thought it is just the way I feel—or felt at this moment. . . . I wanted to give her my commitment. And I think
we both were lucky that she said no afterwards.

By the time of our conversation, the two of them had been together for ten years. It was Tina's first serious relationship since she
left Ike, and she was quick to chime in with her own view of their romantic attachment.

TURNER: Erwin and I don't feel that we need a marriage. We
are as married now as if it was legal.
WALLACE: You're fifty-six. He's forty. Now, that could be
trouble.
TURNER: But he's really sixty, and I'm really fifteen. He's—he's
much more mature. . . .
WALLACE: So you don't push Erwin around?
TURNER: Oh, no. But I— I wouldn't like it if I could.

The big event in Turner's career that summer was the start of an
ambitious fifteen-month world tour that grossed over a hundred million dollars in Europe alone. Our visit to her home came during a
brief break in the tour, and we then arranged for our *60 Minutes* team
to accompany Tina and her entourage on a flight to Budapest, the site
of her next scheduled appearance. It was there that I finally broke my
rock-concert maiden, as they say at the racetracks. I was fully aware
of Turner's reputation for giving over-the-top performances in front of
live audiences. But the spectacle I witnessed on that Hungarian stage
was even more electrifying and sexually provocative than I had been
led to anticipate, and after it was over, the two of us talked about the
way she let it all hang out.

WALLACE: Your public persona is wild, to a certain degree.

TURNER: Raunchy.

WALLACE: Sexy, raunchy—exactly. And yet you say that you're—that you're not really that way, and that you like only to pretend that you're sexy. True?

TURNER: Yes. Let me just tell you how I am about that. What I give off on the stage, any man would approach me, "Hey, Tina, baby." And I—I never like it. But I can't correct it, because that's what I do onstage. It's my work. I think people don't take singers as serious as they do actresses. Some actresses do worse things than I've ever done onstage, and they're treated with respect.

I was so taken by Tina Turner's warmth and vitality that when she launched another world tour in 2000, I suggested that we do an update of our 1996 profile. She was now sixty years old, and her latest romp across concert stages hither and yon was being billed as her farewell tour. When I interviewed Turner in the summer of 2000, most of our conversation dealt with her personal life and some of the values that had shaped it. She was still living in France with Erwin Bach, and I wanted to know why such a prominent African-American performer preferred being an expatriate.

WALLACE: You live in a white world. You do.

TURNER: Hmm.

WALLACE: Live in a white country with a white guy.

TURNER: Hmm.

WALLACE: Your work is mainly like those of white rock bands.

TURNER: Hmm.   \

WALLACE: Correct?

TURNER: Yeah, yeah. Mike, this might be hard for you or people to understand, but I don't think about color or race. I don't think I ever thought that much about the difference, even when I lived in the South.

WALLACE: You mean back in Nutbush, Tennessee, and beyond?

TURNER: Yeah. Going to a back door never bothered me. I don't remember ever being— I don't remember being called a nigger. But a few times when it happened, I just kind of feel, "Well, yeah, I'm black. I—I am considered a nigger." So it never bothered me.

WALLACE: You know, what makes me ask about this is you said to me that you felt that you, in a sense, belonged now over in Europe, more than in the United States.

TURNER: Yes, it's true.

Turner's decision to live in Europe placed her firmly in the tradition of prominent African-American artists who chose to become expatriates. One of them was the esteemed author Richard Wright; although his most famous novel was titled *Native Son,* Wright turned his back on his native land because he found the racial and political climate in Europe more tolerant than the hostile conditions he had encountered in America. That was also the case with James Baldwin, another renowned black writer who spent years living as an expatriate. Europe has long been a haven for many jazz performers, whose music—like Turner's—is deeply rooted in the African-American experience. Yet when I put the question to her directly, asking her if she thought it was "more comfortable for people of color to live in Europe," Turner's reply was more ambiguous than the one I had anticipated.

"Mike, I've never bothered about my color," she said. "I never had that thing about being black. If the whole world was like that, maybe there would be more harmony and love. Maybe. I don't have a problem with being black in a white country. . . . It's— I'm okay where I am."

The profile of Tina Turner was my one and only plunge into the clamorous world of rock music. Though I enjoyed the experience, I was acutely conscious of being outside my natural comfort zone. By way of contrast, I felt completely at home in the company of movie stars, for I had long been acquainted with luminaries of film and theater. There were several other actresses I did stories on over a span of five decades. Among them were such grande dames of stage and screen as Tallulah Bankhead and Gloria Swanson, whom I interviewed in the 1950s, and Helen Hayes and Bette Davis, who were subjects of *60 Minutes* stories in the 1980s. In the years since then, I've done pieces on Oprah and Julie Andrews and Candice Bergen and the seductive French actress Jeanne Moreau. (Our title for that story was, inevitably, "Femme Fatale.")

A recent newcomer to this distinguished gallery was Hilary Swank. My profile of her ran on *60 Minutes* in late January of 2005, just one month before she received an Academy Award—her second Oscar in five years—for her riveting portrayal of a female boxer in *Million Dollar Baby*. In spite of her rapid rise to the pinnacle of Hollywood fame, Swank did not behave like a diva; I was utterly captivated by her casual, unassuming manner. As I said in my on-camera introduction to our story, Swank "is unlike any other movie star I've known. Beautiful but somehow short on glamour; unaffected, down-to-earth; she's intelligent, articulate, yet she's a high school dropout; sophisticated, worldly, but she grew up in a trailer park. We found her fascinating."

She *was* fascinating, and so, too—each in her own way—were the other gifted performers I've mentioned. But to me, at least, there was something extra-special about the quartet I've chosen to focus on in this chapter. In fact, I can't think of a more stimulating treat than to have dinner some evening with the four of them. I would relish the chance to hear Streisand and Turner compare notes about performing. Or to hear MacLaine and Redgrave share their opinions about politics and the film industry. Or to hear all four of these strong-willed women expound on the various issues that inflame their passions. I'd be happy just to sit there and listen and, for once, keep my own mouth shut.

NINE

. . . And Other Celebrated

Characters

(MARILYN MONROE)

NORMAN MAILER

ARTHUR MILLER

I NEVER HAD THE PLEASURE of interviewing Marilyn Monroe. I never even met her. But she was the costar of a *60 Minutes* story I did in 1973, when the celebrated author Norman Mailer wrote a book about Monroe that featured his own bizarre twist on what brought her life to an end in August 1962. In the book's final chapter, Mailer made the outlandish suggestion that Monroe had been murdered by Kennedy-hating conspirators from within the CIA and/or the FBI, and he did so without a shred of solid evidence to back up his speculation.

Needless to say, his idiosyncratic take on Monroe's death provoked a storm of criticism, and to a large extent, he welcomed the controversy that swirled around him in the summer and fall of '73. That came as no surprise to those of us who had followed his career, for over the years, no one had enjoyed a spirited public scrap more than Norman Mailer. He had been courting conflicts and disputes of one kind or another since 1948, when, at the age of twenty-five, he made a big splash with his first novel, *The Naked and the Dead,* which was inspired by his combat experience in the Philippines during World War II.

Other successful books followed, and Mailer eventually proclaimed himself the top literary lion on the contemporary American scene, the king of a lush and creative jungle that encompassed both fiction and nonfiction. (Although he achieved his early fame as a novelist, Mailer won his first Pulitzer Prize and National Book Award in 1969 for *The Armies of the Night,* a deeply personal and intuitive piece of journalism about an antiwar demonstration in Washington; he received his second Pulitzer eleven years later for *The Executioner's Song,* a "true life novel," as he called it, about the Gary Gilmore case in Utah.) He also liked to boast that he was the reigning heavyweight champion of machismo, the aggressive, masculine attitude that aroused the ire of feminists, who labeled it male chauvinism. Given his macho sensibility, it was no doubt inevitable that Mailer would be drawn to the challenge of writing about a mythic sexual goddess like Marilyn Monroe (Aphrodite as observed by King Kong), and it was perhaps just as inevitable that I would welcome the opportunity to do a story on the project that had brought these two icons into each other's realm.

This was not the first time Mailer and I had confronted each other on television. Our initial encounter took place back in 1957, when I interviewed him on *Night Beat.* At that time, the big hero in his life was Ernest Hemingway, who, with his passion for bullfighting, big-game hunting, and other blood sports, had preceded Mailer as the chest-thumping master of machismo, at least in literary circles. Mailer had recently proposed in a newspaper article that Hemingway run for president, "because this country could stand a man for President since for all too many years our lives have been guided by men who were essentially women." One of my first questions in our *Night Beat* interview was about that article.

> WALLACE: What do you mean by that, "men who were essentially women"? Who among our leaders is so unmasculine that you regard him in that light?
>
> MAILER: Well, I think President Eisenhower is a bit of a woman.
>
> WALLACE: What do you mean by *that*?
>
> MAILER: Well, he's very passive. . . . If we're entering a crisis, he's not exactly the kind of man, I believe, who would have any imagination, any particular grasp of how to change things.

Inasmuch as Dwight Eisenhower was a former five-star general who had been the supreme commander of the Allied forces in Europe during World War II, it was patently absurd to characterize him as "a bit of a woman"—and Mailer knew it. He later admitted that he had expected me to quote what he had written about the effeminacy of our male leaders, and he had planned to make the remark about Eisenhower merely to create some mischief and get my reaction. It worked, for when he said it, I nearly fell out of my chair. Mailer later compared my facial response to "the wince of a wounded Indian." Although this was still fairly early in his career, he already was going out of his way to play provocateur.

I interviewed him again in the fall of 1960, when he was on the verge of announcing his candidacy in the upcoming race for mayor of New York City, a decision based entirely on chutzpah, since he had no visible base of support and no political credentials whatsoever. Still, I decided to humor him and his ego trip, so I asked him questions about various local issues, as though his views on such matters were worthy of serious consideration. I brought up the concern over a recent rise in teenage violence, and Mailer was quick to offer a bold and imaginative remedy. The kids, he said, should not be disarmed, because to a male adolescent, "the knife is an instrument of manhood." After extolling the heroic spirit of the Middle Ages, he proposed holding modern "jousting tournaments" between teenage gangs in Central Park. In the meantime, I had noticed that Mailer was sporting a black eye—a real shiner—and when I asked him how he got it, Mailer replied, "Oh, I was in quite a scrape Saturday night."

That was true enough, but it wasn't the whole story. Mailer neglected to mention that when he came home from that Saturday-night scrape, he had quarreled with his wife, Adele, and stabbed her with a three-inch penknife. Our interview was taped on Monday, and while Mailer nattered on about the knife as "an instrument of manhood," his wife was undergoing intensive care following an emergency operation at a nearby hospital. Shortly after the interview, Mailer went to a police station and turned himself in. Only then did the press—and the public—learn about the incident. Adele recovered, but even Mailer recognized that being exposed as a wife-stabber was not a promising way to launch an election campaign. He put his political ambitions on hold until 1969, the year he made his maverick run for mayor of New York. Although his hope of capturing city hall was utterly doomed from the start, his quixotic campaign was stimulating, boisterous, and hugely entertaining.

So here it was, four years after his foray into politics, and he and I were once again crossing swords, this time over what he had written in his latest book. The flap over his biography of Marilyn Monroe was a new kind of controversy for Mailer. He was accustomed to detractors who, over the years, had disparaged him for his raucous behavior, his public displays of bravado, and other excesses that were so much a part of his expansive personality. But even his critics (or most of them, anyway) had acknowledged that at his best, Norman Mailer was one of America's most gifted writers, and his reputation had been enhanced by the highly charged, intensely personal works of journalism that became his forte in the 1960s.

But now, in 1973—and for the first time in his colorful career— serious questions were being raised about Mailer's professional integrity. Most of the criticism of his biography centered on the sensationalism of the final chapter, with its lurid speculations about Monroe's death, but that was by no means the only objection. Mailer wrote the book at a frantic pace (he bragged about having dashed it off in a mere two months), and in doing so, he did not take the time to do any fresh reporting of his own. He gathered almost all his information from previously published books and articles, and he borrowed so heavily from those sources that he was charged with plagiarism. Finally, both Mailer and his publisher, Grosset & Dunlap, were accused of crassly exploiting the tabloid gossip about Monroe and the two Kennedy brothers so they could cash in on the reputations of three deeply admired American legends who were conveniently dead and in no position to respond to all the scandalous stories. That charge of exploitation was uppermost in our minds when we chose to call our *60 Minutes* piece "Monroe, Mailer and the Fast Buck." When I interviewed the author at his home in Brooklyn Heights, I began with a question about his own motives.

"Why did you write the book?" I asked.

"I started to write it as—to do a preface, to pick up a sum of money," Mailer replied. "It was a book which was a commercial venture for me. I needed the money very badly. And then what happens? I fell in love with the material."

As I pointed out to our viewers when we broadcast the story in July 1973, Mailer had never met Monroe, and the material he "fell in love with" was her films and various books and magazine articles that others had written about the actress. Later in our interview, I asked him to explain how he came up with his off-the-wall theory about the cause of Monroe's death.

MAILER: All Hollywood was gossiping about Marilyn having an affair with Bobby Kennedy . . . which I believe in fact she was not having. Although they were dear and close friends. So, if she could be murdered in such a way that it would look like a suicide for unrequited love of Bobby Kennedy, it would be a huge embarrassment for the Kennedys. And there were people around in those days, in the CIA and the FBI, who hated the Kennedys. . . . I'm saying that some of them may have decided it wouldn't be the worst thing in the world to knock off Marilyn Monroe.

WALLACE: You don't believe that she was murdered, though, really. Down bottom.

MAILER: Well— No, I don't know. I didn't know her.

WALLACE: I say you don't believe it.

MAILER: If you ask me to give a handicapper's estimate of what it was, I'd say it's ten to one that it was an accidental suicide. Ten to one, anyway.

WALLACE: At least.

MAILER: But I would not—I could not ignore the possibility of a murder.

WALLACE: And do you believe that Bobby Kennedy was there, had been with her that night?

MAILER: It's possible.

WALLACE: I'm asking you again.

MAILER: I don't know.

WALLACE: Handicap it!

MAILER: I'd say it's even money.

Elaborating on the uncertainty of it all, Mailer insisted that it was impossible to know for sure what had happened to Monroe because "no one's talking, and no one's going to talk about that night."

Mailer was wrong about that. Someone was willing to talk about that night, and she happened to be the one person who could refute his convoluted theory about Monroe's death. Eunice Murray was Marilyn's housekeeper at the time, and prior to my interview with Mailer, I talked to her about the night her employer died. I asked her directly if Monroe could have been murdered.

MURRAY: Definitely not.

WALLACE: You say definitely not. Why?

MURRAY: Impossible. Because I was alone there with her, the doors were locked, we had been— We had gone to bed and there wasn't any— No one was around. . . .

WALLACE: Bobby Kennedy was not there that night?

MURRAY: No.

WALLACE: You were?

MURRAY: That's right.

WALLACE: In doing his research for the book, Norman Mailer never got to you?

MURRAY: That's right. I think it was reported that I was in hiding.

WALLACE: Yes, it was.

MURRAY: It's very funny. My name is in the telephone directory, and I have never made any effort to hide.

I had to conclude that the only reason Mailer couldn't find Eunice Murray was because he didn't really try, and I later stressed that point in my interview with him.

WALLACE: It's as though you and your publishers didn't want too many of the facts, but were more anxious for the controversy, for the mystery . . . a mystery on which a considerable amount of light could be shed by the simple expedient of picking up a telephone and calling Eunice Murray.

MAILER: No, no, no, wait a moment. We obviously discussed the possibility of calling Eunice Murray. . . . I vetoed it because I hate telephone interviews. And I do. As a writer, I hate them. I hate that way of getting facts.

WALLACE: Then you get on a plane and go to Los Angeles—

MAILER: I told you, I had a choice. I was coming down to a deadline. I had something like twenty thousand words to finish in the last week—

WALLACE: But facts, Norman!

MAILER: Now, wait a minute, Mike. Let me just give you my attitude on it. What I knew was I was sailing into a sea of troubles, and I said, "Fine, that's what we're going to sail into." Because the alternative was this: I did not have the time to do both.

Mailer was thoroughly flustered. He clearly had not expected me to grill him about his slipshod reporting methods or the deeply flawed judgments he had set down in the last chapter. I must say, that surprised me. After all, Norman Mailer was hardly one of those reclusive, academic writers who had spent most of his life in the pristine confines of some ivory tower. He was known to be an astute and savvy media warrior who had long been accustomed to mixing it up on television shows; even more to the point, this was not the first time he had been interviewed by me. Hence, he should have been much better prepared to deal with my line of questioning.

When the piece ran on *60 Minutes* and Mailer saw how defensive and unconvincingly he came across in our interview, he was hopping mad. A few days after it aired, he was quoted as saying that the next time he saw me, he was going to beat me up. Ever the macho man, Mailer specified that he would confine his assault to body blows, because "Wallace's face is already so ugly that there's no point in doing any damage to it." That lively remark was passed on to me by a reporter who called to get my reaction to Mailer's threat. I just laughed and said, "Ah yes, that sounds like Norman. What would we do without him? The man's a national treasure."

It was no laughing matter to Mailer. He nursed his grievance against me for many years thereafter, and invariably, when I ran into him, as I did from time to time, he would look at me like I was a hair in his soup.

Marilyn Monroe was also a prime topic of conversation when I interviewed another famous author in 1987. Except on that occasion, the writer also happened to have been her last husband—the esteemed playwright Arthur Miller.

The three men who married Monroe had almost nothing else in common. She was only sixteen and was still known by her real name——Norma Jeane Baker—when she tied the knot with her starter husband in 1942. His name was Jim Dougherty, and his sole claim to distinction was that he was the first mate of the woman who went on to become Marilyn Monroe. Their marriage lasted four years, but during most of that time, Dougherty was away at sea, serving in the Merchant Marines.

In 1954, not long after her big burst to stardom, Monroe married Joe DiMaggio, who was, if anything, even more of a living legend than she was. To their millions of fans, the bond between the Yankee Clipper and the Blond Bombshell was the great storybook romance of the age. Alas, what began as a starry-eyed liaison soon turned into a star-crossed mismatch: Their marriage lasted only nine months. Brief though it was, it produced a terse comment that must be regarded as one of the most telling rejoinders in the history of American pop culture.

While Mr. and Mrs. DiMaggio were on their honeymoon in Tokyo, Marilyn was persuaded to make a brief visit to South Korea to entertain U.S. troops stationed in that grim, battle-scarred country. (The Korean War had come to an end just a few months earlier.) Although DiMaggio did not go with her, the trip was a howling success. To no one's surprise, the GIs greeted the appearance of this stunning glamour queen in their midst with thunderous applause and frenzied screams of rapture. When Monroe returned to Tokyo and her new husband, one of the first things she said to him was "Oh, Joe, you've never heard such cheering."

To which he replied: "Oh, yes I have."

After her divorce from DiMaggio, Monroe was more determined than ever to prove her worth as an actress, and toward that end, she moved to New York and began taking lessons at the Actors Studio. Her mentor was the longtime guru of that famous workshop, Lee Strasberg, and guided by his influence, she began to hobnob with the intelligentsia of the Broadway theater, a social path that led her into the arms of Arthur Miller.

Miller had his own considerable reputation as one of America's finest dramatists, a man who wrote plays that were relentlessly serious. His masterpiece, *Death of a Salesman,* was nothing less than an audacious attempt to create a drama that would be viewed as a modern counterpart of the classical tragedies that dominated the theater of ancient Greece and the Shakespearean tragedies that were the glory of the Elizabethan Age. *Salesman* and some of Miller's other plays were built around his concept that the common man could be as much of a tragic hero as the kings and princes of yore. Moreover, his personality reflected the gravity of his work. In almost every respect, Miller projected the image of an earnest intellectual who brooded over the fate of mankind. As such, he didn't seem at all like the sort of fellow who would wind up with Marilyn Monroe.

At the time of my *60 Minutes* interview with Miller, whom I had known when both of us were students at the University of Michigan, thirty-one years had passed since the day in June 1956 when he and Monroe were married. I recalled how the two of them were portrayed in the tabloids as "the odd couple" long before Neil Simon chose that phrase for the title of one of his comedies. And not only in the tabloids, for even in those days, Norman Mailer couldn't resist commenting on Monroe's love life. He described her marriage to Miller as a union between "the Great American Brain and the Great American Body." That was among the reactions I had in mind when I interviewed Miller three decades later.

WALLACE: You know that people said at the time that you were together, what in the world is Arthur doing this for? Arthur is an innocent. What in the world—Arthur Miller and Marilyn Monroe?

MILLER: That is exactly the point. She also in a way was moving in a world she knew nothing about, a world of getting up in the morning, making breakfast, and living in a— That was an innocence there.

WALLACE: Did she want that, do you think?

MILLER: With part of herself. She wanted it with part of herself, yes.

WALLACE: And with the rest?

MILLER: She wanted to be a great star.

When we broadcast our profile of Miller in the fall of 1987, he had just published an autobiography called *Time Bends: A Life,* in which he set down some observations about the Marilyn Monroe he knew. I quoted some of them in our *60 Minutes* story.

"I never saw her unhappy in a crowd," Miller wrote. "Her stardom was her triumph, nothing less. It was her life's achievement. The simple fact, terrible and lethal, was that no space existed between herself and this star. She was Marilyn Monroe, and that was what was killing her." That led to the following exchange in our interview.

WALLACE: You knew that it was doomed?

MILLER: I didn't know it was doomed, but I certainly felt it had a good chance to be.

WALLACE: You said to her, "I keep trying to teach myself how to lose you, but I can't learn yet." And she says, "Why must you lose me?"

MILLER: Well, it just shows you the power of instinct over what's left of your brains at such moments when you're being drawn to someone, and you sense that it may not work, and you can't stop it anyway. . . .

WALLACE: Those were tough years. Wonderful years, and terrible years.

MILLER: Sure. They were. Oh, there was a lot of pain, cer-
tainly for her, and certainly for me.
WALLACE: Why? What did it do to you?
MILLER: Well, it's a defeat. It always is.

Miller devoted so much time and energy to the uphill struggle of
trying to make a success of his marriage to Monroe that he all but
abandoned his work. During the five years or so that they were together, his only creative achievement was a screenplay for *The Misfits,* a film he wrote primarily as a vehicle for his wife. In the movie,
Monroe played an ex-stripper and recent divorcée who falls in love
with an aging, washed-up cowboy and accompanies him and his bud-
dies on a roundup to corral wild horses. As the story unfolds, she is
appalled to learn that the captured horses are to be slaughtered and
sold to a dog-food company. Miller created the character to give Marilyn the opportunity to play the kind of sensitive and vulnerable
woman he knew her to be. But the project turned out to be the couple's melancholy swan song. By the time *The Misfits* went into production in 1960, the Miller-Monroe marriage was falling apart, and
they were divorced the following year.

I reminded Miller that from the time he hooked up with Monroe
until their divorce, he neglected his life's vocation to such an extent
that he did not write one stage play. And I asked him if, in light of
that fact, he agreed with friends and admirers who viewed his marriage to Monroe as a terrible waste of his time and talent.

"Well, you could say that, I guess," he replied. "At the same time,
she was a great person to be with a lot of the time. She was full of the
most astonishing terms and revelations about people. She was a
super-sensitive instrument, and that's exciting to be around until it
starts to self-destruct."

Marilyn Monroe was Arthur Miller's second wife, and by the time they broke up, he was moving toward his third marriage. While *The Misfits* was being shot on location in Nevada, a group of photographers from the Magnum agency was on hand to take pictures of the production. One member of the Magnum team was a thirty-seven-year-old Austrian woman named Inge Morath. She caught Miller's eye, one thing led to another, and they were married in February 1962, six months before Monroe's death.

When it came to marriage, the third time was the charm for Miller. With Inge Morath, he found the happiness and stability that had eluded him in his previous matrimonial ventures. (One longtime friend sardonically observed that what distinguished Morath from his two other wives was that "she was a grown-up.") In 1987, the year we did our profile of Miller, he and Inge celebrated their twenty-fifth wedding anniversary.

What was more, it was surely no accident that after his marriage to Morath, he resumed writing plays. In 1964—nearly a decade after his last work had appeared on Broadway—a new Miller play called *After the Fall* opened in New York. It was a transparently autobiographical drama, with the character of Maggie, a deeply neurotic and destructive woman, obviously based on Marilyn Monroe.

Miller went on to write more plays, and although none of them measured up to the tragic heights of *Death of a Salesman,* some were worthy additions to his growing oeuvre. When I interviewed him in the fall of '87, he was still turning out plays with impressive regularity. Yet Miller was, by then, seventy-two years old, and since he had exceeded his biblical allotment of threescore and ten, I raised a question I almost never asked an interviewee.

WALLACE: You ever think about an epitaph?

MILLER: Epitaph? Never gave it a moment's thought.

WALLACE: Give it a moment.

MILLER: The first thought that occurs to me is "He worked awful hard." But that's hardly a recommendation. Everybody does, or a lot of people do.

WALLACE: And what did he work for?

MILLER: Oh, some little moment of truth up on that stage that people could feel made them a little more human.

And that's what virtually all his obituaries said when he died at the age of eighty-nine.

JOHNNY CARSON

I SUSPECT THE REASON I asked Miller about his epitaph was because it was around this time—the mid-1980s—that the question was being put to me with some regularity. My customary answer on such occasions consisted of three simple words: "Tough—but fair." A bit laconic, perhaps, but that pretty much captures how I would like my life's work to be remembered. A couple of decades have come and gone since I first came up with that response, for, like Miller, I have been blessed with longevity, and like him, I have been one of those obstinate octogenarians who refuse to stop working. In my case, I've kept at it simply because the challenge of doing stories for *60 Minutes* continues to give me a profound satisfaction that I'm sure I never could have found in retirement.

When Miller died in February 2005, it was just a few weeks after the passing of Johnny Carson, whose death brought to mind the adroit answer he once gave to the question about one's own epitaph. At the time he addressed the subject, Carson was a mere boy of fifty-two who still had twenty-seven years of life ahead of him. (I mention this to make the point that we geezers aren't the only ones who have to deal with that intrusive query.) The year was 1977 and the place was Harvard University, where he was being honored as the Hasty Pudding Club's "Man of the Year." During a news conference at that event, a young reporter asked him, "What would you like your epitaph to be?"

"Well," Carson replied, "I'd prefer not to have one at all, where it never got to that point." Then, after a perfectly timed pause, he said, "I think something like 'I'll be right back.'"

That was exactly the kind of response we would want from a man who, even before he began his long association with *The Tonight Show,* had made his living as a host on television programs, a job that by definition entailed frequent breaks for commercials and other interruptions. Carson was then in his fifteenth year as the host of *Tonight* and was at the height of his reign as the king of late-night television. As it happened, a *60 Minutes* camera crew was on hand to record his reply to the epitaph question, because we were planning to include his acceptance of the Hasty Pudding Club award in a piece I was doing on him.

Carson had to be coaxed into giving his consent to a *60 Minutes* profile, and that did not surprise me. It had long been known that behind the genial facade he presented to the millions of viewers who tuned in to *The Tonight Show,* he was a deeply private man who had a reputation for being standoffish. In particular, he was wary of reporters who tried to pry into his personal life. So getting him to go along with our proposal was a hard sell, and even then the sale did not go through—or at least it did not go through at the time, as planned. Shortly after the event at Harvard, and before I had a chance to interview him, Carson sent word that he had changed his mind; he was no longer amenable to being the subject of a *60 Min-*

utes story. He offered no explanation, and we didn't press him for one. His decision left us with no choice but to abandon the project, and that was how matters stood for the next two years.

In March 1979, I was a guest on *The Tonight Show,* and I seized the opportunity to rag Carson—in his own domain—about the way he had "chickened out" on us. I challenged him to reconsider his decision. "What are you afraid of?" I asked in a teasing tone. "What are you trying to hide?"

I really didn't think that my lighthearted effort to shame him would work, but it did. Not long after my appearance on *Tonight,* Carson changed his mind again and gave us the green light to do a profile. When I interviewed him that spring at his home in Bel Air, I asked him about his flip-flop reaction to our entreaties.

> WALLACE: Why are you doing this now?
> CARSON: Doing what?
> WALLACE: This. You walked out on us once before. . . .
> CARSON: Well, I understood that you were paying me a large amount of money for this.
> WALLACE: You're wrong!

Much of my work at that time dealt with the misdeeds of rogues and con men, like the ones I wrote about in Chapter Six. I was so deeply immersed in investigative journalism that it had come to be regarded by many as my raison d'être on *60 Minutes.* Carson was well aware of that (he claimed to be an avid viewer of our show), and it was his turn to have a little fun at my expense.

> CARSON: Why are *you* doing this now? I'm not running a boiler-room operation. I have no phony real-estate scam. I'm not taking any kickbacks. I did steal a ring from Woolworth's

once when I was twelve years old, and I think that's why
you're here.

WALLACE: We're doing this because you're a national treasure.
That's what they tell me, you're a national treasure.

CARSON: And you know what the dollar is worth nowadays.

As the interview progressed, we talked about his reputation for
being aloof and unfeeling.

WALLACE: There's a stereotype of Carson. You know there is.

CARSON: Well, what is it? What is it?

WALLACE: Ice water in his veins.

CARSON: I had that taken out years ago. I went to Denmark
and had that done. It's all over now.

WALLACE: Shy, defensive.

CARSON: That's probably true. I can remember when I
was in high school—if I pulled out my old high school annual book and read some of the things, people might say,
"Oh, he's conceited. He's aloof." Actually, that was more
shy. When I'm in front of an audience, you see, it's a
different thing. If I'm in front of an audience, I can feel
comfortable.

WALLACE: Why?

CARSON: I'm in control.

More than anything else, it was Carson's nightly monologues
that gave his program a distinctive edge over other talk shows. They
were sharply written, and he delivered them with a crisp and precise
timing that was one of his comedic strengths. The objects of his wit
were not always amused by his put-downs, but he took care to keep

the ridicule within certain parameters, and he had an unerring sense of where to draw the line. When I asked him about that, Carson cited the example of Congressman Wilbur Mills. Five years before our interview, Mills—who was then the chairman of the powerful Ways and Means Committee—made a fool of himself when he got drunk and went on a moonlight romp in Washington's Tidal Basin with a striptease dancer named Fannie Fox—aka "The Argentine Firecracker." That escapade made Mills fair game, a most inviting target, and Carson put the wood to him in several monologues. But, as he made clear in our conversation, he abruptly stopped making fun of Mills when he found out that the congressman "was an alcoholic and had emotional problems and, in fact, was dependent on alcohol."

Carson himself was known to have had some excessive encounters with the sauce, so when he alluded to Mills's alcoholism, I couldn't resist making the connection.

WALLACE: Of course, it takes one to know one.

CARSON: Ah, cruel. You're cruel.

WALLACE: But there was a time—

CARSON: What?

WALLACE: Come on. There was a time when—

CARSON: I used to have a little pop? I sure did.

WALLACE: That's right.

CARSON: I don't handle it well . . . I found that it's probably
best for me to not really entangle with it, because I just found
out that I—I did not drink well. And when I did drink, rather
than a lot of people, who become fun-loving and gregarious
and love everybody, I would go the opposite. And it would
happen (Claps hands) just like that.

Even though two years had passed since Carson's award from Harvard's Hasty Pudding Club, we chose to end the piece with our footage of that event. Being honored by that citadel of Ivy League prestige had to be a heady experience for a fellow who had attended the state university in his native Nebraska in the late 1940s. In his acceptance remarks, Carson acknowledged that in his droll and cavalier way.

"This is really lovely," he told his Hasty Pudding hosts, "but more important than that, I want to thank the club for letting me and my wife stay in the master's residence last night at Elliott House. You really don't know what that means. It's the first time I've scored with a chick on a college campus since 1949."

We repeated our profile of Carson in May 1992, when, after thirty years on the throne of late-night television, he finally passed the crown to his successor, Jay Leno. We broadcast the piece just a few nights before the cheery and familiar introduction—"Here's Johnny!"—was heard for the last time. In the years since then, Carson steadfastly shunned the limelight, including the one that emanated from *60 Minutes*. I tried on several occasions to persuade him to let us do an update of our 1979 story, one that would allow us to take a look at what he'd been doing with his life since he left *The Tonight Show*. His replies were always courteous, even cordial, but the answer was always the same: Thanks, but no thanks. Once he crossed over into retirement, Johnny Carson became an even more vigilant guardian of his privacy.

MEL BROOKS

I'VE INTERVIEWED SOME OTHER COMEDIANS over the years, from Steve Allen in 1957 to Billy Crystal in 2002. I discovered early on that interviews with comedians can often be erratic and mercurial, and that's the main reason I've been inclined to avoid them or at least approach them warily, with my guard up and all my reflexes on full alert. A good interviewer does his best to control the verbal exchange, to follow the agenda he has put together for the occasion. But comedians resist that. They live for humor and revel in distraction. Being compulsive jokers, they will say or do almost anything to get a laugh, even (or perhaps especially) if it's at the expense of the poor souls who are trying to interview them.

As I noted a few pages back, when I interviewed Carson in 1979, he had gentle sport with me for my heavy concentration on investigative stories. It was really quite harmless, but beneath the whimsy, there was a tacit message. In effect, what Carson was saying to me was this: I'm wise to your tricks, Wallace, so don't try to probe too deeply into *my* life. I'm not one of your crooks or con men.

Twenty-two years later, when I sat down with Mel Brooks, he quickly took control. The interview was designed to be the centerpiece of a *60 Minutes* profile of Brooks to be broadcast just before the Broadway opening of his musical *The Producers*, based on a 1968 movie he had written and directed. At first, when I tried to talk about the show, he preferred to focus on my jewelry and wardrobe.

WALLACE: Tell me something. The show—

BROOKS: Is that a hundred-dollar watch? Let me see that watch.

WALLACE: It's about a forty-dollar watch.

BROOKS: It's a beautiful watch.

WALLACE: Isn't it?

BROOKS: Yeah, I love that.

WALLACE: It's a forty-dollar watch.

BROOKS: Really?

WALLACE: Yes, lights up in the dark.

BROOKS: What a cheap son of a bitch you are.

WALLACE: You got that right. You're a great judge of character. Tell me this—

BROOKS: What did you pay for your jacket?

WALLACE: I don't know. This is hopsack.

BROOKS: Hopsack is like fancy burlap, right? Am I right?

WALLACE: That's exactly right. That's exactly right.

BROOKS: It's like burlap shrunk down. Did you know that six months ago, that your jacket carried coffee beans? Do you realize that? And I'm telling you, that came from Colombia full of coffee. Wait a minute. (Sniffs Wallace's sleeve) He reeks of Colombian coffee!

I didn't mind playing straight man to Mel Brooks. As a young man, he was one of the gifted writers who created skits for Sid Caesar's television show, a stable of talent that included such once-and-future hotshots as Carl Reiner, Neil Simon, and Woody Allen.

He eventually moved on from television to film, writing and directing such loony, over-the-top comedies as *Blazing Saddles* and *Young Frankenstein*. But his boldest and most outrageous movie— and one that many critics and fans regard as his best—was his first feature-length film, *The Producers*.

The movie's two main characters are a has-been producer and his accountant, who come up with a scheme to bilk thousands of dollars out of naive investors, most of whom are elderly widows just a few gasps away from their final breath. In order for the swindle to work, the new show for which they're raising wildly excessive funds must be a surefire flop, a guaranteed loser. Their search for such a property leads them to an unreconstructed Nazi who has written a play called *Springtime for Hitler,* an engaging and nostalgic look at the leader of the Third Reich and his fun-loving cronies. The twist comes when, in the production of the play, *Der Führer* is portrayed as such a bumbling buffoon that the audience responds to him with gales of laughter and applause. As a result, the show is a hit, the scam is exposed, and our two heroes are sent off to prison.

Brooks received an Oscar for that year's best original screenplay, and although *The Producers* was not as big a box-office success as some of his later films, it did become a kind of cult classic. And that was that until three decades later, when he decided to revive the story as a Broadway musical.

When I interviewed Brooks in 2001, I asked him about his decision to depict one of the most evil men who ever lived as a goofball. This was his reply:

"Hitler was part of this incredible idea that you could put Jews in concentration camps and kill them. And how do you get even? How do you get even with the man? There's only one way to get even. You have to bring him down with ridicule. Because if you stand on a soapbox and match him with rhetoric, you're just as bad as he is. But if you can make people laugh at him, then you're one up on him. And one of my lifelong jobs has been to make the world laugh at Adolf Hitler."

Throughout his long career, Brooks has worn his Jewish heart on his sleeve. There have been other Jewish comedians who almost never drew attention to their ethnic identity—Jack Benny and Mort Sahl are just two who come to mind—but Brooks's brand of humor has always been driven by a Jewish sensibility, even when the material was not overtly Jewish. Much of the time, his comedy has had a hard cutting edge; some of his silliest pranks and broad slapstick routines have revealed his lifelong resentment of the way Jews have been persecuted down through the centuries. Still, I never heard Brooks address the question in a serious vein until our interview. When I asked him about his seeming obsession with Jews and Jewishness, his mood suddenly grew dark, and his voice snapped with indignation.

> BROOKS: Maybe because I'm angry. Who knows? It may be a deep-seated anger at anti-Semitism. Yes, I am a Jew. I am a Jew.
>
> WALLACE: Yeah.
>
> BROOKS: What about it? What about it? What's so wrong? What's the matter with being a Jew? I think there's a lot of that way down deep beneath all the quick Jewish jokes that I do.
>
> WALLACE: You've never suffered for being Jewish.
>
> BROOKS: Oh, and I was in the army. "Jew boy, out of my way. Out of my face, Jew boy." This guy called me Jew-something, and I—I walked over to him. I took his helmet off. I said, "I don't want to hurt your helmet, 'cause it's GI issue." And I smashed him in the head with my mess kit.

That outburst really caught me by surprise. Here was a man who had spent his life making jokes about almost everything, and now, in a dramatic turnabout, Brooks was giving our viewers a rare glimpse of the pain and rage lurking behind the mirth.

The two of us are from roughly the same generation (Brooks is eight years younger), and as I sat there listening to his grievance, I was struck by the contrast between the tribulations of his young manhood and my own experience. It is hardly surprising that I had no direct contact with anti-Semitism when I was growing up in Brookline, for in that heavily ethnic community, most of our friends and neighbors were Jewish. But I left Brookline when I was seventeen and spent the next several years in the Midwest, first as a student at the University of Michigan and then as a broadcaster at radio stations in Detroit and Chicago. After that came a two-year hitch as a naval officer in the Pacific during World War II. Neither then nor at any other time in my life did I try to conceal the fact that I was Jewish, and yet I never personally felt the sting of anti-Semitism.

This is not to suggest that I lived in some kind of Pollyanna bubble. I was fully aware that there were some Americans (no doubt more than I cared to admit) who disdained Jews and wanted little to do with us. If there were occasional slights and sneers, they were so inconsequential that I just shrugged them off. I can say for certain that I was never the target of the kind of ugly insults that Brooks had to deal with when he was in the army.

Toward the end of our interview, I observed that the long ride on his blazing saddle was nearing an end, and he had to face the prospect of being put out to pasture.

WALLACE: You realize that *The Producers* on Broadway is the capstone of your career. You're seventy-five.

BROOKS: Stop already with the—

WALLACE: Wait, wait, wait, wait.

BROOKS: I—I don't want to hear that anymore.

WALLACE: It's all—

BROOKS: Stop. Don't remind me. I don't look in the mirror and I don't look in the calendar.

WALLACE: It's all downhill from now on.

I later learned from a mutual friend that Brooks was a sensitive septuagenarian who was furious at me for suggesting that his best years were behind him. "He hated that," I was told, "he hated what you said about it being 'all downhill from now on.'"

At the time, I thought it was obvious that I was merely being playful, one geezer teasing a fellow graybeard, and a younger one at that.

EPILOGUE

A ND NOW A FINAL WORD from the old geezer. As I write
this in the spring of 2005, I realize some people are wondering
when I'm going to retire. But for the moment I continue working because I wouldn't know what to do if I didn't. And I continue to be
given opportunities I can't turn down.

Example? In March of this year, 2005, I got an unexpected call
from Beth Knobel, CBS News bureau chief in Moscow, to tell me
that she'd received a surprise invitation from the Kremlin: They
wanted me to come to Moscow in early May for an interview with
Russian president Vladimir Putin.

What in the world? I wondered.

It turned out Putin was planning a huge celebration for May 9, the sixtieth anniversary of the end of World War II. Leaders from the United States, Germany, and France were coming, along with others from around the world. But President Putin, of course, had no idea what a gift he was giving me with his invitation, because May 9, 2005, was also my eighty-seventh birthday.

The ground rules for our unexpected sit-down, set by his worka-holic press secretary Alexei Gromov? Forty-five minutes with Putin, at least half of which had to be about the sixtieth anniversary cele-bration . . . and half about other questions involving him and Russia.

When Gromov showed up for a pre-interview meeting, I launched into a spiel about how important it is, in order to get a nuanced and fully realized portrait of a world figure like Putin, to have sufficient time with him. Well, we drank a little vodka while Gromov ate and chain-smoked and worked his cell phone. And he wound up doubling my time with Putin.

Putin and I, it turned out, were quite comfortable with each other. He spoke Russian on camera and idiomatic fluent English off camera. He was amiable, savvy, talkative. And neither he nor Gromov asked for my questions ahead of time.

His "democracy," of which he's very proud, is not *our* democracy by any means, but he's made it clear it's a long way from the old Soviet system. Fact is, there's a remarkably free, free press in Russia today—lots of newspapers and magazines and cable shows, with op-position coming from many of them—and opposition on the streets, too. But the Kremlin still controls the news that's seen across Russia on the three major television networks, one of which nightly covers the comings and goings of the president.

Putin, the inscrutable former KGB agent, the tough-guy presi-dent labeled by some a dictator but who calls himself a democrat, had been anointed by Boris Yeltsin as his successor in dealing with the greedy oligarchs who had made themselves billionaires by buying up Russia's natural resources—its oil, its energy, its state-owned industries—at bargain basement prices, with Yeltsin looking on.

Putin surprised me by his willingness to talk about things like the clout of those oligarchs, most of whom are Jewish, and he spoke candidly about the resurgence of anti-Semitism in Russia, which he deplored.

He's now in his second and—according to the Russian constitution—last term as president. In 2008, he'll be out of a job, fifty-five years old and still in the prime of life. What will he do? He says he won't try to amend the constitution in order to stay on. Almost as a joke, I asked him: "What about journalism?" No age limit, the money's good, and he'd get a chance, perhaps, to interview the next president of the United States for Russian television.

I didn't tell him that I myself have never gotten a chance to interview the current president of the United States. Karl Rove wouldn't let me talk to him even when he was merely governor of Texas. So . . . I've interviewed just about every president since Abe Lincoln, including Bush the elder, number 41, but never George W., number 43.

So how about it, Mr. President, isn't it time you gave this old man a break?

ACKNOWLEDGMENTS

TELEVISION JOURNALISM IS PERFORCE A collaborative undertaking—reporters, producers, researchers, cameramen and -women, sound technicians, film and tape editors spending days and nights traveling, bird-dogging in pursuit of something they (we) believe is useful, important, and, ultimately, satisfying.

If you've watched *60 Minutes* with any regularity, you've seen their names roll by too fast on the credits at the end of each broadcast. There's no way to adequately recognize them here. Many of them are not simply coworkers, they're my friends, and I am in their debt.

INDEX

A&E, *20th Century* series, 85
Abbas, Mahmoud, 121
ABC Television
  executive decisions in, 10–11, 78, 164
  Mike Wallace Interview on, 5–6, 68, 78,
    159, 164–67
Actors Studio, 258
Aesop's fables, 32
Afghanistan, Soviet invasion of, 131
African-Americans
  in Birmingham, 80
  Black Muslims, 86–91, 93, 98
  black power, 82
  black separatism, 88
  "by any means necessary," 88, 92
  Civil Rights Act, 81
  de facto segregation in the north, 81
  Eastland interview, 70–72
  economic plight of, 83–84
  Edwards interview, 68–70, 80

Elijah Muhammad, 87–88, 89–90
Emancipation Proclamation, 79–80
Farrakhan, 93–98
Faubus interview, 74–75, 166
"I Have a Dream," 80
and integration, 72–73, 80, 81
Jim Crow laws, 68, 76
King, 76–85, 91–92
King assassination, 84, 91
King interviews, 78, 79–80, 82–84
Ku Klux Klan vs., 68–70
and legislation, 79
in Little Rock, 73–75
Malcolm X, 87–92, 93–96
militant activists, 81–82, 85–92
Million Man March, 96
Montgomery boycott, 76–77, 84
nonviolent protest, 77, 78, 80, 83, 84
Organization of Afro-American Unity, 89
Parks, Rosa, 76

African-Americans (*continued*)
  and Philip Morris Company, 71
  and presidential politics, 74, 78–81
  segregation of, 67–85
  and Supreme Court, 70, 71, 72–73, 75,
    76, 77
  and urban riots, 81
  voter registration, 81
  white backlash, 82
After the Fall (Miller), 262
Allen, Steve, 268
Allen, Woody, 270
Al Qaeda, 131, 132
American Jewish Congress, 98, 103–4, 108
American Legion, 138–39
Anderson, Marian, 39–40
Andrews, Julie, 247
Anti-Defamation League, B'nai B'rith, 69
Apartment, The (film), 222
Apple, R.W., 189
Arab oil embargo (1970s), 47, 101, 122
Arafat, Yasir, 107–8, 113–22
  aging and death of, 119–20
  and Camp David accords, 114
  and Carter, 114–15
  courage of, 120–21
  eyes of, 113–14
  and Middle East peace efforts, 116–19
  MW interviews with, 114–15, 118–21
  Nobel Peace Prize to, 116
  and Oslo Accords, 116, 117, 119
  Redgrave's support of, 229
Arendt, Hannah, 107
Arkansas National Guard, 73
Armies of the Night, The (Mailer), 250
Art Students League, 144
Asphalt Jungle, The (film), 159
Assad, Hafez al, 101, 102
Atlanta Constitution, The, 69
Atlanta Journal, The, 69
Autobiography of Malcolm X (Malcolm X and
  Haley), 91–92

Bach, Erwin, 243–44, 245
Baker, Norma Jeane
  and Dougherty, 257–58
  see also Monroe, Marilyn
Baldwin, James, 246
Bankhead, Tallulah, 247
Barak, Ehud, 117, 118
Barasch, Philip, 177–78

Baryshnikov, Mikhail, 157
Bassett, Angela, 242
Beatty, Warren, 222, 225
Bedell, Sally, 195
Beethoven, Ludwig van, 151
Begin, Menachem
  and Camp David accords, 109–10,
    112–13
  and guerrilla warfare, 107, 108, 113
  MW interviews with, 105–9, 114
  Nobel Peace Prize to, 113
  and Sadat, 109–10, 112–13
Belafonte, Harry, 93
Bennett, Tony, 174
Benny, Jack, 204, 226, 271
Benton, Rita, 147
Benton, Thomas Hart (artist), 144–48
  America's heartland reflected in work of,
    144
  death of, 148
  and Martha's Vineyard Arts Association,
    147–48
  MW interview with, 145–47
  reputation of, 144–45, 146, 147
Benton, Thomas Hart (senator), 144
Bergen, Candice, 247
Bergman, Lowell, and Tobacco War, 206–9,
  211, 212, 214, 215–16, 218–19
Bernstein, Carl, 176
Bernstein, Leonard, 157
Beschloss, Michael, 23, 24
Better Government Association (BGA),
  176–77, 184
Betty and Bob (radio), 52
Bingham, Wade, 181
bin Laden, Osama, 132
Birmingham, Alabama, 80
Black Muslims, 86–91, 93, 98
Boies, David, 198, 202
Bonanno, Bill, 172–74
Bonanno, Joe, MW interview with,
  171–74
Bon Soir, New York, 233
Boston Globe, The, 60
Bostonians, The (film), 232
Bradley, Ed, 158, 241
Brando, Marlon, 173
Brenner, Marie, 218
Brice, Fanny, 236
Britt, May, 80
Brookline, Massachusetts, 7–9, 273

Brooks, Mel
  as comedian, 269–70
  Jewish heart of, 271–72
  MW interview with, 269–74
  and *Producers,* 269, 270–71, 273
Brown, Edmund G. (Pat), 54
Brown & Williamson, 207–12, 213, 219
Brown v. *Board of Education,* 72–73, 77
Buchwald, Art, 51, 147
Buckley, William F., 194
Bullock, Annie Mae, *see* Turner, Tina
Burrows, Abe, 142
Burt, Dan, 197–98
Bush, George H. W., 63, 277
Bush, George W., 131, 277

Caesar, Sid, 3, 270
California Pacifica University, 180–82, 184
Callas, Maria, 157
Camel News Caravan (TV), 204
Camery, James, 179
Camino, The: A Journey of the Spirit
  (MacLaine), 226–27
Camp David, and Oslo Accords, 117–18
Camp David accords, 109–10, 112–13, 114,
  117
Canaday, John, 145–46
Capital Legal Foundation, 197–98
Capone, Al, 82, 171–72
Carmichael, Stokely, 82
Carson, Johnny, 263–68
  death of, 263–64
  at Hasty Pudding Club, 264, 268
  MW interview with, 264–68, 269
  privacy sought by, 264, 266, 268
  and *Tonight Show,* 264, 265, 266–67, 268
Carter, Jimmy
  and Camp David accords, 109–10, 112,
  114
  loss to Reagan, 59
  and Middle East, 105–6, 109–10, 112,
  114–15, 127
  MW interview of, 47–49
  post-presidency of, 51
  problems during presidency of, 47, 48
  rise to power of, 45–46
Carter, Rosalynn, 45
  and First Lady's roles, 46–47, 51
  helping others, 51
  and mental health programs, 50–52
  MW interview with, 49–50

Castro, Fidel, 113, 170–71, 229
Catholic Church, 134–36
CBS News
  documentaries, 82, 88
  Hewitt's creativity with, 30
  on influential people, 63, 137
  in-house probe by, 195, 196–97, 203
  and Jewish lobby, 103
  libel suit against, 197–99, 202–3
  Morning News, 82, 89, 90, 188
  MW's assignments for, 13, 24, 100, 167,
  206
  news vs. corporate culture in, 211–13,
  215, 217
  and Tobacco War, 211–15, 217
  20th Century, 85
  and Vietnam, 199
  and Westinghouse, 213, 217
CBS Reports, 82
  responsibility for, 196
  Westmoreland documentary on, 187,
  190–96, 202
Channel 5, New York
  eleven o'clock news, 1
  Night Beat, 1–3, 160
Channel 13, New York, MW interviews on,
  78, 87, 88
Charlie Rose Show, The (TV), 217
Chicago Sun-Times, 177
Christian Tennessee University, 180
Churchill, Winston, 137
Cicero, Illinois, 82
civil rights, *see* African-Americans
Civil Rights Act (1964), 81
Civil War, U.S., as Mr. Lincoln's War, 22
Clifford, Clark, 10–12
Clinton, Bill, 43
  in Arkansas, 76
  and impeachment, 45
  and Oslo Accords, 116, 117
Clinton, Hillary Rodham, 44–45
Close Encounters (Wallace), 3
Cohen, Mickey, 6, 159–65
  as florist, 160
  as killer, 161–62
  MW interview with, 161–63, 165, 166
  remarks about Parker by, 162–65
cold war, end of, 62
Collingwood, Charles, 100
Con Men (Jackman), 185
Connor, Bull, 80

Cook, Greg, 179
Copland, Aaron, 157
Counsel to the President (Clifford), 12
Cravath, Swaine & Moore, 198
Crile, George, 190–96, 202
Crowe, Russell, 218
Crystal, Billy, 268

Dalí, Salvador, 140–43
  autobiography of, 142
  immortality of, 143
  MW interview with, 142, 143
  Persistence of Memory, 140
  and surrealism, 140, 142, 143
Daly, John Charles, 165
Daughters of the American Revolution
    (DAR), 39
Davis, Bette, 247
Davis, Edie, 52–53, 54, 60
Davis, Loyal, 53
Davis, Nancy, 53, 55; *see also* Reagan,
    Nancy
Davis, Patti, 59
Davis, Sammy, Jr., 80, 222
Dayan, Moshe, 100
Death of a Salesman (Miller), 259, 262
Desert Storm, 132
Devotion, Edward, 8
Dickson, Harry Ellis, 149
DiMaggio, Joe, 258
Dougherty, Jim, 257–58
Douglas Edwards with the News (TV), 204
Dukakis, Kitty Dickson, 149
Dukakis, Michael, 149
Duncan, Isadora, 228

Eastland, James, 70–72
Ed Sullivan Show, The (TV), 150
Edwards, Eldon Lee, 68–70, 80
Egypt
  British occupation of, 111
  and Camp David accords, 109–10,
    112–13
  and Israel, 109–10, 111–13
  Sadat, 109–13, 130
  territories of, 100
Einstein, Albert, 107, 153
Eisenhower, Dwight D.
  Eleanor Roosevelt's views on, 38
  Mailer's remarks about, 251
  and Nixon, 24, 41

presidential elections, 42
  and race, 74, 79
  Wright's views on, 138
Eisenhower, Mamie Dowd, 43
Emancipation Proclamation, 79–80
Emerson, Faye, 3
Ernst, Max, 143
Executioner's Song, The (Mailer), 250

Farouk, king of Egypt, 111
Farrakhan, Louis, 93–98
  anti-Semitism of, 97–98
  and Elijah Muhammad, 93, 94
  and Malcolm X, 93–96
  MW interviews with, 94, 95–98
  and racial hatred, 93–94
  travel to Africa, 96–97
Faubus, Orval
  and integration, 73–76
  MW interview with, 74–75, 166
  and reelection, 75, 76
FDR Memorial Commission, 42–43
Fiedler, Arthur, 149
First Lady, roles of, 40, 43–45, 46–47,
    51
Fishburne, Laurence, 242
Fonda, Jane, 228, 229
Ford, Gerald R., 14, 46, 48, 55, 56
Forster, E. M., 232
Four Lads, 174
Fox, Fannie "The Argentine Firecracker,"
    267
FOX News Sunday, 60
Fratianno, Jimmy "The Weasel," 167–71,
    174
  book by, 167
  as killer, 168–69
  MW interview with, 168–71
Freud, Sigmund, 140
Friedman, Thomas, 119
Funny Girl (Broadway musical), 236

Gabor, Zsa Zsa, 6
Gandhi, Mohandas K. (Mahatma), 137
Garment, Len, 25–26, 28, 30
Gilmore, Gary, 250
Godfather, The (Puzo), 171, 173
Goldenson, Leonard, 164, 165
Goldin, Marion, 179, 184
Goldwater, Barry, 54
Goodman, Ellen, 183

Gorbachev, Mikhail, 62–63
Gore, Al, 198
Gorin, Norman, 184–85
Great Depression, 39
Great Society, 20, 22, 24, 44, 62, 85
Greene, Bob, 183
Grosset & Dunlap, 253
Guggenheim Museum, New York, 140

Haley, Alex
    and King, 91–92
    and Malcolm X, 88, 91–92
    MW interview with, 91–92
Hamas, 118
Hamill, Pete, 225
Hammett, Dashiell, 229
Haney, Carol, 222
Harvey, Terrel, 182
Hasty Pudding Club, Harvard University,
    264, 268
Hawkins, Gains, 192, 202
Hayes, Helen, 247
Heifetz, Jascha, 149, 151
Hellman, Lillian, 229
Hemingway, Ernest, 251
Hertzberg, Rabbi Arthur, 104
Hewitt, Don
    and CBS News, 30
    as executive producer, 17
    and Jewish lobby, 103–4
    and LBJ Library tour, 17, 18–19, 20
    and MW's career, 216
    reputation of, 30
    and 60 Minutes, 30, 175, 212, 216
    and special edition, 183–84
    and Tobacco War, 211–12, 213–17
Hill, Clint, 14–17
Hitler, Adolf, 137, 271
Hooks, Benjamin, 57
Hoover, J. Edgar, 214
Horowitz, Vladimir, 152–57
    comeback of, 155–56
    fiftieth anniversary of, 152, 153
    MW interview with, 153–56, 175
    "Stars and Stripes Forever," 156–57
    withdrawal period of, 155
Horowitz, Wanda, 154–56
Howards End (film), 232
Humphrey, Hubert H., 27, 32
Hussein, Saddam, 131–32
Huston, John, 159

I, Tina (Turner), 242–43
I Can Get It for You Wholesale (Broadway
    musical), 236
"I Have a Dream" (King), 80
I Love Lucy (TV), 151
In Search of Identity (Sadat), 111
Insider, The (film), 218–19
Iran
    and Afghanistan, 131
    anti-Western theocracy in, 130–31
    hostage crisis in, 47, 127–29, 132
    and Iraq, 131–32
    Khomeini, 127–31
    nuclear energy program in, 131
    and oil embargo, 122
    revolution in, 126–27, 130, 131, 132
    SAVAK in, 124
    Shah, 122–27
Iran-Contra affair, 60–61
Iran-Iraq war, 131–32
Iraq
    as "axis of evil," 131
    Desert Storm, 132
    and Iran, 131–32
    U.S. assistance to, 132
Iraq-Gate banking scandal, 206
Irgun Zvai Leumi, 107, 108
Irma La Douce (film), 222
Israel
    Begin interviews, 105–9
    and Camp David accords, 109–10,
        112–13
    and Egypt, 109–10, 111–13
    and guerrilla warfare, 106–8, 118
    Knesset in, 105, 109
    occupied territories, 100, 102, 112, 115,
        116, 117, 119
    and Oslo Accords, 116–17
    and Palestine/PLO, 114, 115, 116,
        117–19, 121–22
    Redgrave's views on, 230–31
    relocation to, 105
    right to exist, 115, 116
    Six-Day War, 20, 100, 101, 106, 112, 116
    War of Independence, 107, 116
    Yom Kippur War, 101, 111–12

Jack: The Struggles of John F. Kennedy
    (Parmet), 13
Jackman, Ian, 185
James, Henry, 232

Jewish Defense League, 229
Jewish lobby, 98, 101, 102, 103–4, 108,
    114, 125–26, 229–30
Jim Crow laws, 68, 76
Johnson, Lady Bird, 18, 19–20, 44
Johnson, Lyndon B., 12, 17–24
    achievements of, 20, 21, 22, 24, 44, 62,
    85
    on the burdens of the presidency, 22
    and civil rights, 81, 85
    and Hoover, 214
    LBJ Presidential Library, 17, 18, 20
    and LBJ ranch, 18–19
    political career of, 45, 46, 54
    and Vietnam War, 18, 20, 21, 22–24, 32,
    84–85, 192
Jordan, territories of, 100, 112
Julia (film), 229, 232
Just for the Record (Streisand), 236

Kaden, Ellen, 211, 213, 217
Kaplan, Marvin, 201, 202
Kennedy, Jacqueline Bouvier, 15, 43–44, 158
Kennedy, John F.
    assassination of, 13–17
    in Brookline, 8–9
    and integration, 79, 80
    and New Frontier, 61
    and Pearson interview, 7, 9–13
    political career of, 9–10, 46
    presidential election (1960), 25
    and Profiles in Courage, 10–13, 42, 164
    and Vietnam, 22, 24
    in World War II, 9
Kennedy, Joseph P., 8, 9–10, 12
Kennedy, Robert F., 10, 223
    assassination of, 14
    Mailer's conjectures about, 253, 254–55
Kennedy, Rose, 8
Kennedy family
    in Brookline, 7–9
    counsel for, 10, 11, 12
    lawsuit threat from, 11–12
Khomeini, Ayatollah Ruhollah, 127–31
    MW interview with, 128–30
    and revolution, 130–31
King, Larry, 50, 64
King, Rev. Martin Luther, Jr., 14, 76–85
    assassination of, 84, 91
    on the economic plight of the Negro,
    83–84

Haley's views on, 91–92
"I Have a Dream," 80
influence of, 137
and militant activists, 81–82
ministry of, 76
MW interviews with, 78, 79–80, 82–84
MW's admiration for, 84, 85
Nobel Peace Prize to, 81
nonviolent protests of, 77, 78, 80, 83, 84
and presidential politics, 78–81
threats and violence aimed at, 77, 84
Knobel, Beth, 275
Korean War, as Mr. Truman's War, 22
Kovacs, Ernie, 1
Kowet, Don, 195
Kraft, Robert, 8–9
Krips, Alfred, 149
Ku Klux Klan (KKK), 68–70
Kuwait, Iraqi invasion of, 132

Lancaster, Burt, 234–35
Lando, Barry, 127, 128, 184
Last Mafioso, The (Fratianno), 167
Last Year at Marienbad (film), 180
Lawford, Peter, 222
LBJ Presidential Library, 17, 18, 20
Lebanon, 115
Lee, Spike, 91, 92
Lenin, Vladimir Ilyich, 137
Leno, Jay, 268
Leonard, Bill, 60
Leonardo da Vinci, 142
LeRoy, Mervyn, 55
Lewinsky, Monica, 45
Life, 175
Lincoln, Abraham, 22
Lincoln Memorial concert (1939), 40
Little Rock, Arkansas, 73–75
Lloyd's of London, 166
Lomax, Louis, 86–87, 88
Long Day's Journey into Night (O'Neill), 232
Longfellow, Henry Wadsworth, 8
Lorillard, 212–13
Louis X, see Farrakhan, Louis
Luciano, Lucky, 172
Lucky Strike, 204
Lund, Peter, 214

MacLaine, Shirley, 221–27
    as actress, 221–22, 225
    as dancer, 221–22

MW interviews with, 223–24, 226–27
and political causes, 223, 227
and Rat Pack, 222–23
spirituality of, 223–24, 226–27
Madison, James, 22
Mafia
capo don of, 171
Capone, 171–72
Castro plot of, 170–71
ceremony of, 169
and *Godfather*, 171, 173
hit men for, 167–69, 171
membership in, 174
omertà code of, 171
Sicilian vs. American culture in, 172
Mailer, Adele, 252
Mailer, Norman, 249–57, 259
book about Monroe by, 249–50, 253–56
controversy welcomed by, 250, 251–52
MW interviews with, 250–51, 252,
253–57
political campaigns of, 252
Pulitzer and National Book awards to, 250
Malcolm X, 14, 87–92
assassination of, 91, 93, 94–96
autobiography of, 88, 91–92
"by any means necessary," 88, 92
and Elijah Muhammad, 89, 94
family of, 94–96
and Farrakhan, 93–96
Haley's views on, 91–92
influence of, 88, 92, 93–94
magnetic presence of, 88
MW interviews with, 88, 89, 90–91
and Nation of Islam, 88, 89, 95
and Organization of Afro-American Unity,
89
pilgrimage to Mecca, 89
respect accorded after death of, 91
Malcolm X (film), 91
Man of Honor, A (Bonanno), 171
Mansfield, Jayne, 6
Martha's Vineyard Arts Association, 147–48
Martin, Dean, 222
Mary, Queen of Scots (film), 228
McChristian, Joseph, 191, 192, 202
McClure, Bill, 101, 123
McGovern, George, 223
McKellar, Kenneth, 6–7
McKenna, Siobhan, 3
McNamara, Robert S., 22

Mead, Marikay, 128
Medicaid, 176–77
Menuhin, Yehudi, 151
Mexican War, as Mr. Polk's War, 22
Middle East
Afghanistan invasion, 131
Al Qaeda, 131, 132
Arab oil embargo, 47, 101, 122
Camp David accords, 109–10, 112–13,
114, 117
Desert Storm, 132
Egypt, 109–13
freedom fighters/terrorists in, 107–8,
116–19, 132
Iran, 122–31
Iran-Iraq war, 131–32
Iraq, 131–32
Israel, 105–9, 116
and Jewish lobby, 98, 101, 102, 103–4,
108, 114, 125–26, 229–30
Oslo Accords, 115, 116–18, 119
peace efforts, 99–100, 109–10, 112–13,
114, 116–19, 121–22
PLO and Arafat, 107–8, 113–22
radical Islamic groups in, 118
Six-Day War, 20, 100, 101, 106, 112, 116
Syrian Jews, 101–5
Yom Kippur War, 101, 111–12
Mike Wallace Interview, The
at ABC, 5–6, 68, 78, 159
cigarette commercials on, 205
end of, 78
guest list on, 6
legal watchdog for, 166
libel suit threats to, 6, 11, 12, 164–67
live broadcasts of, 162–63
national audience of, 6
Miller, Arthur, 258–63
autobiography of, 260
as dramatist, 259, 261, 262, 263
Monroe's marriage with, 257, 258–62
MW interview with, 259–61, 262–63
Million Dollar Baby (film), 247
Million Man March, 96
Mills, Wilbur, 267
Mirage Tavern, 177–78, 184
Misfits, The (film), 261, 262
Monroe, Marilyn
and DiMaggio, 258
and Dougherty, 257–58
Mailer's views on, 249–50, 253–56

Monroe, Marilyn (*continued*)
  and Miller, 257, 258–62
  in *Misfits*, 261
Montgomery, Alabama, bus boycott, 76–77, 84
Morath, Inge, 262
Moreau, Jeanne, 247
Morgan (film), 228
Muhammad, Elijah, 87–88, 89–90, 93, 94
Murdoch, Rupert, 60
Murray, Eunice, 255–56
Murrieta Hot Springs, 178–80, 184, 185
Murrow, Edward R., 205, 217
My Turn (N. Reagan), 63

NAACP, 57, 69, 87
Naked and the Dead, The (Mailer), 250
Nasser, Gamal Abdel, 111
Nation, The, 78
National Guard, 101st Airborne Division, 74
Nation of Islam, 87–88, 89, 93, 94–95
Native Son (Wright), 246
Near East Report, 104
Negroes, *see* African-Americans
New Deal, 37, 39, 40
New England Patriots, 8
New Frontier, 61
Newsweek, 87
New York *Daily News,* 217
New York Philharmonic, 152
New York Times, The
  on Black Muslims, 87
  on CBS self-censorship, 217
  on Faubus interview, 75
  on Ku Klux Klan, 69
  ownership of, 126
Nicholson, Jack, 225
Nicoli, Frankie, 168
Night Beat
  controversial topics covered in, 3, 160, 165, 250–52
  format of, 2–3, 5
  idea for, 1–2, 201
  popularity of, 2–3
Nixon, Pat Ryan, 34–35
Nixon, Richard M., 7, 24–35
  Eleanor Roosevelt's views on, 41
  MW interview of, 32, 33
  New Nixon, 25–26, 27, 32
  personal traits of, 27, 34–35
  and the presidency, 33–34, 46

presidential campaign of, 24–30, 31, 32, 33, 35
  as "Tricky Dick," 25, 32
  as vice president, 24–25
  and Vietnam War, 22, 32, 34, 46
  and Watergate, 29, 34, 46, 55, 176
Nolte, Nick, 239
North Korea, as "axis of evil," 131

Ober, Eric, 211–12, 213, 217
Olivier, Laurence, 228
Onassis, Aristotle, 157
O'Neill, Eugene, 232
Organization of Afro-American Unity, 89
Oslo Accords (1993), 115, 116–18, 119
Out on a Limb (MacLaine), 223

Paar, Jack, 233
Pacino, Al, 173, 218–19
Pahlavi, Shah Mohammad Reza, 122–27
  and American hostages, 127–28
  as anti-Communist, 130
  and Jewish lobby, 125–26
  MW interviews with, 123–26
  and revolution, 126–27, 130, 131
Pajama Game, The (Broadway musical), 222
Palestine
  British rule in, 107
  guerrillas of, 106–7, 115, 118, 120–21
  homeland of, 105, 114
  and Israel, 114, 115, 116, 117–19, 121–22
  and Middle East peace, 114
  and Oslo Accords, 116
  self-rule, 116, 117, 121, 122
  stateless refugees of, 113
Palestine Liberation Organization (PLO), 107–8
  Arafat, 113–22
  intifada of, 115, 118
  Redgrave's film about, 229
Palestinian, The (film), 229
Pall Mall cigarettes, 204
Palme, Olaf, 226
Parker, William H., 162–65
Parks, Rosa, 76
Parmet, Herbert, 13
Patterson, Eugene, 183
Pavarotti, Luciano, 158
Pearson, Drew
  MW interview of, 9–10, 166

and *Profiles in Courage,* 10–13, 42, 164
  reputation of, 6–7, 11
Pegler, Westbrook, 40–41
Peres, Shimon, 116
Perlman, Itzhak, MW interview with,
  150–52, 175
Perlman, Toby, 152
Persistence of Memory, The (Dalí), 140
Philip Morris Company, 71, 77, 166,
  204–7
Picasso, Pablo, 143–44, 147
Plummer, Christopher, 219
PM East, 233–34, 235, 237, 238
Polk, James K., 22
Pollock, Jackson, 144
Power Peddlers, The, 103
Previn, André, 151
Prince of Tides, The (film), 237, 239, 241
Private Dancer (Turner), 242
Producers, The (Brooks), 269, 270–71,
  273
Profaci, Rosalie, 173
Profiles in Courage (Kennedy), 10–13, 42,
  164
Public Broadcasting System (PBS), 78
Putin, Vladimir, 275–77
Puzo, Mario, 171

Quill, Mike, 3

Rabin, Yitzhak, 116–17, 118, 121
Raft, George, 170
Rahman, Ahmed Abdul, 120
Ramrus, Al, 161
*Reaching for Glory: Lyndon Johnson's Secret
  White House Tapes* (Beschloss), 23
Reagan, Nancy
  book by, 63
  children of, 59, 60
  MW friendship with, 52, 54, 56, 58–59,
    64–65
  MW interviews with, 55, 63–64, 65–66
  personal traits of, 56
Reagan, Ron (son), 59
Reagan, Ronald
  achievements of, 62–63
  as actor, 53, 54, 55
  Alzheimer's disease of, 65–66
  as California governor, 53–54
  Carter's views on, 48–49
  death of, 66
  MW interviews with, 56, 57–58, 60–61
  and Nancy, 53, 56, 61, 65–66
  personal traits of, 61, 62
  and the presidency, 61–62, 63
  presidential candidacy of (1968), 28, 29,
    54; (1976), 55–56
  presidential election (1980), 47, 56, 59
  problems during presidency of, 60–61
  on Vietnam War, 57
Reasoner, Harry, 30, 158
Reclining Figure (drama), 142
Reconstruction era, 68
Redgrave, Michael, 228
Redgrave, Vanessa, 227–32
  as actress, 228, 231–32
  MW interview with, 230–31
  political views of, 228–31, 232
Regan, Donald, 63
Reiner, Carl, 270
Republican Party, conservative wing of, 53,
  54
Revere, Paul, 8
Rhodes, James A., 28
Riano, Rosalba, 182
Rockefeller, Nelson A., 27, 28, 29
Roe v. Wade, 136
Roman Catholic Church, 134–36
Romney, George W., 26, 27–28
Rooney, Mickey, 234
Roosevelt, David, 42
Roosevelt, Eleanor, 37–43
  and Anderson concert, 39–40
  critics of, 40–41
  and DAR, 39–40
  death of, 42
  influence of, 40, 41, 42, 43, 44, 45,
    137
  MW's interview with, 38, 40–41
Roosevelt, Franklin D., 6, 46
  death of, 37
  influence of, 37–41, 63, 137
  memorial to, 42–43
  and New Deal, 37, 39, 40
  and World War II, 22
Roosevelt, Theodore, 63
Roots (Haley), 91
Roselli, John, 170–71
Rove, Karl, 277
Royal Shakespeare Company, 228
Rudd, R. J., 179–80, 185
Russell, Richard, 23

Sadat, Anwar, 109–13
    assassination of, 130
    autobiography of, 111
    and Begin, 109–10, 112–13
    and Camp David accords, 109–10,
        112–13, 114
    Khomeini's views of, 129–30
    MW interviews with, 110, 111–12
    Nobel Peace Prize to, 113
Safer, Morley, 148, 158, 185, 217
Sahl, Mort, 271
St. Cyr, Lili, 6
St. Patrick's Cathedral, New York, 139
St. Valentine's Day Massacre, 172
Salant, Dick, 167, 206
Sales, Soupy, 1
Sandefur, Thomas, 209, 210
Sanger, Margaret, 6, 133–37
    and birth control, 133–36
    and Catholic Church, 134–35, 136
    influence of, 137
    MW interview with, 134–35, 166
    and women's rights, 134, 136
Saudi Arabia
    and bin Laden, 132
    and oil embargo, 101, 122
Sauter, Van Gordon, 195–96, 197, 203
SAVAK, 127
Screen Actors Guild, 55
September 11 attacks, 132
Shabazz, Attallah, 94–96
Shabazz, Betty, 94
Shales, Tom, 197
Sharon, Ariel, 118–19, 120, 121
Shaw, George Bernard, 3
Siegel, Bugsy, 160
Sills, Beverly, 158
Simon, Neil, 259, 270
Sinatra, Frank, 173, 222
Sinclair, Ernest, MW interview with,
    181–82, 184
Six-Day War (1967), 20, 100, 101, 106,
    112, 116
60 Minutes
    "between you and me," 178
    Brooks interview, 269–74
    Carson interview, 264–68, 269
    Carter interview, 47–49
    comedians interviewed for, 268–69
    debut of, 24, 31, 175
    detractors of, 183–85

Farrakhan interviews, 94, 95–98
guests' discomfort on, 64
Horowitz interview, 153–56, 175
investigative journalism of, 183–85,
    265
LBJ Library tour, 17, 22
magazine format of, 30, 175
Mailer interview, 253–57
Malcolm X retrospective, 91–92, 94
Middle East issues, see Middle East
Miller interview, 259–61, 262–63
Mirage Tavern interview, 178
Murrieta Hot Springs story, 179–80
MW's nervousness on, 152–53
Reagan interviews, 55, 60–61, 65–66
Redgrave interview, 230–31, 232
sham diploma story, 180–82
special edition of, 183–84
Streisand interview, 236–40
taped broadcasts of, 162
Tobacco War, 206–20
Turner interview, 243–47
validating the crooks, 185
and Watergate, 175–76
Some Came Running (film), 222
Sorensen, Ted, 11, 13
Southern Manifesto, 73
Soviet Union, collapse of, 62
"Stars and Stripes Forever, The" (Sousa),
    156–57
Steinem, Gloria, 35
Stern, Isaac, 151
Stevenson, Adlai E., 42, 138
Strasberg, Lee, 258
Streisand, Barbra, 233–41
    on Broadway, 236
    as movie star, 237, 239
    MW interview with, 236–40
    personality of, 234, 235–36, 237
    on PM East, 233–34, 237, 238
    as song stylist, 233–34, 236
Student Nonviolent Coordinating
    Committee (SNCC), 82
Styron, William, 51, 147
Sulzberger family, 126
Supreme Court, U.S.
    and abortion, 136
    and birth control, 136
    and race, 70, 71, 72–73, 75, 76, 77
Swank, Hilary, 247
Swanson, Gloria, 247

Syria
  Jewish community in, 101–3, 104–5
  police state in, 102
  territories of, 100, 102, 112

Taliban, 131
Terms of Endearment (film), 223, 225
Terry, Luther, 206
Thatcher, Margaret, 137
Time Bends: A Life (Miller), 260
Time magazine, 63, 74, 137, 146
Tisch, Andrew, 212–13
Tisch, Laurence, 213, 214, 217
Tobacco War
  and anti-smoking movement, 219–20
  and CBS management, 211–15, 217
  congressional hearing in, 209, 212–13
  and fire deaths, 206–7
  fire-safe cigarettes, 207
  and First Amendment, 212, 216
  and health hazards, 208–10
  impact boosting, 210
  Mississippi civil action in, 218, 219
  movie about, 218–19
  MW interviews in, 208–10, 213,
    214–15
  and news vs. corporate culture, 211–13,
    215, 217
  and nicotine as addictive drug, 209–10,
    212, 220
  Project Hamlet in, 207
Tonight Show, The (TV), 264, 265, 266–67,
  268
Touhy, William, 189
Treyz, Oliver, 10–11, 164, 165
Trinity Christian College, 180
Truman, Bess, 4
Truman, Harry S, 6, 12, 22
Turner, Ike, 242–43
Turner, Tina, 241–48
  autobiography of, 242–43
  and Bach, 243–44, 245
  early years of, 242
  marriage of Ike and, 242–43
  MW interviews with, 243–47
  as rock star, 242, 244–45
TV Guide, 194–95, 196, 203
TV journalism
  effect of Watergate on, 176
  entrapment charges against, 184
  formats for, 30

investigative methods in, 183–85
responsibility in, 196
20th Century, 85

Ugarte, Mario, 182
Uniform Code of Military Justice, 191
United Nations, 40
University of Texas at Austin, 20
Urban League, 71
USA Today, 198

Vanity Fair, 218
Vanocur, Sander, 225
Vietnam War
  antiwar protests, 32, 192
  escalations of, 188, 192
  failure of U.S. mission in, 199
  and Johnson, 18, 20, 21, 22–24, 32,
    84–85, 192
  as Mr. McNamara's War, 22
  MW's tour of, 188–89, 192
  and Nixon, 22, 32, 34, 46
  order of battle in, 193
  public deception about, 190, 191,
    192–94, 195, 202
  as quagmire, 189, 203
  and Reagan, 57
  Tet offensive, 190, 194
  and Westmoreland story, 187–99
Vineyard Gazette, 148
Voting Rights Act (1965), 81

Walcott, Louis Eugene, *see* Farrakhan, Louis
Wallace, Chris, 59–60
Wallace, Frank and Zina, 7, 39
Wallace, George, 14
Wallace, Helen, 157
Wallace, Lorraine, 200–201, 226
Wallace, Mary Yates, 200–201, 226
Wall Street Journal, The, 217–18
War of 1812, as Mr. Madison's War, 22
Washington, Denzel, 91
Washington Post, The, 176, 197
Watergate, 29, 34, 46, 54–55, 175–76
Weizman, Ezer, 108
Westinghouse Corporation, 213, 217
Westmoreland, William C., 187–99
  CBS investigation of story about, 195,
    196–97, 203
  and *CBS Reports* documentary, 187,
    190–96, 202

Westmoreland, William C. (*continued*)
  and libel suit, 187, 197–99, 202–3
  military assurance of, 188–89, 190, 199
  MW interviews with, 190, 191, 192, 193,
    196
  TV Guide story on, 194–95, 196, 203
What's Love Got to Do with It (film), 243
Wigand, Jeffrey, 207–20
  and anti-smoking movement, 219–20
  confidentiality agreement of, 208, 211,
    212, 219
  harassment of, 219
  movie about, 218–19
  MW interviews with, 208–10, 213,
    214–15
  named as whistle-blower, 217–18, 219
  research conducted by, 207–13
Wilkins, Roy, 87
Williams, John, 149
Wilson, Woodrow, 22
Winfrey, Oprah, 247
Winston cigarettes, 204
Witness Protection Program, 168
Woodward, Bob, 176
Workers' Revolutionary Party, 231
World War I, as Mr. Wilson's War, 22
World War II
  Kennedy in, 9

  as Mr. Roosevelt's War, 22
  and Vietnam, 188
Wright, Frank Lloyd, 6, 137–40
  on church architecture, 139
  death of, 140
  Guggenheim Museum, 140
  MW interview with, 138–39, 166
Wright, Richard, 246
Wylie, Philip, 6

Yamani, Ahmed Zaki, Sheik, 101
Yates, Mary (Wallace), 200–201, 226
Yates, Ted
  and Cohen's allegations, 163
  death of, 2, 200
  and Eastland interview, 70, 71
  and *Mike Wallace Interview,* 70, 78, 160,
    205
  and MW's career, 216
  and *Night Beat,* 1–2, 5, 201
  personal traits of, 2
Yeltsin, Boris, 276–77
Yentl (film), 237
Yom Kippur War, 101, 111–12

Zekman, Pam, 177–78
Zionism, 102, 108, 126, 230
Zoloft, 202

A leading force behind *60 Minutes*, CBS's seminal newsmagazine, MIKE WALLACE has won countless awards for his work (including the Robert F. Kennedy Journalism Award, three Alfred I. duPont–Columbia University Awards, three George Foster Peabody Awards, a Robert E. Sherwood Award, and a Distinguished Achievement Award from the University of California School of Journalism) and has been inducted into the Television Hall of Fame.

GARY PAUL GATES is the author or co-author of four previous books on media and politics—three of which were national bestsellers—including *Close Encounters*, his 1984 book with Mike Wallace.

Visionaries, rabble-rousers, con men, presidents, criminals, cultural icons, and world leaders all have one confidant in common—Mike Wallace. Now, in this candid and revealing book, Wallace tells behind-the-scenes stories from his remarkable sixty-year career, including how he first got an interview with Martin Luther King, Jr.; the account of the Secret Service agent who felt responsible for not saving John F. Kennedy; a poignant interview with Nancy Reagan concerning her husband's Alzheimer's; and many more illuminating stories about Richard Nixon, Malcolm X, Eleanor Roosevelt, Salvador Dalí, Yasir Arafat, Itzhak Perlman, Shirley MacLaine, Barbra Streisand, Arthur Miller, Johnny Carson, Mel Brooks, and more, as well as reflections on his childhood, his professional friendships, and his battle with depression. Mike Wallace's challenging and perceptive questions often evoked reactions from famous figures that have sometimes changed minds and—occasionally—history. *Between You and Me* gives readers a behind-the-scenes look at one of the great broadcast journalists of our time.

"A fascinating read because of Wallace's personalized style and his ongoing involvement with a universe filled with fascinating individuals."
—*Rocky Mountain News*

"Wallace's equally hard-nosed approach with presidents, crooks, celebs, and himself proves fascinating."
—*Entertainment Weekly*

U.S. $14.95 Canada $18.95

ISBN 13: 978-0-7868-8843-6
ISBN 0-7868-8843-1

51495

9 780786 888436

Memoir / Journalism
Cover design by GTC Art & Desig
Cover photograph by Andrew Eccl

HYPERION
www.HyperionBooks.com
Also available on Hyperion AudioBo